Flame and Fortune: How the Fire Service (almost) Killed Me

Rick Bucher

Published by Rick Bucher, 2023.

FLAME AND FORTUNE: HOW THE FIRE SERVICE (ALMOST) KILLED ME

First edition. March 1, 2023.

Copyright © 2023 Rick Bucher.

ISBN: 979-8215894200

Written by Rick Bucher.

Table of Contents

This is for those brave souls who put their own lives on the line every day so that others may live. It's for those who put their safety at risk to protect the property and possessions of others. And it's for everyone whose mental health has been sacrificed in exchange for the opportunity to live a life in the service of strangers. Surely there's no more noble or worthwhile pursuit, and I'm proud that you're about to hear my story.

RB

Preface

Let's get this out of the way up front. For the most part, this is not a "happy" book. It exists because of tragedy, because of loss and because of a brush with death so close that even I can't seem to understand it sometimes. This is the story of how I became a firefighter, how I grew as a man and how the traumas of my life affected me. You're about to run calls with me. And you're about to see a portion of what life in a fire station is like. But you're also about to see what the business of saving lives and property costs those who participate in a fire service career. Hopefully you're about to laugh, but certainly many people cry when they hear some of the things you're going to be exposed to. Don't worry, I'll be right here with you the whole time!

It is my hope that sharing this story can not only shed light on the current and growing problem of firefighter mental health, but that it will also bring some comfort to those brave souls who feel absolutely and completely alone in their own mental health struggles.

You are not alone. People love you and are counting on you. If you are having unhealthy thoughts, please seek professional help before you irreversibly change the lives of those around you and potentially erase any good that you can do for yourself and others in the future.

Chapter 1
"And In The Beginning..."

IN FALL OF 1992 I WALKED into my local fire station and asked, "Are there any jobs here?"

I was going to the local community college, getting core class requirements out of the way for a business degree I didn't want so I could get a job doing something I wouldn't like doing. But that's the way my dad had guided me, so I went. I had felt lost for months heading down this path, but didn't have any other plan to follow. Fortunately, that would soon change.

I'd been a bicycle road racer since my early teens and a BMX racer before that. I supported my passion for racing by working at a local bike shop first as a bike builder, then a mechanic, salesman and eventually as a key-holding manager. That was great, because I had access to and got a discount on all of the latest and greatest bike equipment and a pretty loose schedule. Bike shop managers love having a kid working for them who races because it gives the shop some street cred when someone comes in looking to spend a ton of money on a race bike. What it gave me in return was a schedule that allowed plenty of time to race and train.

Hugh, one of the part-time guys at the shop I worked at, was a Phoenix Firefighter, and one day he invited any of us who were interested to come do a ride-along, which is an informal public education opportunity designed to expose the public to what life in a fire station is like. The only one who took him up on his offer, I showed up one afternoon when Hugh was on shift. The crew gave me a tour of the red brick fire station and the truck, and then we headed to the grocery store for dinner supplies. From the moment we left the station in the truck, it was clear to me that this would be no ordinary grocery run. A fire engine is a massive beast, and once you've climbed up the steps to get in and sit down, you realize just how tall it is. Your ass in the seat is well above the rooftops of the cars next to you and there's a commanding view of the road ahead. Even without our lights and siren on, other drivers yielded to us while their kids waved fervently from the back seat. And when we got to the grocery store, we parked right up front in the fire lane because it did after all have our name on it. Then there were the other shoppers in the store. They all looked at Hugh and the crew of Engine 27 with reverence and respect, engaging us all in conversations, which mostly started with, "Whose turn is it to cook tonight?" or "What time's dinner, I'm coming over!" The crew all pitched in money for groceries and we headed back to the station.

Nothing of real interest happened until a working fire call came in well after the dishes from dinner were done and I was about ready to leave after hours of inactivity. Everyone (myself included) ran to the truck and before I knew it, we were driving on the wrong side of Thunderbird Road, forcing oncoming traffic to pull over with an air horn and a wind-up Federal siren which is absolute music to not only every firefighter on the planet, but also to those who call in an emergency; it means that help is on the way. My friend Hugh and his partner were sitting in the backward-facing seats getting their turnouts on and strapping on air packs which would let them breathe fresh air even in the unknown environment of the awaiting inferno. I'd watched the television show "Emergency" all through my seventies childhood years, but the stars of that show, Johnny and Roy, had nothing on this because THIS was REAL!

The engine company came to a stop in a cul-de-sac in front of a model home with smoke pouring from the front door. Something was burning in there, and Hugh and his partners went in to put it out. Steam expansion from them hitting the fire with water forced heavy black, then grey/white smoke from the front door and nearly as quickly as it had begun, it was over. I vividly remember thinking to myself at the time, "I think I just found what I really want to do with my life!" But the ride-along experience had done something surprising to me. It had left me with more questions than answers. "What do they carry in the pockets of their turnouts?" "What's it feel like to drive a fire truck?" "How do they cook for so many people in the station?" "What's it like to save someone's life?" I was asking questions, yes, but not the right ones. There was no way for me to even begin knowing how little I knew about this profession or those who choose it.

This simple Saturday ride along set me on a path that would forever shape who I would become and how I would think, feel and act as a man, despite the fact that at the time, I wasn't even old enough to drink. My pursuit had begun.

Chapter 2
"Are there any jobs here?"

THIS BEING A TIME BEFORE the Internet had really caught on, there was no looking at a website for postings about job openings. So if you wanted to work somewhere, you'd usually just go there and ask if they were hiring. I was living in my first apartment, about ½ mile from Fire Station 19 in Scottsdale, Arizona with only a 1992 Honda Nighthawk motorcycle for transportation. Realizing that there exists somewhat of a stigma surrounding motorcycles and those who ride them, I decided to walk down and see what I needed to do to get hired.

I went in the front door of the tri-level, tile-roofed station and was directed to the Captain's office. The on-duty company officer that day was busy with some paperwork at his desk and when called in, I simply asked, "Are there any jobs here?" He replied, "Maybe, are you an EMT?"

I said, "No, I'm not."

"Well, then go to Scottsdale Community College (yes, the school I was already attending) and get certified."

So I walked back home, got on my motorcycle and headed to school to sign up for the upcoming fall semester of EMT class. When it began a few weeks later, the group of people in class was a mixture of mainly young kids in their 20's like me, and most of them seemed to be simply exploring a career option. But it was different for me. I was on a mission to become a firefighter and this was the first real, committing step.

A Scottsdale Firefighter Paramedic named Rob taught the class. He was socially awkward, stuttered a bit when he spoke and stood uncomfortably in his shoes. Of slight build, I thought to myself that if this guy can handle the physical requirements of the job, I sure as hell could. But Rob really seemed to know what he was teaching and I had respect for that. He had a certain funny way of blending what was presented in the two-inch-thick textbook with his own real-world experience. What I had no way of knowing at the time was that I would work extensively with Rob in the future. The class was difficult and required mastery of a multitude of patient care situations including medical emergencies, trauma, airway management, bleeding control, childbirth and a litany of other skills. Rob and his assistant instructors did a great job preparing the class for the final hurdles. Two separate exams stood between the students and National Registry certification as Emergency Medical Technicians: a long written test and a practical skills evaluation. Earlier, my school experience and performance were limited by a genuine lack of interest in most classes I ever took all the way from elementary school right up to the accounting class at SCC that I had dropped out of the semester before. When I found interest in a class, I dedicated the time and effort to learn the material. If uninterested, I'd mostly sit in class imagining whatever else I'd rather be doing. I excelled at things that were science or language-related. I had an interest in the natural world and how things worked. Communication always fascinated me and I had a passion for competition. And when the time came, I passed both EMT exams and got my Arizona State and National Registry certifications, along with an "A" and a top-3 finish in the class.

So back to Station 19 I went. I headed back upstairs to the Captain's office and found the same officer there as I had before. Looking up from his desk, he asked if he could help me. I said that I'd gotten my EMT certification and that I'd like to apply for a job. In a monumental moment of déjà vu, he asked me, "Have you taken any Fire Science classes?"

My next goal was set right then and there, and off I went again to register for the only Fire Science class left open for the upcoming semester, Fire Hydraulics and Apparatus. I couldn't help thinking that if he'd asked me that the first time I'd visited the station, I could have taken fire science classes along with the EMT class I had just finished last semester. But I was undeterred and continued on. Complicating my only choice of class was the fact that this one is intended for experienced firefighters who are preparing to take over the role of driving fire trucks, and I was nowhere near being that person yet.

The instructor, Randy, also worked for Rural/Metro in Scottsdale and had recently been promoted to the rank of Battalion Chief. He reminded me of the actor Sam Elliot with the cowboy way he had about him. He was country before country was cool. And having been raised in Ft. Worth, Texas until age 14, I thought *that* was cool. On the first day of class after everyone's introductions I realized that the demographic was much different from my EMT class in that it was occupied primarily by about 20 currently employed firefighters who all seemed to know one another. After class, Randy pulled me aside and asked incredulously, "So this is your FIRST Fire Science class?"

"Yes it is." I replied.

"Well, you're kind of putting the cart before the horse, but let's see how you do." The horse reference was most definitely not lost on me. I found the class fascinating and was easily able to conceptualize the physics involved with the flow of water through a pump, hose and nozzles. And I got another "A".

And back to the station I went. This time I'd randomly shown up on a different shift and met with John, the new "B-shift" Captain at station 19. I said that I had my EMT certification, had just finished a Hydraulics and Apparatus class, and was wondering if they were hiring. He said that he'd just taken over the Central Scottsdale Reserve Firefighter Program and had some positions open. I wasn't even sure who these "reserves" were or what they did, but it sure sounded like a job opportunity to me, so I listened carefully. I was then invited to come back to see reserve drill the following Tuesday evening and before I knew it I was performing hose rolls with the reserves in front of the station. They all had red shirts on that said "Recruit" on the right chest, but were otherwise outfitted just like full-time firefighters with navy pants, black leather belts and steel-toe boots with yellow firefighter helmets. I couldn't stop seeing and becoming interested in the finest of details, like the way they had applied lettering stickers indicating their last name to the back of their helmet, or how polished their boots were. I watched how they held the rolled 1 ¾" hose before briskly tossing and unrolling it. Several of the group of seven or eight were getting the 100' section of cotton-jacketed line to extend fully at the end of the throw, but many were not. I think I had to borrow a pair of gloves to do it, but my first ever hose throw fully extended beautifully, as if in slow motion in my mind. "Nice job, come back Thursday", said the new Captain and I went home with a mile-wide smile on my face.

On Thursday of the same week, I met with Captain John at the station, and then went for a urine drug screen and background check. After passing both, I returned to the station to pick up a uniform voucher and then signed some paperwork, including a W-2 form for taxes. I went to Martin's Uniforms in downtown Phoenix, then to the Red Wing boot store to pick up my first pair of steel-toe zip-up duty boots. If I'd known what the soles of those boots and a couple dozen other pair would see me walk through during my fire career, I bet back then I wouldn't have batted an eye. I probably would've been happy and excited about it. But as I write this now, over 27 years later, my current self would have had some second thoughts.

My gear ensemble wasn't complete yet. I was fitted for turnout gear that would protect me in a fire, including a Nomex[1] hood and thick fire gloves, which felt more like oven mitts than something you'd actually be able to work in. And by "fitted", I mean standing in the storage shed out behind the station with one of the full-time guys in front of a pile of old, mismatched yellow turnout coats, pants and boots. "Here, try this one." "Nah, too big." "Here, try these on." It was laughable by today's standards, but it's the way it was. And it was the way they'd all started out long before I showed up. The one new thing I received was a helmet. My brand new yellow helmet couldn't have sat for more than a few hours before I'd proudly emblazoned "BUCHER" on the back in black stickers. This was getting real.

And just like that, it began for me. In the modern fire service, there are commonly hundreds or thousands of people who show up just to pick up one of a limited number of applications for the position of firefighter and after that, very few of them make it through the background check, written test, physical skills course and interview processes. Being a firefighter is one of the most coveted, revered and honored career choices anyone could ever dream of making. Kids and even many adults fantasize about what it'd be like to do the job. The love for and adoration of firefighters all over the world by the public is well known. But what the day in and day out operation is like, and what *really* happens at the station and at the end of those code-3 runs with lights and siren remains a mystery to all but the brave few who dare to make their dream a reality. I'd made my decision after just one ride-along with my friend Hugh that night several months earlier. My desire was that strong to go after something that looked to be more fulfilling than any career path I'd ever considered. I was in for the ride of a lifetime, and I felt ready.

Reserve firefighters supplemented full-time staffing for Rural/Metro in Scottsdale by responding to fire incidents from home and by eventually getting "shift qualified" so that they could work 24-hour shifts to fill in for people off on vacation, sick or injury leave. But as a recruit the work was limited to helping pick up hose and putting gear back on trucks at fire scenes. Tools and equipment were color-coded with unique paint marks, which identified what truck they belonged to. I still remember that station 19 was purple, 14 was brown and 10 was red. The other five Scottsdale stations at the time slip my mind. If you found an axe with a purple stripe on it, you knew it was from 19. Ladder with a red stripe? That would be 10's.

Now comes the question, "How did reserves know they had a call?" One day, early after I had all my fire gear, Captain John called me in and handed me a small grey plastic box with two knobs and a button on top that said "Motorola Minitor II" on the front next to a small speaker, a charger for the device and a map of the City. This was the radio pager I'd be summoned with for the next three years when there was a fire or a need for a reserve response. He said that one setting was for channel 2, which was for dispatch. When turned on, the unit would silently listen or "monitor" for the correct radio transmission calling reserves and then alert with a beeping tone. To me, that tone eventually began to mimic the sound of slot machines in a casino when it went off, as I knew I'd be heading out to make some money. Captain John also told me that the other setting was for channel 4. This was the fire ground tactical channel, which I'd change over to on the way to a fire or other incident so that I could have an idea of what was going on when I got there. I used to keep a pen and paper under the Minitor belt clip because in those days, we had to write down the address for the call when the dispatcher said it over the air. As he handed me these items he said that I could respond to reserve call-outs and to not speed or run red lights along the way to incidents. He also said I could help out on fire scenes, but specifically said, "Don't go inside any burning buildings for as long as you wear that red shirt."

Oddly, the first fire I can remember being called to was a brush fire. I had zero idea what was going on at the scene, but followed along in the dark as everyone stirred up dirt around burned out stumps and piles of grey ash, which used to be brittlebush or creosote bushes. I didn't even have a headlamp yet to see what I was doing and remember having to work in the beam of another firefighter's light. I recognized one of the other red-shirt reserves there from my reserve program and followed his lead the whole time. The entire one-acre landscape had been reduced to ash, save for the larger mesquite and Palo Verde trees standing like gnarled, blackened hands with palms facing skyward as if to plead, "Why me?" Hours later that night, I returned home smelling like a campfire and looking like a coal miner, but feeling ecstatic that I'd finally been to a fire. A tradition exists in fire stations everywhere which states that any time a firefighter has a "first" anything, they have to buy ice cream for the entire crew. On the one hand it's a celebration of that first event, whether it be a structure fire, cardiac arrest or TV appearance. But on the other hand it's more an opportunity for senior firefighters to score some free desert. The reality is that it's payment tendered by junior firefighters in exchange for the wisdom passed down by older, experienced mentors. I had no idea the tradition even existed until long after my first fire experience that night. For the first time ever, I'd be paid for my services on an emergency scene. Those two hours of work would earn me a whopping $6.50. And that was before taxes were taken out. The truth is I'd have done it for free, just for the excitement.

Emergency call-outs weren't the only way to make money as a reserve firefighter in those days. The reserves did all manner of fire department support tasks, such as shuttling trucks or equipment around the city and any other task deemed too unimportant for regular full-time crews to handle. Another option was to do ride-alongs at stations and go on calls with the crew. In those days, Rural/Metro fire trucks in Scottsdale were staffed with three and in a few cases, only two crewmembers per truck. Most of the trucks could hold four people, so having a reserve along wasn't usually any sort of inconvenience and most crews liked having another set of hands around to help out. Further, if a particular crew didn't care for reserve riders, you were unlikely to learn anything of real value from them anyway and they were avoided. I wasn't paid for just being at the station, but did get an hour paid for every call I ran. The $3.25/ hr. pay sounds absurd in retrospect, but I was having a ton of fun and learning a massive amount in the process. I could feel myself starting to become a firefighter.

At the time, I was still working at a local bike shop, racing, training and had started waiting tables at a Mexican restaurant. I was hustling heavily to make enough money to pay rent, my motorcycle payment and have enough left over to eat. An American Express card entered the frame and saw an immediate balance thanks to a new pair of skis and boots. The waiter position eventually made me more money in a shorter time than the bike shop job, so my days of building, selling and repairing bikes and managing the shop came to a close. This freed up time to do more ride-alongs, so that's what I dedicated myself to. And by the way, I was doing all of this with only a motorcycle for transportation. I grew up in a "not while you're in this house" motorcycle situation. Within a week of moving out several months earlier (and without a car), I enrolled in a Motorcycle Safety Foundation Basic Rider Course hosted by a company called TEAM Arizona. Two and a half days of training later, I had a motorcycle license. A week after that, I rode a new 1992 Honda CB750 Nighthawk home from the dealer and started making my first vehicle payments. It cost me $4,400 out the door and was paid off in three years. Rain or shine (mostly shine in AZ), I rode everywhere on that black beauty. I'd bought a massive black nylon duffel bag for my fire gear and would strap it to the back seat with two bungee cords in an "X" across the 50-lb. load. I loved riding, got 40 mpg and received a discount on insurance in exchange for getting the rider training. A couple months later, I signed up for and took both the Intermediate and Advanced Rider Training classes with TEAM AZ. At the end of the advanced class, the instructor offered me a job with them. If the timing were right, I'd have done it, but I'd just eliminated one job from my list and didn't need another to sway me from my fire service dream. I didn't know it at the time, but that opportunity would present itself again later in life and lead me down another beautifully twisted road.

As a reserve, I was able to ride at any station in the city. But there were stations that were notoriously hard on reserves. Station 10 at Miller and Thomas on the south end of town was one such place and ran more calls than any other in Scottsdale. My motivation to ride there was two-fold. If they were busy, I'd get paid for more calls. And if I had my skills together, I'd be able to prove myself in front of the most critical audience available. That week at reserve drill on Tuesday night, no more than four or five weeks into my "reservedom", I asked Captain John if it'd be okay to ride at station 10. He replied, "Call the Captain down there first thing to make sure it's okay, stay busy in the bay learning about their trucks and memorizing where all the equipment is, don't pick your nose and I'll pay you at least an hour for every call you run, just write down all the run numbers and times." To the side, I'd spoken to several of the other reserves in my program that night who thought it was crazy to go to station 10 so early into being a reserve. I was nervous, but definitely not scared. I'd been doing ride alongs at station 19 for weeks, with only a limited number of calls under my belt and I wanted to see, learn and do more. I needed action.

The next morning, I called 10 and went for my first ride along there. To my surprise, the officer at the station that day was Captain Eric, one of the most egotistical, over-inflated men I'd ever meet in all my life. He was also the very same captain who'd sent me off to school from my stops at station 19 to inquire about work. Twice. He'd recently transferred to station 10 and would become a mainstay there for many years. I identified myself as a central Scottsdale reserve and asked if it would be okay to ride that day. "Fine, come down." then the line clicked. I hung up the pay phone at the gas station down the street from station 10 where I had placed the call. Station 10 was about 30 minutes from my apartment and I didn't want to waste a second, so I had driven toward South Scottsdale before the crew had even done shift change for the day. This was it. Out of the pan and into the fire, so to speak!

The department had recently hired around twenty Paramedics in order to staff the ambulances (we called them Rescues) that Rural Metro was putting into service in town. Rural hurried the Medics through a very basic fire academy and set them up for failure right away by rushing it. Keep in mind the fact that Rural was out to make money and you'll understand why most of the companies executives would probably have rather just put these well-intentioned people through a one-hour class on how to properly fill out ambulance billing paperwork and handed them a box of pens instead of providing them with any sort of fire service training. But the situation was more complex than that. Rural was selling itself on being able to provide fire protection in addition to ambulance service and that was what got them the contract with the city when it came time for the old ambulance provider to renew. In a way it was a win-win, but not necessarily for the crews who staffed the new rescues or for the citizens they protected.

Station 10 was closest to the south training yard, site of the makeshift fire academy currently being held. And the trucks from station 10 went to the yard for drill on the day that I did my first ride-along there. We did a few training evolutions with the new medics and I was feeling confident in my performance. That's right about when the yelling started. Everyone was standing in a circle when Captain Eric went off about the academy class not being able to pull hose correctly. Their poor skills were on display for all to see and despite being new at this, I could tell that most of them really did suck at being firefighters. Before I knew it, the short-tempered Captain had me by the elbow and was pulling me out into the middle of the circle of 30 or so people, asking how long I'd been a red-shirt. "Six weeks, sir." He then said, "He's only been on for six fucking weeks and pulls hose better than all of you!" My face surely turned as red as my shirt, but I knew I'd just proven something to him and to myself. I got the feeling that the medics weren't big fans of mine, though!

And so it went as a red shirt recruit for several months, until finally one day it was announced that there would be a Firefighter I&II academy held for us. This is a few months of classroom and practical instruction that culminates in qualification through the State Fire Marshall's Office as a Firefighter. It was not the hardest thing I'd ever done, and as we made our way through the IFSTA[2] textbook "Essentials of Firefighting", the groundwork was laid for everything else I'd learn over the course of my career. Our live fire training was pretty darn rudimentary, with some of it actually held in an old metal shipping container with wooden pallets burning in one end while we sat and roasted in the other. It got us hot enough to get first-degree or small second-degree burns on our shoulders where the turnout coat was pressed tight by our SCBA[3] straps and on the tops of our ear lobes. Nonsense like that was a sign of bravery that would never be seen as acceptable training in the modern fire service, but it was what we had. As a class, we ran many miles, "threw packs" (put on SCBA's for time) and went through all manner of "evolutions" where we'd lay different configurations of hose and equipment for specific fireground circumstances. One great thing about those days was the fact that we got to take turns on evolutions pumping the truck, or acting in an engineer role by driving and operating the valves required to make water flow. I fell into that position quite naturally, considering that I'd just taken a college course on the subject and have always been very mechanically inclined. Always entertaining was the race that occurred during evolutions where the engine would stop at a hydrant or "plug" for a firefighter to connect to. After the firefighter had wrapped the 4" yellow, rubber-jacketed hose around the plug, he'd yell "Ready!" signaling the engineer to start "laying line" or paying out hose from the top of the bed as the truck drove toward the fire scene. The race involved the hydrant person trying to make their connection and begin opening the hydrant before the engineer had stopped at the fire, set the parking brake, put the pump in gear and gotten out to place a clamp on the hose lying on the ground behind the truck. Without the clamp in place, water was free to flow into the remaining hose up in the bed on top of the truck, causing a tangled accordion of epic proportions, which I still find funny to this day.

Fortunately, it never happened to me. And in the hydrant position, I had many opportunities over the years to charge a slow engineer's hose bed, but could never bring myself to do it to anyone. I just didn't believe in causing that level of embarrassment in order to make myself look better than others.

Quick historical note:

In early times, water was actually carried through hollowed-out logs to supply water in cities for firefighting purposes. Along the run of logs, holes were drilled, and then plugged. When the horse-drawn steam fire apparatus were brought to a fire, firefighters would "take the plug" out of the log and place an intake hose for the pumper to draw water out. I wonder what they did in those days to embarrass one another by making a quick attachment!

Once I'd graduated from the FF[4] I&II academy, I'd never have to wear a red "Recruit" shirt ever again and as a class, we had a shirt-burning ceremony to bid them goodbye. The other thing I'd never have to do again was wait outside of a burning building while the "real" firefighters worked inside. It didn't take long. One night my pager went off for a fire at an industrial area on the far south side of Scottsdale in an unincorporated section of Maricopa County that we called the "River Bottom". It bordered the normally dry Salt River bed and was a conglomeration of seedy, run-down auto shops and warehouses. One of the shops called "Earl's Fiberglass" was burning, and there was still plenty of fire left to fight when I showed up, 30 minutes into the call. I reported to the Incident Commander and was pointed to a hose line where two other guys were about to go through a side door to the shop. I got into third position on the line and in we went. The room we went into struck me right away as beautiful, with flames dancing across the floor and over shelving units to the tall ceiling. It appeared as a kaleidoscope of colors, and the entire three-bay shop was awash in flames. Looking back, that wide variety of flame colors means only one thing: Hazardous Materials, known as "HazMat" were burning. The chemicals and supplies involved in fiberglass layup are highly dangerous and when burning put off toxic gasses which appear in wildly different colors such as blues, greens and purples. Take a look at a campfire's flames next time you're near one. That's what a "normal" fire looks like. HazMat looks like an interpretive art painting.

After we'd controlled the fire, we exited the building, coated in sticky, stinking residue from the chemicals inside the shop. As I walked past one of the fire trucks at the scene, I noticed a firefighter not only getting out of his turnouts, but his shirt also, with a concerned look on his face, which by the way held one of the most impressively sized moustaches known to the department. Being as green as the flames I'd just fought, I didn't realize that Gene, the man in the back of the truck, had been exposed to the same HazMat I now carried with me on my gear. As the fire scene wound down, I assisted in rolling and loading hose and tools, and then strolled off to start the commute home with my first real firefight under my belt. I got home, showered, and thought little of the tingling feeling I was having on my skin and turned in for the night after putting my gear outside on the apartment balcony to air out. The next day I got a phone call and was told to bring all my gear to Station 10. Once there, they told me to bag everything up in a large, opaque trash bag and label it as "contaminated". They issued me some old spare turnouts for the time being and had me provide a urine sample for testing for chemical exposure. I never heard anything back, but still wonder if some day I'll be reminded of that first real firefight by some sort of cancer diagnosis. So strong was my desire to be a firefighter that I was willing to look right past the possible consequences of my decision. Such was my desire to serve, and this was only the beginning.

Chapter 3
"Things Get Wild"

———

AND THEN THERE WAS wildland. One of the great things about the department back then was the availability of training. For all their shortcomings, Rural/Metro really did a good job of providing training and it was free for the taking. Much of that training probably revolved around the fact that we had to do more work with fewer people on calls than neighboring departments. But we were at least competent about what we were busting our asses doing. When a S-130/S190[5] class was offered in-house, I signed up right away. Being an avid outdoors enthusiast, I took to the study of fuel, weather and topography immediately and was fascinated to learn how fire could quickly travel through a landscape, the path it would most likely take and how to stop it. The class included a "Pack Test", where each candidate had to carry a 45lb-weighted backpack over three miles of flat ground in 45 minutes or less. That averages to 15-minute miles with a heavy pack, and wildland firefighters all over the United States take the test every year to get a red card which qualifies them to fight fire outdoors in a mind-boggling variety of terrain and fuel types. The test is challenging, but I passed it every year that I took it with time to spare. Picture hiking as fast as possible without running and you have an idea of the pace required to pass the test. With red card in hand, I was now federally qualified to travel out of the city in order to fight fire when paged to do so. What I soon realized was the fact that fires on different public and private lands paid differently, with "Fed Fires", or those on federal lands like national forests paying the best. I made decent money toward the end of my first year as a reserve fighting wildland fires carrying a shovel on a "hand crew" and was soon qualified to operate not only the small 4x4 "Type 6" wildland fire trucks in our fleet, but the big, 3,000 gallon water tankers or "tenders" as well. Keep in mind the fact that at the time, I thought $7.50/hour was "good money"!

My 4x4 vehicle operator class was the first time I had really driven anything off-road, and sparked an interest in something I still enjoy doing today. But the big water trucks were the most challenging rigs in the fleet to drive, as they had 10-speed split-range manual transmissions, which were a nightmare to learn. Once mastered, there are few driving experiences more rhythmic and entertaining to perform. All that throttle blipping and double clutching is quite artful, almost like dancing. And whenever one was requested at a fire, I'd always be first to pick it up at the station. The driving experience wasn't the only reason I was King of the Tenders. Those trucks were consistently held at wildland fire scenes hours longer than other units because they were many times the only consistent supply of water. And that meant more scene time and money for me.

Being able to contact the station or the alarm room quickly after a page for manpower went out meant that I'd be the one to get the hours. To that end, I got my first cell phone, a Motorola "Brick". Google it and find the grey one; that was mine. When you think of a truly old school cell phone, this is what comes up. I carried that thing everywhere, including to fires, where I was able to keep in touch with people while out in the field. Funny that I can still remember the phone numbers to many of our old fire stations to this day, having dialed them as quickly as possible dozens of times over those first years in the service. It was a delicate balance though, because back then we paid by the minute for cell service. Consequently, those calls were usually quite short!

Another supplemental form of income became working for the Tonto National Forest[6] as a seasonal wildland firefighter, manning one of their type-6 engines. I picked up shifts at Tonto any time I could for two summers. I learned a different level of wildland operations during my time there and gained an appreciation for what it takes to suppress fire in the desert and mountains, which each present their own unique challenges due to different fuel types and topographic layouts.

At some point during a break at a fire scene one summer, I wrote the words "Flame-n-Fortune" on the underside of my yellow wildland helmet brim. That phrase reflected the fact that I was making more money than I ever had in my new life fighting the flames. Unfortunately, the drive to earn more money saw me drop out of my college chemistry class during that second year at school. It was the last class I needed for my Associates Degree in Fire Science. I never went back to finish it, which was a shortsighted mistake I regretted for years thereafter. But working as a seasonal for Tonto was fun. I loved driving the dirt forest service roads, visiting the fire lookout tower on top of Humboldt Mountain and being outside. It was also where I learned to really drive off-road in some very challenging conditions, with lots at stake. And by "off-road", I mean that there wasn't even a dirt trail much of the time, often requiring a spotter to walk through the tall grass in front of the truck, guiding the driver around holes, large rocks and sharp cactus. Those skills stay with me and are practiced to this day when I travel in the backcountry. Working for the forest service wasn't all fun and games, though. Cleaning and painting the campground toilet structures was most certainly NOT fun, and neither was picking up trash or breaking up unwanted campfire rings on our district. But I really did feel like I was contributing to something I cared about and felt like a steward of the land. I learned how to build barbed wire fence, remove a stuck river rock from between dually truck tires with a 20' chain, and quickly wind up hose in a figure eight pattern over my outstretched arms as well as plenty of other interesting outdoor skills.

We did have several brush fires during my time with Tonto, but nothing more than twenty acres or so. What working there did for me back at Rural was give me instant street cred for my experience. But that wasn't enough. I took every single in-house wildland class offered by Rural. I learned everything from how to forecast the weather, to how to drop trees with a chainsaw, from how to operate and maintain portable water pumps, to how to intentionally burn areas of land to slow or stop a quickly spreading wildfire. Eventually I was qualified as an Engine Boss, which allowed me to run as the wildland equivalent of a company officer on a truck, and as a Crew Boss, which meant I could take charge of a 20-person crew of firefighters. And I was 22 years old. Think about that for a moment.

In July of 1995, Scottsdale experienced its to-date largest wildland fire ever. The "Rio Fire" charred 23,000 acres of desert at the far northeastern corner of the city, as well as unincorporated county land and even some acreage in the adjoining Tonto National Forest.

It was mid-afternoon on July 7th when my pager went off, and the situation sounded really bad on the radio. Captain Hal, one of our most experienced wildland company officers, was there first with his engine company, Engine 18. The fire had started with a lightning strike from a passing monsoon storm. Many times, these strikes are quickly extinguished by subsequent falling rain. But this was a "dry strike", with nothing to stop it and only strong winds to fan the flames. It quickly built up size and strength, storming its way south toward Rio Verde Drive, a 40' wide paved road which ran east-west across the fire's path. Hal knew that stopping it at the road was the only chance they'd have before this monster reached Scottsdale's preserve land and eventually the worst possible outcome:

multi-million dollar homes on the south and west sides of the McDowell Mountains. The words "It just jumped Rio Verde Drive. This thing is runnin' like you haven't seen." crackled across my radio pager as I drove up Pima Road on my way to pick up Tender 18 at the station. Finding the tender already gone, I drove to the scene and parked near a few fire department vehicles, including engines, command vehicles and even a couple of ambulances which served as a bit of a grim reminder to actually be careful on this one. There was a full-on dust storm happening at the same time as an exponentially growing wildfire, which was oddly beautiful. In a way it reminded me of my first fire at Earl's Fiberglass, but the bright blues and greens of those flames were now replaced by a full range of browns through oranges and yellows, with the sky turned a deep, menacing red. The apocalyptic chaos of the scene was palpable at an existential level. Scenes like that make one think that this could be what it looks like when the world is coming to an end.

Things get a little foggy at this point, but I had made my way with a brush truck crew to some houses that were on the east flank, to the side of the fire. After confirming that several of them had been evacuated, we prepared to make a stand at a dirt road between the houses and the main body of fire, which was still about 100 yards west of us. There was no time to run when a dramatic wind shift turned the direction of the fire's travel from south to east, directly at us. The crew of three was widely spread out and not in direct communication with one another, and the fire was burning in desert grass, Palo Verde trees and Creosote bushes. The flames were about 20-30' high, far beyond qualification for direct-attack firefighting tactics. I had about 10 seconds to decide between going back to the engine for a drip torch or fusees[7] in order to start burning out the fuel next to the road or going for the houses and possible shelter, but it was too late. The fire was moving faster than I could run. When

I got within 50' of the truck, the smoke hit me. I crouched, and then laid down flat on the dirt road and it happened. I got burned over. The heat wasn't any worse than what I'd felt in that training cargo container at the yard, but now only my green Nomex pants and a long-sleeve yellow Nomex brush shirt protected me and I could tell that my protective gear was nearing its limit. I didn't look up, but I'm sure there was a tall wave of flames cresting over the road I was laying facedown on. I knew that if it got much hotter, I'd be seriously burned or worse. I desperately wiggled my wrists to cover the gap of exposed skin between my shirt and work gloves as I felt the skin on each wrist burning. More intense was the smoke. I was suffering smoke inhalation, but not airway burns yet. Normally in this situation without an escape route or a safety zone, the only option is for a wildland firefighter to deploy a fire shelter. I had been trained to do so, but in the moment, there actually was no time to mess with the foil pup tent that we nicknamed an "EZ-Bake." Our crew had been working so feverishly that we had violated multiple established wildland safety procedures that have been put in practice after various tragedies took place over the years. These were all covered extensively in that initial training I'd had just two seasons prior. The operational pace of the fire was higher than any I'd been involved with during my short tenure, but as the most experienced person on that crew, I learned a valuable lesson that day. Someone has to take charge and I had failed at doing so.

There's a special type of panic that overcomes a person who can't breathe, whether it's by drowning, choking or gagging on smoke; the feeling of helplessness is exquisitely pure. There's a sensation of panic so primal and visceral that it obstructs the desire to do anything in the world other than take a good, clean breath of fresh air; the kind of breath one takes after making it to the surface after a nearly-too-long period underwater. I'd felt that before after being thrown around in the churning Gulf Coast surf as a kid, and I did it again after nearly being overcome by smoke at the Rio Fire. The difference between the two is that when I finally could take a deep breath while still laying there in the dirt, that breath was still contaminated by smoke! It was what's referred to in the fire service today as a "near miss." Our crew of three had very narrowly missed a catastrophic outcome, but there was no time to ruminate on the fact. I'm sure there are firefighters out there who would have called it quits immediately after such an experience, if not from the career, at least from the Rio Fire scene. But this was a fight, and as long as I could still function, there was no way I was going to stop slugging it out with the largest wildland fire many of us had ever, and would ever, see. Miraculously, the fire didn't jump the 30' dirt road or burn any of the homes we'd set up to protect. There were small "spot fires" ignited here and there by flying fire brands and embers in the neighborhood, which we put out easily after searching for them like so many Easter eggs hidden in the brush around the houses. The rest of the firefighters operating in that same area took a good hit of smoke as well, but also kept on working. Word got back to incident command about the close call that had happened on the road and we were called to respond to the command post. When we showed up, we were sent as a group to a waiting ambulance for evaluation. Jay, a Paramedic I knew from the south part of the city, checked my lung sounds and vitals. My heart rate was just shy of 160, my respirations nearly 30 per minute, and my blood pressure was through the roof. I think he looked at me and said, "Dude..." I remember looking back at him, shaking my head and saying, "I'm fine, and I'm not leaving." I rested for a bit and was reassigned to head back out. Such was the nature of the fire service then, and to some extent necessarily, still is. When bad things are happening and when lives and property are in jeopardy, someone has to stand in the way and put a stop to it. Someone has to take the smoke, heat and risk and keep working. Someone has to do the things that no one else is qualified, trained or equipped to do. I learned how unforgiving fire could be that afternoon, but I also learned a lot about myself and what I'm capable of as a man. It was one of the first times that I really felt like a superhero at work. And it felt DAMN good. I spent three days coughing and hacking like a lifelong smoker while working on the Rio Fire, but it was eventually contained.

No structures or lives were lost, but thousands of acres of high-dollar real estate had been charred black and nearly looked like a moonscape, devoid of anything living. The north aspect of the McDowell Mountains, which had several rock climbing areas that I'd grown up on, looked like a massive camp fire ring. The desert would recover, but it would take many decades to even partially grow back. One thing I realized then was that no matter what, all fires eventually go out. They even go out without human influence. And there will always be more. Unfortunately, the bravery of wildland firefighters doesn't get enough press until there's a tragedy. And if you bring up courage, sacrifice and honor to any firefighter, they're most likely going to tell you the same thing I would: "I was just doing my job." While true, those things are part of the job; they only just begin to scratch the surface of what it means to be a firefighter.

Chapter 4

"Are you ready to work?"

THE EVOLUTION OF MY fire service career took me away from the wildland arena and back into town, because the ultimate goal was to get hired full-time and wildland work didn't do much to help me in that area. During all that wildland training, I was also working on getting "Shift Qualified". Reserves with this to their credit were able to start working 24-hour shifts in firefighter positions within the city when full-time staff were sick, injured or off on vacation. This was a huge money-saving measure for Rural, as they were paying reserves low wages and weren't providing any benefits. I remember actually paying more each month for health insurance than I was paying for my motorcycle payment. But it was the gateway to a full-time position as a firefighter, and they knew that those who really wanted to be firefighters would do anything to get there. I ask myself now if it was fair. The answer is that although ethically questionable, it was fair at the time. But it was hard, tough work and in my opinion those who made it had a level of grit that's notably absent in firefighters who are hired off the street and sent through an academy right away. A few years of wanting something and working toward it through on-the-job training generally make for better, harder-working firefighters and full-time Rural/Metro firefighters seemed to have had a different view of the value of their careers. They'd all fought for what they had.

Then the call came from the Battalion Chief in charge of scheduling. He asked if I was ready to start working some shifts, and he knew that I'd recently been checked off to do so. I said I was ready for anything he had and he laid it on me. My first "shift" was with something called "ATS", or "Alternative Transport Services". Rural had their hands in the ambulance service and were trying out non-emergency transportation of patients between medical facilities. They bought several vans and sparsely equipped them with a gurney and a wheelchair lift. My first shift wouldn't be on a fire truck or fire department rescue. And it wouldn't even be in Scottsdale. I drove to an ambulance station in central Phoenix and met up with a partner there. We were dispatched from one nursing home or hospital to another, acting as a glorified taxi service for people who were not ambulatory enough to ride in a private car or cab. While it served a purpose, I found it to be demeaning and definitely NOT what I had signed up for. I also had no training for it, so I was learning the ropes as I went. The shifts were eight or ten hours long, so at least I was making steady money for the week or two that it lasted. Then a different Battalion Chief called and offered me a "real" shift at a fire station in Scottsdale. From that day on, I worked up to 18 shifts per month, sometimes for four days straight and quit my job at the Mexican restaurant for good. I'd never hear a complaint about salt on the rim of a Margarita glass or the wrong tacos on a plate ever again. For the first time, I really felt like I was on my chosen career path with a bright future. I felt proud.

Shifts came and went, calls came and went and like all reserves, I mostly worked on the Rescue unit if there was one at my station assignment for the day. These were ambulances with one Firefighter/ EMT (me) and one Firefighter/Paramedic. We carried turnout gear, SCBAs and some basic forcible entry tools, allowing us to function on fire calls and vehicle accidents as well as the normal "EMS" emergency medical service calls. The rescue shifts afforded a certain amount of freedom in the fact that there was no way for the alarm room to know where we were at any given time, and there was no company officer or captain on the unit. So as long as we stayed in our "first due" area where we were expected to respond first to calls for service, we could do what we wanted. Add that to a good partner and it equals a really fun 24 hours. But spend that same quantity of time with a partner who isn't motivated, has a bad attitude or just really stinky feet and you're not going to have a great day!

As a reserve, you were expected to handle all the cleaning and chores around the station and to keep busy any time you were in quarters. I was good at that. I didn't sit in a recliner for the first few years and instead took up a chair at the day room table with something to study if there was no physical work to be done. I took every Fire Science class and in-house course that was offered. And I felt like I was getting pretty dialed in on this whole fire service thing.

One of those in-house classes was Rope I&II[8], which addressed the basics of technical rescue involving rope use. It was similar to the starting point I had with my wildland training. Having been a rock climber for six or seven years at that point, I was a natural. Over the course of several months, I acquired other technical rescue courses including trench rescue awareness, water rescue and confined space rescue. I began attending the technical rescue team drills each week and took part in the evolutions, first as their "victim", but eventually even getting to ride in and then rappel out of the Maricopa County Sherriff's Office helicopter. If I thought I had a good handle on being a firefighter, I was getting a great handle on being a rescue tech. I had no idea at the time back then in 1994 that the groundwork for what would become one of my life's passions had been laid.

Part of being a reserve back then included getting hazed in a wide variety of ways by full-time firefighters. Reserves who showed vulnerability or made themselves easy targets always bore the brunt of it, and anything that came my way was mostly a way of showing respect, though I didn't understand that at the time. This happened much the same way a fourth-grade boy slugs a female classmate in the shoulder to show that they like them. It was also a way of injecting humor into the day between calls. Typically taking place in the evening, the most basic form of hazing always involved water. At station 10, as at several other stations, it was common practice for guys to sit out in front of the apparatus bay and smoke cigars when the Arizona weather cooperated. Conveniently, the layout of the bay at station 10 allowed easy access to the roof via a ladder. I'd always wondered what the rope hanging next to that ladder was for, but never found out until one night when I was invited to take part in the "code red" of another reserve. After a full-timer had climbed the ladder, he had me tie a mop bucket to the rope so he could haul it to the roof, where he filled it with a garden hose. The other reserve was invited to the front apron for a cigar. Surely he didn't recognize the fact that none of the others was sitting anywhere close until it was too late and seven gallons of water were dumped onto his head all at once. The crew erupted in laughter, as did the people in cars waiting for the light to change at the nearby intersection. Water pranks weren't always that involved, though. There was the one where a firefighter would follow someone into the bathroom and pretend to use the next urinal over, then from behind the divider, pull out a 20cc syringe and spray a stream of water onto the other guy's foot and say, "Oh, sorry dude." Or the week or two during one summer when stations were having water fights with each other regularly. One day heading back from drill, I couldn't understand why one of the guys in the back of the truck with me had brought the PW can[9] into the cab with us. We were heading up Hayden Road when we pulled up next to another truck going home. Our guy motioned for the back seat guys in the other truck to roll down their window and when they did, unloaded the contents of the extinguisher at them from the next lane over. Most all of these things were done in good fun, but things did get dangerous on occasion. I'd heard of a guy making a fireworks setup that looked like a bomb in another guy's locker. That gave me an idea that I'd hold onto for another year or so for just the right time to come.

It was always interesting to see what kind of day I'd have, based on what station and what shift I was working on. But I kept motivated and had a positive attitude regardless of whom I was working with. This was easy at the time because I always knew that I'd be working with a different crew the next time I showed up for duty.

There was just one Battalion Chief per shift for the entire city of Scottsdale when I started. Battalion Chiefs serve a supervisory role in day-to-day operations, and take on an Incident Command role during fires or larger medical incidents such as car accidents with extrication, TRT or HazMat[10] calls, etc. Soon after I came on, a second BC was added to each shift. Two of them really stand out in my memory. One was Chief Bryce, on B-shift. He promoted from Captain at station 10 downtown to the position, and I'd had a small run-in with him the year prior during a ride along before I'd gotten shift qualified. A dumpster fire call had come in and I ran out to Engine 10 and started putting my turnout gear on. The truck was only staffed with three full-time people during the day until a fourth came on in the evening after performing fire prevention duties. Three of us were in the truck waiting for Captain Bryce when the driver turned around and sent me back into the station to find him. As it so happened, I went in one door to the bay while he came out the other door at the same time at the other end of the station. Making a quick sweep and heading back to the truck, I climbed in and found him sitting in the right-front seat. As we pulled out of the bay, Bryce turned around and said, "You need to get on the ball a little better and get your shit together." The driver quickly said over the headset,

"I actually sent him inside to find YOU." There was silence for the rest of the call. What I didn't know at the time was that there was nearly a full-on mutiny going on with Bryce's crew, based upon his management style. He never said anything about mistakenly calling me out for not getting to the truck quickly, but it didn't matter much to me. What I did think was pretty great was the fact that a full-time firefighter had stood up for me and it felt awesome to feel like someone had my back. Bryce and I had a relationship of mutual respect for the rest of my career from what I gathered later on.

One of the other Battalion Chiefs was the legendary Fred Lighte. He stood (not very) tall in his position and had consistently high expectations of his crews and particularly of his engineers. In the Rural days, there was no formal engineer position, but the term was regularly used to describe whomever was in charge of driving the fire truck for the day. Chief Lighte worked on A-shift and would commonly call one or two stations first thing in the morning to respond to some location for pump drill. Typically, one or two firefighters would pull hose and start flowing water while the engineer would establish a supply of water from a hydrant and set the pump discharges to the correct pressures. There is an orchestra of tasks that go on behind the scenes of any fire operation, and Chief Lighte was the maestro. He demanded perfection and had a temper if he didn't get things done his way. I remember seeing grown men cry at the pump panel with him standing there yelling at them to set the correct pressures or establish a supply to the truck before the on-board water tank ran dry. The trick with him was to do everything perfectly at least once. From that point on, he'd always leave you alone. At some point I did just that, and he and I also had a mutually respectful relationship from then onward throughout my career. To this day, "Fred Lighte Drill" still means getting together with neighboring stations to flow water. To the untrained eye, this may just look like an opportunity for a supervisor to wield some power. But looking back on it now, pumping a fire for real never presented nearly as much stress as one of his drills. And meeting with neighboring units always fostered camaraderie and brotherhood in the ranks. That's usually not done enough in today's fire service.

There are a seemingly infinite number of shift structures used to staff fire departments. Back then Rural used an A-B shift, which alternated every day between two different crews. There was something called a "Kelly Day", which was one day of the week that you always had off. For example, if you had a Tuesday Kelly Day, you had every other Monday through Wednesday off and this yielded a 13-day working month. If you took a vacation day on Sunday or Thursday on the right week, you'd have five days in a row off. This was the first work schedule I'd be exposed to. Soon after I started working shifts, a "kicker" day was added, which effectively added that extra day once a month and provided one three-day period off followed by a five-day period two weeks later, for a total of 12 days on duty each month. Being a reserve, I had no set schedule but instead worked when called or when I was placed on the schedule ahead of time. Having full-time firefighters on kicker days was great because it meant more work for me. Remember, these were days before the Internet and what that meant for me was showing up at a station just before the first of the month and leafing through the paper schedule, which was delivered via interoffice mail. I'd write down all my shifts on my personal calendar and work any extra days in between that I could. It was hard to say "no" for two reasons; I'd be losing potential earnings and the scheduling chief didn't like having to make more calls every morning than necessary to fill open positions in the city. So I became one of the "yes men" who could be relied upon to work pretty much all the time. I regularly worked over 18 or even 20 days each month.

At about this time, I decided that the motorcycle-commuting thing was getting to be a bit much and started shopping for a car. I scoured the Auto Trader magazines available at gas stations for an International Scout, but couldn't find one. In the same section though, I saw a 1968 Toyota FJ40 Landcruiser that was within my limited budget. The owner lived in Scottsdale and I set up a time to check it out. It was a faded blue with a white top and the interior looked like a rat's nest, which matched the condition of the engine compartment wiring nicely. But it started right up and ran. During our conversation, it came up that I was a firefighter and the owner cut me a deal. $2,500 later, I was driving the old "'Cruiser" down the road back to my apartment. That $2,500 came from the sacrifice of my beloved Honda Nighthawk, but I knew that it just wasn't practical to own right now and made the difficult decision to sell it.

I had a limited set of tools and just a little auto mechanic experience at the time, but I was no stranger to spinning wrenches, as I'd done that plenty in my days working in bike shops over the years. Little by little I fixed that truck up and it became a reliable daily driver. I kept my turnout gear, uniforms and bedding in the back of it, ready for a shift or a reserve call-out. There were times when the interior of that truck smelled like a house fire, which I loved. That goes far from the currently accepted practice of strictly keeping dirty turnouts at the station and sending them out to be laundered commercially and never bringing contaminated duty uniforms home under any circumstances. My how times change, mostly for the better. The 'Cruiser was the first real 4x4 I ever owned, and it was quite capable off-road. I explored nearly all of the Sonoran desert in and around Scottsdale in it and it never let me down. Until one day the head gasket let go. I replaced it myself with instructions from the shop manual. But when the block finally cracked, it was time for a complete overhaul. It wasn't until a few years later that I decided I needed something safer for towing a trailer that I sadly and reluctantly sold it. I can still remember watching as the new owner drove her away, as I very nearly changed my mind just as it went out of sight behind station 19.

At this point I was working steady shifts, getting my life organized and acting like an adult on most days. Stability was coming.

Chapter 5
"Full-Time Follies"

———

ALTHOUGH ALREADY QUALIFIED as a firefighter, getting hired into a full time position with a fire department is the first massive step in a fire service career and requires another academy to do so. Thousands of people regularly show up just to get an application to try for one of the coveted positions in a fire department, and those thousands may be competing for only a dozen spots. But Rural had a different way of going about hiring full-time personnel, and did so almost exclusively from its pool of reserve Firefighters. This process usually takes a few tries before one is successful in getting a full-time position, and often a job opens up in a different city than the one you want to work in.

The first chance I'd get at a full-time spot in Scottsdale finally came in around late 1994. They were hiring about six people and there would be a few dozen interviewing. I failed to plan my interview well and should have sought help from the last graduating class of the academy in order to know what to expect when I sat in front of the interview board, which was made up of a firefighter, a battalion chief and a HR representative. It was clunky and worse, insincere. My closing statement was overconfident and came across as cocky, but I thought that's what they were looking for. After all, this was the fire service and we should be strong figures, right? I actually said in my closing statement that I was "technically and tactically proficient". I really think that saying those things, as a relatively inexperienced reserve was what blew the interview process for me that time. And I honestly felt like I was doing pretty well up until that point. Needless to say I didn't get hired for a full-time position on that go-around.

But the guys who played baseball with one BC did. And the guys who helped another BC build a patio on his house did also. I was discouraged by the process, but soldiered on. The "good old boy" network was pretty strong, but I preferred to let my work do the talking and that cost me more than once over the years when hiring or promotion opportunities happened.

The neighboring community of Fountain Hills was next to put on a full-time hiring process. They're only a few miles away over a small mountain pass, but were worlds away in terms of leadership and firefighter quality, and not in a good way. They contracted with Rural Metro also, but were governed by a fire board and thus much of the operation was seasoned with a healthy amount of politics. They had just one rescue unit, and when that truck transported a patient to the hospital, a Scottsdale rescue was placed on "move-up", sent to cover their area until they returned. One night while on move-up to Station 23 in Fountain Hills, I sat down at the computer desk in their office and right there in front of me was a written list of the upcoming interview questions. I ran a copy of it, put it in my pocket and scheduled an interview for a Fountain Hills position the following week. Most of the questions were general fire service oriented items, but there were two that no one in their right mind would ever think of to study. The first had something to do with the Town of Fountain Hills and the Fire Board, but the other was unimaginably specific. "What are the dimensions of the HazMat 704 diamond?" The 704 diamond is a placard that's placed on the exterior door of a building containing hazardous materials, advising firefighters of the type of hazards contained within. I knew the answer because I'd read it on the list. When the question showed up the next week in the interview and I said, "7 ¼" by 7 ¼", the oral board got a collective quizzical look on their faces. Clearly, the few Fountain Hills reserves that they wanted to hire had the interview answers. But I was an outsider and had just nailed their interview.

Three days later, I was asked to respond to admin for a meeting with two chiefs. One gave me a dose of intimidation, asking questions about how I had studied for the interview. He was a large, imposing figure in the department, but I had no respect for him as a leader or as a man because I'd seen how he treated his people with disrespect while kissing the ass of any figure in the department or Scottsdale leadership that could possibly advance his career. And I also didn't fear him because I'd surmised that he was a bit of an insecure coward, based on a few stories I'd heard in the stations. I handled his questions pretty easily. The other, who was a Scottsdale battalion chief, asked how and where I'd learned about the dimensions of a 704 diamond. This one was pretty on the nose and to the point. Thinking on my feet and without hesitation, one of my proudest moments followed. I replied, "I learned all about the 704 diamond and HazMat in general in the class you taught at SCC last semester, chief. Remember?" I'd turned the tables on two chiefs in just a moment and it felt great, despite the fact that I'd cheated on an interview and been suspected of it. On the other hand, I realized that there had been another overly specific question on the Scottsdale interview just a few weeks earlier and knew that the people hired had been handed the answers. I was dismissed and they went ahead and hired Fountain Hills reserves for all of the full time positions anyway. This was the second time I had experienced something I refer to as a "lock and key" interview process. The hiring board holds the lock and the keys are granted to the candidates they want. On it went, and it seemed a Scottsdale opportunity would never open up for me again unless I were to start swinging a bat or a hammer with the right group of guys.

The next hiring process went on for Rio Verde, another small community nearby which was also serviced by Rural Metro. Not knowing what would be on the interview this time, I crashed in a big way. They actually asked candidates to name all the fire board members in the town by first and last name. I had no idea, and no chance at getting hired. No matter, because taking a spot out there in Rio Verde would have spelled the end for any chance at excitement in the fire service due to the fact that they ran very few calls and even fewer fires. The keys weren't mine for that one either. I'd keep working shifts in Scottsdale and hope for another hiring process to present itself. But one thing was becoming clear. If I were willing to go to the extreme of cheating on an oral board, I was showing signs of desperation to get hired full-time.

I still attended reserve drills on Saturdays if I hadn't picked up a shift. One morning during a reserve drill, a mountain rescue call came in nearby. We all responded to the call as a group and found two kids in their late teens up on a mountain where they had hiked off-trail to smoke some pot and watch the sun come up. One was stuck on a ledge about 50' above the ground and the other was lying about 100' below, where he'd come to rest after falling off the cliff and rolling downhill a bit further. He was dead on the scene, so efforts were focused on getting the other kid down safely. My friend Gerry, also a rock climber, made access above the patient on the ledge and helped him to safety. Now it was time to recover the body, which was still on the mountain. But before we could move him, the police wanted pictures for their investigation. The officer was in no physical shape to climb up the mountain, so I volunteered to take her camera up with me and do the job because after all, I had photography experience and it was a hobby of mine. I hiked up and took pictures of the scene and the body. The sight of the boy's face is still readily visible in my mind. I'd never seen that sort of facial trauma before and it struck the 22 year old me in a way I hadn't expected. I handed the camera back to that officer and never talked to anyone about what I'd seen through the viewfinder that day. I'm writing these words 27 years later.

During my days as a reserve, I ran dozens of amazing calls that were exciting, scary, fun, funny and fulfilling in ways I couldn't even begin to understand at the time. Overturned vehicles, house fires, drownings, car-pedestrian accidents; you name it and I was knee-deep in it. And I loved every minute, because I was starting to practice my craft.

In December of 1996, another full-time interview process was held in Scottsdale. At this point, I'd been a reserve for almost three years and was working far more hours each week than even the full-time guys. I felt like a full-timer without the title or the pay and benefits, but I loved what I was doing more than ever. I went about the hiring process differently this time around. I sought advice from others and studied the proposed interview material feverishly. It was my goal to get hired without ill-gotten gain. And when the day came, I performed well. I answered the board's questions honestly and with sincerity. And then it came time for my closing statement. A closing statement allows the candidates a chance to wrap things up with the interview board and it's the one and only real chance you get to tell them what makes you different from all the other people who have been interviewed and why you deserve the job more than any of them. The movie "Backdraft" had just come out and I 'd watched it the night before. It's a cheesy Hollywood version of the fire service, but it was entertaining. If you ever watch the movie, notice how there's never any smoke in any of the interior fire scenes. I'm sure that's because they used gas-burning props, but it was also that way so that a viewer could see the actors. I made a reference to Kurt Russell's character being told by his wife that day or night, on-duty or off, he was always a firefighter. I told the board that that was how I felt now, always a firefighter. I also brought up living in Scottsdale and how I felt there was great value in living in the city that you protect. Without knowing, I'd made an impact on Captain Eric, who sat on the interview board. At the time, he lived about two blocks south of fire headquarters. That explained the enthusiastic nodding from him after I had made that statement. I finished second in that interview to my good friend Greg and our full-time academy began about a week later.

It was a rainy Monday when about twelve of us walked into the first classroom session of our full-time academy. And by "rainy", I mean that it was dumping rain and the roads and washes were flooded. We were missing one guy, Gil. What you need to know about Gil is that he'd been the whipping boy for senior firefighters in the department for years. A red-head of then slight stature and mousy disposition, Gil was frequently the target of station pranks and once was even taped to a spinal immobilization backboard and propped up in front of station 10 in south Scottsdale. Then there was the story I heard about him getting soaked with water, then doused with flour by the crew. These were all common hazing practices "back in the day" which would not only cost you your job now, but perhaps bear legal consequences as well. Once, Gil had gotten word that some senior guys were going to give him a "code red", which usually involved being soaked with water from the roof of the station or in some other creative way. That day, he hid in the city water pump station next to station 10 for over an hour as the story goes. Gil was late for the first day of our academy and when he walked in, the class leader, Captain Beech wasted no time in opening up on him. He told Gil to wait outside while we, as a class, decided his fate. It was hinted by the staff that he should not be permitted to continue. I felt for him and knew how important this was to all of us. I suggested to the group that Gil be required to write an essay about why he should be allowed to remain in the academy class. He agreed to do it and was invited back into the classroom to join us. The tension in the room was palpable. The day's first instructor, Chief Sachs arrived and talked first about turnout gear inspection. He knew I'd recently been issued another fresh turnout coat and asked if I'd inspected every stitch of every seam on it. He also asked the class if everyone had a pocketknife or a multi-tool with them. A few guys didn't have either and he said that he'd call each of them "Sally" until they did. With even more tension building in the room, Sachs turned a corner and asked if anyone spoke any Spanish. The guys knew I was fairly fluent, having worked in a Mexican restaurant for some time and sold me out right away, "Bucher does!" When asked to say something in Spanish by the chief, I didn't miss a beat. "Donde está el donkey show?" flowed freely from my mouth and with a pretty impressive accent if I do say so myself. Everyone in that room, including Chief Sachs erupted into laughter. The ice had been broken. But more importantly and unbeknownst to the others, I'd gained a boost in self-confidence that would last throughout the academy. I felt empowered somehow by making the group laugh and it was great to break up the tension that had been building in the room after the Gil situation.

The next months were filled with mornings of running and "P.T." or physical training, classroom time and "grinder drills" where we pulled hose, raised ladders and did all manner of firefighter tasks, plus learned the department's Standard Operating Procedures (S.O.P.s) intimately. And the injuries started to happen to the class. One morning after a long run, my buddy David was limping pretty heavily. I sat down next to him on a curb where he was taking off his shoes and socks. Full-length blisters on both feet were starting to lose their skin and he could barely walk. But he didn't complain, and didn't quit. This was the chance of a lifetime and he wasn't going to give it up. Another guy in my class had to ride a bike at the back of the group after a week of running had inflamed his knee so badly that he could barely walk either. Another of our guys wound up requiring surgery and was out for the remainder of the academy, later returning on crutches. We found a walker in a bus we were using to travel from the academy to training sites around the city and gave it to him as a gift. Seeing the toll all of these injuries took on us as a group and individually, I took on a bit of an informal leadership role during my academy and got great at making up cadences, or verbal call-and-response phrases during our class' morning runs to help the time and miles pass. I was able to think on my feet and use my quick whit to not only entertain everyone, but to make those long miles of suffering seemingly fly by.

"I don't know but I've been told"

"Jimmy Long is mighty old"

"Creakin' knees and achin' back"

"When we fail, he pulls our slack"

They just flowed like that, one after another and I loved doing it. But I hated running then and to this very day I still do. It's my belief that running is for people who don't have bikes, and that it should only be done if someone is chasing you!

After three years as a reserve, the full-time academy truly was just a technicality I had to go through along the path to a permanent position. I had been working full-time hours (or many more) for well over a year at that point and felt confident in my skills as a firefighter, so my attention during the academy shifted toward the position of engineer and the associated responsibilities. My thoughts were somehow drawn to those paramedics I saw at the yard during their fire academy. It's been said that you can make a firefighter into a medic, but not a medic into a firefighter and in general, I agree. My buddy Greg was one exception to this, as he was the only paramedic in our academy class. Everyone else was "just" an EMT. But Greg's fire skills were sharp from having been a reserve in a neighboring city for some time before he started working for Rural as a reserve in Scottsdale. He and I spent much of our time together during the academy and grew to be friends. Several people even said that we looked like brothers, being the same height and body type with the same facial features. Our close-cropped academy haircuts helped matters, too.

At the end of it all when graduation day finally came, I got the news. I had finished first in the academy class and would be assigned to station 15, home of the Technical Rescue Team (TRT). It was a dream come true and a position usually reserved for senior firefighters to bid on in the rare event that a spot opened up. I had been selected by the command staff to fill the position. It's extremely rare for a probationary firefighter to make the TRT team and I realized that there was a good chance I could spend the rest of my career doing technical rescue work if that's what I wanted. My hard work and all those classes and training I'd taken part in were paying off and I was extremely proud and excited to have the opportunity. Greg finished a close second in the academy, although I thought he'd done better in class and admired his knowledge and ability as a firefighter and as a paramedic. We shared the same sense of humor and quick whit, which got us into hot water more than once along the way. I later had the good fortune to be assigned to the same station with Greg for a period of time after paramedic school, which helped to shape me as a firefighter and as a paramedic for the rest of my career.

During our graduation ceremony we were sworn in and were pinned with our firefighter badge. It was a proud moment, for sure. While a slide show was shown, the Metallica song "Fuel" played. The lyric "Gimme fuel, gimme fire, gimme that which I desire", struck home with each of us. In that moment, we each were hungrier to practice our craft than ever before. We wanted the whole world to catch fire so we could be the ones to put it out. That desire to use one's training, to pull 200 feet of hose toward a smoky doorway, to hold your breath and listen carefully for the cries of someone trapped or to wait until you actually see fire before opening the nozzle are the skills we had. They're the skills that thousands of firefighters the world over had. And we had just joined their ranks. We were real, live, smoke-eating, dragon-slaying, ass-kicking firefighters with the training required to perform a very special job in a very demanding career. The only thing we lacked was the vital years of experience needed to round out the package and make us all of those aforementioned things, plus wise, compassionate and safe.

The real training was about to begin.

Chapter 6
"The Training Wheels Come Off"

STATION 15 WAS SLOW from a fire and EMS standpoint, but we had more than our fair share of TRT calls. At that time, our station handled not only the technical rescue response for Scottsdale, but also for a large portion of Maricopa County because Rural/Metro was the fire department coverage in all unincorporated county areas. There were mountains, lakes, rivers and all manner of urban hazards. I worked with Leif, Scott, Mack and our Captain, Jim Loper. Unknown to me at the time, I would go on to work with Jim more than any other person in the fire department throughout my career. We were together for over 17 years and he was the leader of the TRT team in Scottsdale for that entire time. He'd actually been one of the first firefighters in Arizona to go through formal technical rescue training and was known as one of the godfathers of TRT. Hundreds of firefighters got their initial rope training from him during State Fire School sessions held every September and I learned an immeasurable amount from him during our time together. Our station housed a three-man engine company, a two-man rescue and the TRT truck, which was responded by one firefighter from either the engine or rescue when a call required it. Unfortunately, I worked primarily on the rescue for much of that first year as a "booter", or probationary firefighter. The name "booter" comes from a tradition of probationary firefighters at least once polishing everyone else's boots in the station. I actually went to polish Jim's boots one day and he said, "Don't ever do that." I think I'd learned lesson number one that day. Jim was a laid-back leader. He expected his crew to know their jobs and do them well, but he was secure enough in his position that he didn't feel the need to flaunt his captain's rank. Hell, Jim worked his first shift as a firefighter when I was two years old. It wasn't that he didn't want me to polish his boots. I feel like it was a desire to have me think more of myself than to feel like I had to stoop to that level of service, as I'd perhaps already proven my worth to him over a few years of technical rescue training and showing up when needed. In the fire service, there's a distinct difference between kissing ass and busting ass. A senior firefighter actually wrote it out for booters to pass on over the years. Essentially, it means letting your work speak for itself. Instead of telling the captain you had just finished washing the truck, you let him notice for himself the wet concrete beneath a sparkling rig sitting out on the front apron of the station, with tires so slick and shiny they looked like mirrors; never mind the bright aluminum 22.5" wheels they were wrapped around. I was an expert at busting ass and staying busy, even at a relatively slow station. Everything was always clean and in its place, which played well with Jim's obsessiveness. He insisted on order, and his crews gave it to him over the years and saw value in finding things where they were expected to be, not only in the station but on emergency scenes as well.

Along with working on the rescue came those move-up assignments into the areas of other stations while they were on calls. That little hellhole called Fountain Hills required endless move-ups over the years, and I've covered more mileage back and forth on Shea Boulevard in Scottsdale than probably anyone but the mailman. But once in a while, we'd get a call out on the Beeline Highway, north of town while on move-up. Those calls were almost always motor vehicle accidents. And they were always gnarly. I'm talking about long responses, sometimes over 30 miles from our station. There were even times that we responded outside of the range of our radios, with no way to call for help if we needed it. It was serious cowboy shit out there in the Arizona desert. And back then, that's

what I loved doing. The worse the call was, the better. T
I could do and see, the more I could learn. I was thirsty
and experience, but what I didn't know or understand at
was the fact that nobody in the department knew or care
about the calls I was running or the trauma I was expose
one of any consequence had any idea unless I told them.
may have been where my habit of busting ass cost me a little
experience did serve me well, but it also carried a price tha
just recently begun to pay.

Arizona's summer and winter are punctuated by two rain
The "monsoon" season happens in the mid to late sumn
characterized by heavy afternoon thunderstorms which co
quickly, sometimes leaving flooded streets and raging whi
normally-dry washes behind. The winter season has longer
rain, commonly lasting for days on end. We were several
winter rain one night when a water rescue call came in n
Valley toward Payson in a creek near a tiny area called Sun
call was at least 35 miles from station 15, up the Beeline H
beyond Fountain Hills. We scrambled out to the apparat
and Mack got into the Engine, Scott and I got into the
Leif got into our support truck, a 70's era Ford which wa
leg. The hulking white truck wouldn't start, and if anyon
that thing running it was Leif. He tried for a long minute
had no luck. Jim made the decision to move some water
from the support truck to the engine and within about
minutes, the engine and rescue were underway. It wa
pouring rain all the way out Shea to the Beeline. We tu
and it didn't let up. Visibility in front of Rescue 15 wa
100'. Then the wind started howling. Barely able to se
in front of us, I thought I saw something hanging off
the truck. My suspicion was confirmed when Scott pi
radio microphone and said, "Engine 15, you're laying lin

actually being blown off the top of the truck. Mack immediately stopped and we all jumped out to put a couple hundred feet of 4" supply hose back on the top of the engine where it sits in a bed. We'd sustained another five-minute delay, and once moving again, were only able to travel at about 30mph in the greatly reduced visibility. And we'd all gotten soaked in the process. After about forty minutes responding, we arrived at a creek crossing I'd driven by a dozen times in the past when heading up to the Arizona high country to camp or enjoy the mountains. The normally dry creek was a raging torrent, with a white, full-sized van sitting ten feet or so from the closest bank and a Jeep Wrangler parked on dry ground in front of it with a tow

strap attached between it and the van. The "Attack Truck[11]" from Fountain Hills was parked along the road about 100' downstream of the incident and we pulled in behind it. The Jeep belonged to an off-duty Sherriff's Deputy who had arrived first and tried to secure the van. What I couldn't understand was if the water was low enough when he got there to attach a tow strap, why he didn't have the six people occupying the van walk to the shore, or even put the Jeep in 4-low and pull them out in one complete package. As I got out of Rescue 15 and walked toward the engine to get a helmet, life vest and throw bag[12], I faintly saw six people sitting on top of the van, with a very strong current of water around it. While putting on my PFD[13] and helmet, I heard screams and turned, just in time to see the van tipping over and people falling into the raging floodwater. I grabbed a throw bag and began a full sprint toward the bank slightly downstream, where I thought I'd have a chance at intercepting the victims. It was raining. It was dark. And I couldn't see the chest-high barbed wire fence that I sprinted into at full speed. Just as I realized what had happened and pushed myself off of the fence, Mack ran into me from behind also at full-speed, pushing me hard into the fence again. Undeterred, we hopped the fence and

continued to the water, probably 100 yards from the engine now. We pulled an adult male and a juvenile male from the water, and then continued to search for the rest. Another male made it out of the water with assistance just upstream from us. Our crew continued to search for the others. Someone brought flashlights down. As I searched as far as ¼ mile downstream, the speed of the raindrops, illuminated by my orange box flashlight, began to slow down for some reason. They'd slowed because it wasn't raining anymore. It had begun snowing. But we kept searching for the other three victims. I was shivering and soaked. It had been at least 30 minutes since the van tipped over and there was little hope left for finding anyone alive in these conditions. I slowly walked the riverbank back up to Rescue 15 to find two battalion chiefs waiting nearby. Chief Bryce looked at me and said, "Bucher, your lips are blue. Get warm and dry in the back of the rescue." I'd stopped shivering at this point because I was hypothermic. A few hours later, we drove back to the station, leaving a few crews on scene to finish the search. I remember nothing at all about that drive home. It would seem I was numb in more than just one way that night. In the morning, we got the news. We'd rescued the only survivors. Two boy scouts and a scout leader were found lifeless in the flooded creek sometime after sunrise when the floodwater began to recede.

During our response to the call, Jim had called for air support from Arizona Department of Public Safety (DPS) and Maricopa County Sherriff's Office (MCSO) helicopters, which initially wound up grounded due to the low visibility. Having aerial illumination and an elevated view may have made the difference that night, but everyone involved was too late. The Chief Pilot for MCSO, a Vietnam veteran with tens of thousands of helicopter flight hours to his credit, decided to make a go of it. The visibility was so poor that for several miles, he was forced to fly just above the pavement of the Beeline Highway to navigate to the call, flying over cars as he came to them.

It finally got so bad that he was forced to land on the highway, wait out the storm, and then head back to the airport where the helicopter was based.

News crews came to Station 15 the next shift for interviews. I saw the footage a few years ago (over twenty years after the incident) and my face told a story of immense sorrow and grief, as well as guilt. For years after that call and to some extent even today, I question why the support truck didn't start that night, why the supply hose had fallen off of the truck, why the Sherriff's Deputy and Fountain Hills crew hadn't gotten the people off of the van, and why that damn fence was in the way. Saving "just" three people wasn't much consolation and no one ever debriefed our crew. I guess we all dealt with it in our own ways, but certainly none were healthy. And none of us spoke very much about that call afterward. That stormy Arizona night put the first crack in my armor as a firefighter. It was the worst thing I'd experienced on duty at that point and truly one of the worst thing's I'd been involved with in my life. I never felt any form of closure afterward. I remember it like it was yesterday even now, decades later. One thing was for sure, and that's the fact that the training wheels had definitely come off. I was a real-deal no bullshit firefighter and rescue worker. I had the training and was getting the experience. I was also just 23 years old.

That call ignited a fire in me to be one thing and one thing only: Better. I wanted to be the best Rescue Tech the world had ever seen from that point forward. I wanted to further master being a firefighter, and I never wanted to lose another patient when there was even the most remote of chances at a successful rescue. It also ignited something new in me: The desire to become a Paramedic.

Chapter 7
"A Higher Calling"

THINGS CONTINUED ON during my probationary year just fine. I kept very busy and was the first in my academy class to finish my probationary packet, which reviewed the entire SOP book and Rural/Metro policies and procedures. While working on the computer, I found a program that taught me how to type. I'd had a typing class in high school, but was of course too distracted by more entertaining things and had no outlet after that to keep my skills up. I was steadily trying to increase my life skills in any way I could find.

Technical rescue drills now included work with the Maricopa County Sheriff's Office helicopter, "Fox 1". We used Fox to "insert", or fly rescue crews into remote areas for patient treatment and evacuation. The ability to make quicker access to isolated areas by not hiking in with equipment on our backs made the difference between a good outcome and something worse more than a few times over my career, but the true value of helicopters was only beginning to be understood by senior fire department leadership. Their use even met resistance for several years until the fire department command staff came to understand that the TRT guys weren't just using them for their own enjoyment. As time went on and as the skills required to pull off effective helicopter rescues became more clear, it was obvious that this would be one of the technical rescue "niches" that I'd be most involved with. Helicopters had been used in very rare circumstances to perform rescue operations as early as the 1940's, but it wasn't until after the Vietnam War ended that helicopters began to be used frequently in the civilian arena. Municipalities throughout the country were using helicopters as effective tools in police work, with a few fire departments using those same platforms for rescue and even wildland firefighting operations.

We flew search and rescue calls all over eastern Maricopa County and did demos at public education events and fire academy classes. I took to it well with my comfort at heights (a result of years of rock climbing), and found it relatively easy to keep a cool head under the pressure, noise and constant danger of spinning rotor blades. I didn't realize at the time how many hours of helicopter training and mission time I'd get to do over the course of my career and how it would shape who I would become as a firefighter and rescue tech. Unfortunately, the key players in the helicopter game at that time and now were paramedics. Their qualification to treat critical patients made them more desirable and helpful than EMT's when there was a choice as to who could fly into a remote emergency situation. Simply put, I was playing second string on the team due to my medical capabilities or lack thereof. Unfortunately, in order to attend paramedic school, I would have to transfer out of my special operations assignment in order to "reduce distractions" for a year and station 28 in Paradise Valley would become my temporary home. It was costly, but a price I would have to pay in order to play the game at a higher level in the future.

Rural/Metro announced an upcoming paramedic class, and three friends of mine held interviews at headquarters for the 20 open spots. One of my partners at the time, Leif, asked why I wanted to be a paramedic. He'd been one for several years at that point after a start very early on in his own fire service career. I told him it was partly for the money and partly to be able to do more work on calls. After a small argument, I internally agreed with him that I should eliminate the monetary motivation and go after this with a higher purpose. He was absolutely right about the fact that being a medic would eventually mean the difference between life and death for a greater number of people than I could have ever imagined back then. When it came to a planned closing statement for the interview, the main thing I wanted to get across was the fact that I wanted to be able to do and contribute much more on EMS scenes than what I was currently capable of as "just" an EMT. When my turn to interview came around, I calmly answered the board's questions and completed two basic skills stations with ease. In fact, during the interview I was so at ease as to ask the board what the paperclip, pen and thumbtack were sitting on the table in front of me for. Chaz, one of my friends, answered that those things were placed there just to see if anyone would fiddle nervously with them or ask about them. It turned out I was the only one who'd asked. And I was accepted into the upcoming class.

There were prerequisite classes announced, so I took Cardiology and Pharmacology in the same semester at SCC. Two more A's went on my steadily growing transcript and medic school started shortly thereafter. There were around 24 of us at the start, mostly firefighters, with some EMT's from one of Rural's sister companies, Southwest Ambulance also attending. The class was horribly inconsistent because there were several changes to the lead instructor position. The first, my friend Chaz, was a medic I looked up to and had worked shifts with. He transferred to another Rural operation in Texas just a month or so into our class. The next lead instructor role was filled temporarily by a forgettable woman who had only a seemingly small amount of teaching experience in a different operation somewhere in the country. Once she'd had enough of us, Gene Bell and Sam Little, two Scottsdale paramedics, shared the lead instructor role. Gene was the firefighter with the legendary moustache from the back of Engine 10 at the fiberglass fire that night of my first interior firefight. Things went well for a few months until Sam seemed to develop a personal vendetta against me and tried to see to it that I was removed from the program.

During medic school, I was assigned to work with a very seasoned medic named Mason Richards. I looked forward to learning from him, and knew him through our mutual involvement in wildland. During one of my normal shifts on Rescue 28, my partner Mason asked if I wanted to patch while we were on a medical call. A "patch" is simply the act of establishing online medical direction from a receiving hospital, and more often than not only required someone to tell the nurse on the other end of the radio what we were coming in with. If needed, medics could ask for orders for medicines or treatments from an attending doctor over the phone or a radio. The patient I was patching on was nothing special, and no orders were needed. All I had done was establish the communication link and advise the receiving hospital of the patient's status and our ETA[14]. During medic school, it was explicitly stated that we were not to practice any ALS[15] or paramedic skill while we were on shift and not supervised by an instructor. Sam got wind that I had patched on a patient while on shift and completely lost his mind. He claimed that I'd practiced an ALS skill while on shift and began campaigning to have me removed from the paramedic-training program. We almost came to blows when he started yelling at me in front of the class about the topic. I stood up and said I thought we should talk about this outside and he jumped at the chance. Two other instructors followed us out and kept us separated while the profanity flowed freely. We stood in the parking lot in an exchange that lasted about five minutes, during which time I found myself focusing on an area of his neck I planned to punch should he come at me first.

When we each had calmed down, we returned to the classroom, which faced the parking lot. Most of the class was still pressed up against the windows trying to see what was going on.

This became my first experience using a union representative for assistance during an incident, and after several interviews and an investigation more befitting a murder case than using a radio, it came to a conclusion. At the end of it, I remained in class but Sam persisted behind the scenes for a few weeks. I was found to be free of any wrongdoing, as patching is something performed by EMTs all over the country every day, proving that it was not an ALS skill. I was right and I stood up for myself because a major step forward in my career had been put at stake. Medic school is hard enough on its own, but being distracted by a seemingly bi-polar fire captain as your instructor presented an unnecessary added amount of stress. My nickname for the remainder of medic school became "Patch."

We did hospital clinical rotations, where we had shifts in Emergency Rooms, Labor and Delivery, Cardiac Cath Lab, and Med-Surgery. We had cadaver labs, where we dissected human cadavers in order to learn more about human anatomy and physiology. I actually got to cut the heart out of a cadaver, then dissect it in front of the class. From that point on, I had an extremely good grasp of why the heart does what it does from both electrical and mechanical points of view. There were vehicular rotations, where we were put into the paramedic role under the supervision of either our instructors or approved field paramedics. During those vehicular rotations, team leadership began to play a part in our functions, and we learned how to document all of the patient information and treatments via handwritten charts. Practical skills testing occurred nearly every class session and gradually increased in intensity and difficulty. And of course, there were tons of written exams.

The pressure was immense, and unlike some paramedic programs, I had to go back to work after class each day and run calls. It was hellish, but also very valuable when I saw things taught in class applied in the real world just hours later. I was part of a study group comprised of the top players in class. We had study sessions, which regularly turned into drinking games and had a great time working our way through it all. Bryan, one of the members of the group even went on to make Assistant Chief in the department years later. It was always hard to take him seriously in the chief's role after having shared days and nights of debauchery with him during class! I finished second in medic school and placed a uniform order for new duty shirts with the white "Arizona Certified Emergency Paramedic" patch on the right shoulder. (I can remember that it was on the right shoulder because medics always believe they're right!) One final thing stood between me and the freedom to practice as a paramedic in Scottsdale and that was precepting. Precepting with an experienced paramedic was the final stepping-stone before the department would staff a position with a new paramedic and still serves as the final opportunity for someone to say, "Yay" or "Nay" regarding turning a student loose on the general public with needles, drugs and a defibrillator.

Soon I'd be able to do more on every call I'd ever run again. Soon I'd be responsible for patient care and transport. Soon I'd be filling a position I'd envied ever since watching Johnny and Roy on "Emergency!" on TV as a kid in the seventies. And soon the way I thought about life and death would gradually begin its irreversible and inevitable change. There is a definite parallel that can be drawn between new firefighters wanting the world to catch fire so they can put it out or rescue techs wanting to practice the craft. The same thing happens with new medics; except they want the world to drop dead so they can bring it back to life. What I thought I wanted was exactly what I would get.

Chapter 8

"Ready or not?"

———

JUST AS MEDIC SCHOOL had ended so had my time at station 28 in Paradise Valley. It was for the best, as the one thing other than good guidance that a new paramedic needs is plenty of calls to put their newfound skills and knowledge to use, solidifying theory into practice. Station 10 at Miller and Thomas in south Scottsdale fit the bill and had a paramedic vacancy with my name on it. Station 10 was far and away the busiest station in the city and the reputation it had earned during my reserve firefighter days continued on when I transferred there as a full-time guy. Returning to station 19 and the Technical Rescue Team would have to wait; I had new skills to concentrate on.

Over the years since it had been built, station 10 had undergone a significant evolution. In the early days, it actually played home to the "Alarm Room" for the city. Before the days of calling "911" for an emergency, residents actually called the fire department directly. Those calls were answered in a closet-sized room in the front of station 10 until a larger dispatch center was built at headquarters in the mid to late '80s. A large variety of vehicles were quartered at the station over the years also. Everything from normal fire engines, ladder trucks and ambulances spent time in the four bays there over the years. Curiously, the first thing resembling a TRT truck spent some time there as well. One day while in the bay at station 10, I noticed that there were a few small pulleys mounted on the rafters above my head. I asked a few of the guys what they were for, but no one knew. Finally, one of them said, "Let's ask John, he knows everything." The "John" they were talking about was Captain John, the officer who'd hired me as a reserve just a few years prior. He came out into the bay, looked up and said, "Oh yeah, those were put in by the angle dangle guys. They used to store a boat up there and lower it down onto the top of the rescue truck when there was a water rescue." He'd affectionately referred to TRT as the "angle dangle" guys in a play on their high-angle rescue capabilities.

During my days at station 10, there was a three-man engine (four after dark), a two-man squad truck, a two-man pumper truck, two rescues and a battalion chief. Yes, that's a total of thirteen people. And no, there wasn't enough room for everyone to sit in any one room together at the same time, other than during dinner when an extra table and chairs were set up in the kitchen. Imagine being the booter there and having to clean up after all those animals! Fortunately there was almost always someone newer than me filling in a vacancy on any given day.

Here's perhaps the craziest thing about the staffing at station 10 when I was there. There was only one company officer assigned to the entire station. Other than the battalion chief, who had his own SUV to drive around, there was only one man in charge of eleven subordinates in the station. It was of course a total zoo and I seem to recall the average age in the station being late-20's to early 30's. I was assigned to A-shift there, and the Captain was none other than Captain Eric.

Looking back on those days now, I know that Eric had to have people he could count on because there was no way he could keep eyes on everything all at once. After all, the widely acknowledged limit to effective span of control is seven things at one time. It looked to many as though he played favorites, but such wasn't necessarily the case. I later began to realize that I very well might have been one of Eric's favorites, particularly after that day in the middle of the circle at the training yard.

As I was there primarily to precept as a new medic, I'd be spending most of my time on a rescue with Ben Jeffson, a salty, soft-spoken paramedic with tons of experience and a sterling sense of humor. He trusted me right away with our patients and I can't remember ever having a call with him that went poorly. He exuded the type of quiet confidence that I not only admired, but also strove to embody immediately. Ben was one of Eric's trusted engine drivers, and having to precept me meant he'd be taken away from his engine shifts to babysit me. But he did so without complaint and I definitely appreciated it. My job was to see as many patients as possible, essentially doing continuous, repetitive tasks in order to make them become second nature until I could be turned loose to work on my own without paramedic supervision.

Transporting patients was the primary role of rescues and we did plenty of it. Most of the time we'd run EMS calls with the two guys on the squad truck and transport to the nearest hospital, Scottsdale Memorial Osborn. But our unfortunate side-job was something called a "general transport". "GT's" as they were known were the thing Rescue crews detested the most, as they were non-emergency transports of patients between medical facilities who were not well enough to go by private vehicle or by taxi. (Remember my first ATS shifts?) Rural/Metro made hundreds of dollars on each of these runs, but what they also did was took us out of the role of emergency care, which was demeaning to every firefighter who was ever dispatched on one. It was not uncommon for each rescue at station 10 to run 12-14 transports in a 24-hour period. Seeing how each one took up to an hour, it's obvious what the term "stand-up 24" means. I actually had shifts where I never put the sheets on my bunk, but just laid there in my uniform for a few minutes until the next call came.

The two rescues had been relocated from station 7 to station 10 at about the time I'd been hired full-time. At their prior home, they were known as Rescue 7 and Medic 7 and were each staffed with one firefighter and one paramedic. On A-shift, Medic 7 had a lieutenant paramedic named Ron Benly. I remember working our first shift together when I was still a reserve and getting an EMS call somewhere up Hayden Road. As we pulled out of the station, a Madonna song came on. I could just barely hear it under the wail of the siren as I drove through traffic. Suddenly, Ron cranked up the music, looked over at me and laughed saying,

"You DO like Madonna, don't you?"

Chuckling, I admitted, "Hell yes I do!"

We've been friends ever since.

One other memory I have of a day at station 7 was the morning of October 9, 1995 when an Amtrak train was derailed by saboteurs in the desert about 40 miles west of town. A call had come in, telling us to stand by for an out-of-town dispatch. Miraculously, there had been only one fatality but there were nearly 100 people with injuries. The unit I was on did not respond, but the other rescue at the station did. My original medic school instructor, Chaz Tucker was on that unit. In retrospect, I'm glad I didn't have to experience a medical incident that big, but at the time I was not only eager to go but disappointed when passed over. A funny thing I remember when driving to a call one shift with Chaz was that he smoked cigarettes nearly all day. Every rescue carried oxygen for patient treatment, and had a silver sticker with red text on the dash stating, "NO SMOKING". Once, while heading to a call, Chaz put his foot up on the sticker, lit up a cigarette and looked over at me.

"What do you think about that?

"Fine with me", I said.

"Cool. Drive faster, this one sounds serious!"

After several weeks under the tutelage of Ben at station 10, I was approved to work alone as a paramedic. It's both thrilling and horrifying to be released "on your own" for the first time as a medic. Not only was I expected to handle patient care and documentation but I'd also be the de facto company officer of any rescue I worked on, in charge of an EMT below me in "rank". I drew on the four years of experience I had at that point working with a wide variety of medics, most of whom impressed me, but also with a few who were disappointing. It was the disappointing ones who unknowingly taught me the biggest lessons and helped mold what I would avoid in my own practice moving forward.

Station 10 remained my official station assignment for the foreseeable future because I'd given up my TRT spot at station 19 when I began paramedic training. That was a big sacrifice, but I needed the training if I was ever going to be the "go-to" guy some day when I returned to the team. Being one of the city's newest paramedics meant that I'd be moved once in a while to other stations when a paramedic spot needed filling due to someone being off for a shift here or there. Fortunately, the scheduling chief kept me in the south part of the city at station 10 or the next one north, station 11 on McDonald Drive. Given the choice, I'd always rather work at 11 than at 10. Both stations were in equal disrepair and none of the eight total apparatus between the two were in what

I'd even call decent condition. But it was the crew that made all the difference, and the leadership in particular. The captain at 11 was a hulk of a man named Jerry Peters. With a reputation as an opinionated, outspoken hard-ass, he and I got along well right away. I again allowed my job performance to speak for itself, kept my head down and stayed out of trouble. In return, I was given some additional responsibility when I worked at station 11, which was staffed by seven people on three apparatus: Two on Rescue 11, two on Engine 11 and three on Ladder 11. The rescue was the same as all others, a box-style ambulance. The engine was another old Ford like the squad and pumper trucks at station 10 and was only staffed with two firefighters, one of whom was a paramedic and the ladder had only three people. One was a captain and the other two were firefighters. At least one of the three had to be a paramedic. Because of the nature of Rural Metro's staffing, firefighters were commonly thrust into de-facto captain's roles and one such spot was the right-seat of Engine 11. Looking back now, it was an absurdly unsafe setup. But like many things, when you're in it, things feel different. Typically, when there was a medic working at the station who wasn't permanently assigned there, it meant a shift on the rescue. But the way things worked out when I was at 11, I did get to work on the engine a fair amount. This was sometimes due to two assigned medics being off, but would also happen here and there when one of the regular guys wanted to get out and run calls on the rescue or was just trying to stay away from Jerry. I worked some of my engine shifts driving the truck and others in the right seat, providing routing, talking on the radio and trying to act as a captain would. It fit me much better than working on the rescue, and I reveled in the chance to feel more like a firefighter than an ambulance jockey.

So back and forth between 10 and 11 I went, most of the time knowing where I'd be working the next shift, but sometimes not. Those last-minute mornings where I'd find out I'd been moved to

Station 11 were stressful, as there were actually times that I'd find out I needed to move only after I'd begun the morning equipment check on one of the units at station 10! I guess it'd be similar to making someone drive a different car to a different job location at the last minute. Sure your job may be the same, but everything else is different. And that's tough to deal with sometimes because not being able to find a vital piece of equipment on an unfamiliar truck could have dire consequences.

When I was at 10, I had the good fortune of working with Greg Heddy, one of my academy brothers. Greg grew up in station 10's first-due area and knew it like the back of his hand. This, along with being a very skilled firefighter/paramedic, meant that he got the driver's seat of Engine 10 frequently. It also meant that we didn't get to work on the same truck very often. But we did wind up on some of the biggest, most memorable fires in the city during that time. Greg was one of those guys who were always ready to help new firefighters who came up through the ranks behind us and I always admired him for his patience, sense of humor and undeniable, unshakeable bravery. Many times, Greg would wind up in some type of a clash with Ron, our administrative EMS Captain at the time. He's the same Ron who loved Madonna, and had taken the department's administrative EMS Captain position along with a pay raise recently. Any time there was some type of trouble with or a complaint from a patient or a member of another agency or hospital, it was Ron who had the unenviable job of playing "bad cop" and tracking down the issue. Greg and I found ourselves on the other end of the phone with Ron frequently enough that after a while, Ron would just say, "Hey, it's me." when he'd call either of us. Somehow, it seemed to draw me closer to Ron, as I understood that he'd stood up for me on at least one occasion and actually helped keep me out of trouble instead of falling deeper into it if there was an issue with someone outside of our department.

As much as Greg and I pushed the limits of what the rules and regulations would allow, we really did both want what was best for the public and our patients. One day, when we were each assigned to the rescue units at 10, something pretty funny happened. Each of our units was dispatched to a nearby nursing home to transport two non-emergency patients to the hospital. Mine was on a ventilator machine and would have to be manually ventilated with a bag-valve-mask (BVM) for the entirety of the transport. In his room, the nurse had disconnected the ventilator from the man and I took over squeezing the bag device to breathe for him. He was conscious, with his eyes open and fully aware of what was going on around him. Clearly, he didn't care for either the rate or depth of ventilation I was giving him or probably both. Improvising, I asked him if he wanted to bag himself. As he shook his head yes, I looked to the nurse, who with shrugged shoulders said to give it a try. The unorthodox idea worked perfectly! Just after wheeling him out into the hallway and beginning our walk out to the rescue, Greg rounded the corner on his way to pick up a different patient on the same floor. He couldn't control his laughter when he saw what I had going on and high-fived me enthusiastically as our gurneys passed one another in the hallway. I'm pretty sure he shared that story at the dinner table that night and for some time thereafter. It remained one of the funniest things I'd ever done on the job.

I missed Greg when he took a position with the fire department in neighboring Mesa, Arizona about a year or two later and we fell out of touch. It shocked me to the core years later in August of 2018 when I learned that he'd taken his own life. Most unnerving was the fact that a person I'd seen as one of the most confident, knowledgeable and courageous figures I'd encountered had done such a thing. I mean, this guy really seemed to have his shit together. I guess we truly don't know what's happening in the lives of others unless they share what's going on. Greg's funeral was such a sad experience for everyone in uniform that day because I'm sure at one time or another, every one of us had some of the same thoughts going through our heads that he'd probably been having. It took a long time for me to come to grips with that and to begin understanding the effect that years in the fire service can have on a person. It was haunting. If this could happen to Greg...

Chapter 9

"Back to Normal?"

IN EARLY 1999, A CAPTAIN'S position opened up in one of Rural Metro's western Maricopa County stations. What that meant to me was that I'd be going back to my TRT position and here's how. When I'd left station 15, a firefighter named Gerry had bid into the open position I created. In the meantime, the TRT resources had been moved from station 15 down the street to station 19. Yes, this was the same station I'd walked into a few years earlier when I was looking for a job. Gerry was on the Captain's promotional list and took the county position as an officer, which meant an opening back at TRT with my old crew and a few changes. I took the spot and would remain assigned to station 19 for the next 13 years. It was a homecoming of sorts for me to be assigned as a full-time firefighter to the station I was based out of as a reserve, and was attractive due to the fact that I had essentially no chance of ever having to move anywhere else due to some sort of random circumstances. Although I wasn't still living in the same neighborhood, I was still close enough to ride my bike to work. Riding to work was a habit that would continue, for the most part, for the rest of my career. The station's new location was mostly a tactical move for the department, as it took the technical rescue team out of the direct line of fire from Fountain Hills move-ups. At least it did so for the engine. Rescue 19 was still first in line to cover our neighbors when their rescue was tied up on a transport to the hospital. I was about to enter the world of fire department special operations for a long, long time.

The station itself had a bit of a unique layout compared to others of its time in that it was a tri-level, with one large bunkroom in the basement. The bunks were separated by shoulder-high walls and measured roughly 7' x 10'. Each bunk had a twin bed and a nightstand, and perhaps a TV if someone had added it on their own. Rural Metro added no real creature comforts to the city-owned stations and only provided the most basic furnishings required in the form of twin beds and living room and office furniture. The rest was always brought in by the firefighters stationed there. The middle level of the station was at ground-height, with three apparatus bays, several offices and a large room which originally housed Fire Prevention personnel, then EMS supplies and finally, a gym over the years. All of those changes were made, and in some cases, funded by firefighters. Odd story: The gym equipment we had was actually donated by the widow of a patient of ours who didn't make it after intentionally setting himself on fire. She wanted the equipment gone and said it was ours for the taking. Upstairs at station 19, there was a day room with recliners and a TV, a large table with chairs for meals and meetings, the kitchen and one more office. One large room upstairs served as an alternate dining area, but at times played host to a ping pong table and in the station's golden age, it actually had full sized craps and blackjack tables from real Las Vegas casinos. Those were brought in by one of the guys who ran a charity gambling gig on the side, Doug. He had lots of gaming equipment and rented it out for charitable events and fundraisers, along with dealers who were mostly all firefighters. Guess where some of them learned how to deal...

Overall, the station was not in the greatest condition, with many unpainted drywall repairs here and there, vestiges of rowdy arguments between crew members during a time before such antics would see people losing their jobs. One interesting appliance in place on each of the three floors was a 2'x2' metal box with vents in and out of it attached to the ceilings. These were "smoke eaters", designed to filter the cigarette smoke from the air inside the station during the early 80's, shortly after the station had been built and in a time before tobacco use was prohibited by our employer.

A couple years after the station change, we got approval for a new support truck for our TRT equipment. Think of it as a giant rolling toolbox filled with everything required for performing technical rescues of all sorts. Replacement of the old truck was influenced not only by the fact that it was produced in 1974, but also by it having a u-joint fail on the freeway one day when my partner Leif was driving it to a public-safety demo on State Route 101. When the component failed, the entire 7' long steel drive shaft was ejected from the underside of the truck, narrowly missing several cars. This was the same truck that wouldn't start on the rainy night of the Sunflower Boy Scout incident. Good riddance.

When the new truck showed up, we configured all the gear we had into compartments arranged by discipline. All the trench rescue lumber was in the back, water rescue gear was front-left, structure collapse was rear left, rope rescue gear mid-right and trench rescue hardware and shoring was right rear. The top of the truck had storage as well, with four "coffin"-type diamond plate boxes housing overflow items from each of the lower compartments. The layout allowed us to go to just one place for all the essential gear required for a particular type of call. I took things further over the years by labeling shelves and where possible, storing gear in a pre-assembled, ready state.

An example of this pre-rigging was the confined space communication set, which allowed hands-free communication capability between members of a rescue crew and the operator on the outside of the space. All the cables were pre-connected, batteries were in place and control boxes were attached. All this was custom-fit into a Pelican hard plastic case with foam cut outs. The goal was to make it efficient, but I wanted it to look kick-ass and professional as well. My shift took the lead with putting new gear in service because our Captain, Jim, did all the ordering of TRT equipment.

The support truck had all manner of specialized gear on it and I mastered the use of all of it over the years. Every time we either trained or ran a call, I would reevaluate the efficiency of our equipment storage and sought ways to improve our operation in both speed and safety. Looking back on it now, I know that losing those three boy scouts that cold night in Sycamore Creek made me never want to sacrifice a single second when someone's life was on the line ever again. The knowledge that no matter what the call was, I'd be ready to work with my tools, gave me much-needed and hard-earned confidence as a rescue tech, and I took great pride in the state of readiness we had achieved.

During the 1990's, the northern part of Scottsdale experienced a big boom in new home and light commercial construction activity. Along with that boom came an increase in trench rescue calls, as nearly every construction site had some sort of trench or excavation dug into it at some point. We were running lots of calls for injuries or even just simple medical emergencies for workers at construction sites. Interestingly, there was a shift happening in the types of incidents. Wildland fires had been the norm up north until this point, but construction was putting an end to the fires and bringing with it a different kind of emergency by eliminating natural fuels from the desert.

A trench rescue call came in at around noon for a collapse on a construction site in a development called Desert Mountain while my partner and I were out and about in Rescue 19. Desert Mountain is a very high-end community in the farthest north reaches of the city, about 20 miles from our station. We immediately headed that direction and arrived on-scene at least ten minutes ahead of the engine and support truck. The scene was chaotic, with a group of men digging feverishly at the base of a pile of dirt at least 30' high. There was a large section of the side, which had clearly just sloughed off, demarcated by an area of soil that was much darker in color than the dirt surrounding it. With small rocks and amounts of dirt still tumbling down the side and another collapse possible, I quickly scanned the area where the men were digging and saw no sign of the coworker they were trying to expose. It looked, and I felt, hopeless. But I by no means felt helpless. There were several more lives hanging in the balance, as a small mountain of dirt hung over their heads while they worked franticly in an area of potential further collapse.

I keyed the mic on my handheld radio:

"Rescue 19 to alarm."

"Rescue 19, go ahead."

"Rescue 19 is on the scene of an excavation collapse with one victim fully buried. Rescue 19 will have Desert Mountain Command. This will be a body recovery operation."

"Alarm copies Rescue 19 with Desert Mountain Command and a body recovery of one victim."

I'd never had to make that call before. A few dozen fire department personnel and apparatus were speeding our direction with lights, sirens and hopes alight and I'd just had to essentially tell them all, "Sorry guys, we've lost this one." I'd also indirectly told that construction worker's parents, wife, children and friends that there was no hope of finding their loved-one still alive because he'd been buried by dirt and rock, which weighs about 100 lbs. per cubic foot. Under such a heavy load, there's no chance for a human to perform the task of breathing, even if there were any air left under there in the first place. If as much as a few minutes pass when someone is buried, chances of survival quickly drop to zero. That knowledge is what I based my decision on, and after the call I was told by people more experienced than me that I'd done the right thing.

The difference between deciding to try and save a man's life and admitting that he cannot be saved is a very big one. It's also an incredibly heavy thing for someone in their 20's to have to bear. I can still smell the gear oil from the heavy equipment and that loamy odor of just-disturbed soil when I think of that call. The construction site that worker had arrived at that morning had effectively become his grave. And unfortunately, we'd have to be the ones to exhume his body.

With my best Spanish, I told the workers to all come out of the trench at the base of the hill and stand to the side. When they didn't react, I remembered the one word the head cook at Ajo Al's Mexican Restaurant would use when his guys were in trouble.

"Policía! Ven aquí, hombres!" which translates to a warning of trouble and a request to "Come here, guys."

The group of six or so panicked workers turned and walked to the side, up and out of the trench via a ladder right away. I picked up a traffic cone and asked one of the workers where he'd last seen his friend. After he'd pointed to the area, I tossed the cone down there as a marker for us to aim for. That would be where we'd concentrate our efforts.

When the engine and support truck arrived, we started digging in shifts lasting 30 minutes, with two guys working at a time. Everyone there knew that this was going to take a while. We wore harnesses and "tag" lines, or rope attached to our backs, which would let our crew find us quickly in the event of another collapse. But we knew that if the wall of dirt collapsed again, they'd be looking for our lifeless bodies as well. An excavator was used to "bench" or make large steps in the hanging mass of dirt before we entered the area. This helped reduce the chances of another collapse and it wasn't but a few moments before I thought to ask myself why they hadn't done this in the first place, before the collapse occurred. Not all workers know or remember the proper way to work on a job site and clearly there were OSHA[16] violations on this one. One huge consideration during a recovery operation is keeping the fire department from violating government regulations themselves in what can be very emotionally charged scenes. Sure, there are times during a rescue operation when we can turn a blind eye and bend the rules, even breaking them in extreme cases where a life hangs in the balance. But during recovery efforts, the rules become set in stone.

The correct way to uncover a buried victim is to dig, laboriously, by hand. If heavy equipment is used, there's just too much risk of tearing the victim apart. Imagine something akin to an archeological dig site, where dirt is gingerly removed one shovel-full at a time until the body is reached. About three hours into our operation, my partner Leif and I started our shift. We hit something right away. It was the victim's back. That movie-scene moment where a shovel strikes something in the ground is real. You really do stop and look at each other when it happens, wondering and at the same time knowing what lies beneath. We cleared dirt for the next 30 minutes, now with small hand shovels and had all but his lower leg uncovered. This is when I learned just how tenacious dirt's grip could be. I dug down to his ankle and Leif and I tried pulling him out, but couldn't because the dirt still had too tight of a hold on him. It was as though the Grim Reaper was lurking there underground, with an icy skeletal fist wrapped around the victim's ankle, preventing us from freeing the body. I dug in a little more and we carried the worker's lifeless body out of the trench 45 minutes into our fourth 30-minute shift. Jim had left us in until the end so we could be the ones to finish the job, and it did serve to give me some closure on the whole ordeal.

By this time, the worker's family had arrived at the scene and stood outside our working area screaming, wailing and crying as we set their loved one's body nearby and covered him with one of those ubiquitous yellow plastic highway blankets that mean only one thing when you see them covering something on the ground. The death of a man is sad indeed, but knowing the effect that loss has on his family has always been worse for me. They'd have to live on without this person in their lives. And that loss, grief and sorrow always affect the living long after the yellow tape is pulled down and the traffic cones put away.

Never did I experience a positive outcome at a trench collapse. The power and weight of dirt, sometimes combined with water, overcome human life with remarkable ease and rapidity. For the rest of my life when I pass a construction site with a trench, I'll always take a look to see if the crew has the proper shoring in place to protect workers who are deep in a hole. That experience also drove me to a more serious place when it came to training, and gave me some practical experience on which to base it. Having actually practiced the skills you go on to teach gives an instructor great amounts of credibility, particularly in the fire department special operations arena.

Other memories from station 19 include Raymond. He tried killing himself by jumping in front of a passing car on Shea Blvd one day. He didn't succeed then, but did when he set himself on fire with gasoline in his back yard a few months later. I was there for the second of those incidents, and that's where our aforementioned gym equipment came from.

And how can I forget the mother who crossed against the walk signal while pushing her baby daughter in a stroller. A passing SUV ran over the stroller and its passenger, right across the street from the hospital.

There was the woman who set her bed on fire (with her in it) while her small children and their friends played upstairs. Crews brought the kids down a ladder out front while Leif and I pulled the mother from a side window at ground level around the corner. I learned how easily burned skin comes off of a victim at that call.

One night, a convenience store worker was shot in the chest during a robbery. The trauma surgeon in the ER opened up the workers chest to operate, only to find two holes that didn't belong in his heart. It was too late to do anything for him.

On a Sunday afternoon, a father found his lifeless son hanging from the ceiling fan in his room. What he didn't notice was the pornographic video still playing on the computer screen when we walked in. I shut off the computer right away. Autoerotic asphyxiation.

Late another night, a young veteran had come back to the U.S. after the Gulf War and, while parked in his church parking lot, shot himself in the right temple. I reached through the shattered driver's side window to open the locked car door, pulling his body out and transporting him to our trauma center. Another one didn't make it.

There was absolutely no shortage of tragedy right from the very beginning of my career, and it just never seemed to let up. I also never dealt with any of it in a healthy way. Alcohol and risk-taking were coping mechanisms I'd use, as well as avoidance and isolation, none of this intentional or therapeutic in any way. The lure of the action at work and the idea that the next best call was just around the corner were what kept me coming back to the station shift after shift. All I thought I wanted was more. More action, more calls, more challenges and along with all of that, more experience. And those all kept coming my way in abundance.

The bothersome thing is that it was all becoming normal to me. The loss, the death and the injury were all desensitizing me under the guise of experience. I thought at the time that the experience I was gaining through all these catastrophic incidents was a good thing and maybe it was, from the standpoint of becoming more capable at the craft of being a firefighter, paramedic and rescue tech. But they were costing me from a mental health standpoint. Retrospectively, the experience wasn't worth the cost, and I couldn't see what precious currency I was paying with at the time.

Chapter 10
"Birth Of A Mentor"

⸻

THE FIRE AND EMS SERVICE relies quite a bit on on-the-job training even to this day. Much of the theoretical craft is learned in school, but putting that which is learned into practical application requires the guidance of experienced people. Ideally, these are people who are willing to make some sacrifices in the name of presenting the student with opportunities to learn. Such things often include spending a longer period of time at the hospital after dropping off a patient while the student refines their documentation skills, taking time out of station life to arrange practical skill stations and being an advocate for the student when they have encounters with patients, hospital staff and perhaps most critically, other firefighters or company officers. I respected my preceptors quite a bit and admired their willingness to spend time and effort when I needed their guidance. That's probably one of the things that motivated me to take on the preceptor role when the opportunity presented itself.

I'd been a Paramedic for about five years when I volunteered to precept new paramedic students for the first time. My first student was a "problem child" from a local ambulance company. His skills weren't great, and his bedside manner was even worse. The program director told me they'd sent him my way because they felt that if anyone could fix him, I could. This was not the supportive, nurturing preceptor role I had envisioned when I started, and clearly I was selected out of the pool because the other preceptors probably didn't want him. About one month into working with him, I'd realized that there was just no putting out this dumpster fire and called the director. I got the go-ahead to have an honest discussion with him about his future as a medic. We stood out in the back parking lot of station 19 and I laid out all of the thoughts I had about his skills and attitude. I was frank with him about where he stood and about what those around him viewed as problems he was having. He turned around, walked into the station to gather his things and then drove away. When I went inside, my crew was sitting around the day room table looking at me, incredulous. Someone broke the silence with, "Dude, did you just make that guy cry?" Knowing what his performance had been like, the guys weren't surprised that his position was in jeopardy and that there was probably no fixing him. So it wasn't a shock when I got the news the next day that he'd withdrawn from class.

You see, there are several metrics by which paramedic students are graded. They have lots of written work, clinical rounds in hospitals and tons of practical evaluations where they treat mock patients following modalities established by local, state and national agencies. That's all very important information for sure. By the time students get to their vehicular time or precepting rotation, all the schoolwork is pretty much finished. It's this time when, to me, the most important evaluation is made. And I always made that evaluation by asking myself one question. Would I want this person to work on my family or me if we were sick or injured? The answer was, with only one or two exceptions, always "Yes". I took great pride in helping new medics get their first bit of confidence under my watch, but I feel like I really did nothing more than what Ben had done for me years earlier. I gave them enough freedom to practice the craft, but was always there as a safety net when needed. There are times however, when a preceptor must take that safety net from under the student and throw it over them in order to reign in a potential problem.

They say that one of the best ways to maintain a skill is to teach it, and I couldn't agree more. In order to guide a new paramedic, you have to not only posses a strong academic foundation to draw upon, but also must have a healthy dose of street-cred and peer respect, which are essential. The best experiences I gave my students were probably at times when other medics would have jumped in and performed a skill, but I'd let my folks work through problems right up until the point where patient care or scene safety could possibly suffer. At that point, I'd always try to give them a hint or two before having them stand back and watch as I performed whatever the intervention was. It was a truly rare occasion when this happened, but it was always clear what the right thing to do was at the moment.

Role-play was always an important learning tool that I'd employ. Performing a patient interview is one of the toughest jobs a medic does, because it's not always intuitive in nature. You have to be an investigator, a translator, a lie-detector and try to remain empathetic during the whole process of interpreting what a patient is telling you, all the while looking at what the patient is showing you, because there are times when they won't be able to tell you that their heart has stopped or their blood sugar is critically low. It's those times, when I'd watch a student kneel down next to an unconscious person for the first time, that I could see if they had what it took to do this paramedic thing or not. There are those who are somehow naturally gifted at looking at the evidence presented to them and those who need work at it. When it's good, it's a beautiful sight to behold. And when it's bad, it's a cringe-worthy shit-show train wreck that you can barely stand listening to. That's where one of the role-play opportunities came in. Back at the station, I'd play the part of the patient and answer my student's questions during mock patient interviews. I'd act drunk, only to have them reveal that I was a diabetic with low blood sugar through the signs and symptoms I provided. I'd wheeze loudly, provoking them to listen to the lung sounds of an apparently asthmatic patient. Or I'd complain of chest pain that came on while I was exercising, prompting them to follow the chest pain protocol. This practice is no different than going to the gym to work out. As one does more sets and reps of a given exercise, they become stronger. I carefully gave my students as many sets and reps of exactly the exercises they needed in order to make them stronger at each particular skill, overwhelming them when they became overconfident, or easing up when they struggled. It was quite simple, really. But I developed a certain wisdom to it and enjoyed seeing my people succeed.

If I were precepting a person I felt I could trust, I'd enact a few rules. One regarded IV[17] starts. Easily placing an IV is one of the hallmark skills of most good medics, and this time in the field was when students got to practice on real people instead of mannequin arms. Mind you, when students practiced on these patients, they were *my* patients. If the student agreed to it, the rule went like this. If they missed an IV start on one of my patients, I'd start an IV on *them* when we got back to the station. You'd be surprised how well people pick up IV skills under those conditions! But there was another side to it. If we were on a call and *I* missed an IV, I'd be getting my own arm poked by the student when we got home from the call. Fair enough, and agreed to by every student I ever had.

Patching, or contacting a receiving hospital to either notify them of an incoming patient or to request a doctor's guidance would commonly trip people up if they'd not at least heard others do it before. Patching practice went like this: When the student was ready, they'd say "Ring, ring." That was my cue to "answer" the patch phone by saying, "Osborn ER, this is Rick, go ahead."

"This is Paramedic Student ______, how do you copy?"

From there, the student would relay the pertinent patient information in a short, organized way and be done with it. I'd have them shoot for one minute or less, and leave the nurse on the other end with no more than one question to ask, if needed, for clarification. If a nurse asked multiple questions, it was usually because the student hadn't presented enough of what they wanted to know.

Trauma reports were a particularly high-stress situation for medic students. Imagine having just responded to a call for a serious traumatic injury like a car or motorcycle accident, treating the patient's life-threatening injuries on the scene in under ten minutes, then riding in the ambulance to the hospital while finishing up any interventions needed, then finally wheeling the patient into the trauma bay in the ER where about a dozen people were standing, waiting to hear what you're about to tell them. And on top of that, they're going to make treatment decisions, based to a certain extent, on what you tell them about the patient. It's intimidating, and the audience includes between one and three doctors, a trauma surgeon, anesthetist, multiple nurses, x-ray technicians, respiratory therapists and maybe even some other students. When smartphones made their debut, I started recording student's trauma reports and patches for them to review later. It's also one of the things I was very good at and I always listened with much pride when my students nailed a trauma report for the first time, especially when a doctor or nurse would tell the student they'd done a good job, sometimes throwing me a nod or wink of approval afterward.

Another fun teaching tool involved me choosing whatever the student's biggest weakness was and requiring pushups any time that thing appeared when treating a patient. The last student I had before I retired was a sparky young lady named Kate. Her self-proclaimed weakness was her sassiness. She could lose her cool and say things at the wrong time to the wrong people on occasion. So when I made a rule requiring pushups, she agreed to watch herself when interacting with hospital staff. One day well into her vehicular rotation, Kate got sassy with a Nurse and I'd heard it. When we got back to the station, I told her that the episode was going to cost her some pushups, which she'd expected. But what I'm sure she didn't expect was for me to do the same number of pushups with her. I could be tough, yes, but I was always fair!

Finally, I'd always give my students a gift with a note at the end of their precepting time. I did this because perhaps without ever knowing it, each of those students made me a better paramedic and a better mentor to those who would pass later and I wanted to show my appreciation for that. Being able to pass my knowledge along to others was the real gift that I received along the way and I feel like I got better at it every time another student passed through my station. It's this never-ending cycle of teaching and learning that makes "practicing" medicine better for everyone involved and I'm grateful for the experience. One of the last things I told Kate after her paramedic graduation ceremony went like this, "Give this job your best, but don't let it get the best of you." I gave her that advice long after it was too late for me to take it myself.

Chapter 11
"The Affect Of 9/11 on 911"

ONE TUESDAY MORNING in September (You know the one.), I awoke in my bunk at station 19 to the sound of someone saying that there'd been a big plane crash in New York City. I headed upstairs to the station's day room and just as I rounded the corner, the TV came into view. That's when the second plane hit. 9/11 and the global war on terror had begun. I sat down at an uncharacteristically silent fire station table and realized along with everyone there that our country was under attack. My crew stayed for a while after our shift ended just to see what would happen next, but gradually we all started to think about and become concerned for our own families, resulting in everyone speeding home a few hours after our normal shift change. The Pentagon crash happened, then the south tower collapsed. Next, flight 93 crashed into a field and then the north tower collapsed. We watched the whole thing unfold on TV over the course of just under two hours. This was my generation's greatest tragedy. It was our Kennedy assassination, our Pearl Harbor, our Great Depression. And everyone knows exactly where he or she was when it was happening. Of the firefighters gathered in station 19 that morning, a few wept, others flew into a rage and others, myself included, sat there quietly wondering what to feel. I was angry, scared, uncertain and vengeful all at once. We lacked an explanation and wanted one immediately.

I drove home in a curious fog that day, and didn't know what was next, just like the rest of the country. I think I watched the news non-stop for most of the day and made sure my guns were loaded. No one knew what could happen here or in any city across the country.

So much changed that day. I put my U.S. flag up outside the house and later in the day saw that nearly everyone everywhere had done the same. This tragedy had instantly united the country. It's a sad fact that one of the things that draws people together stronger than anything is a villain. But in this case, we didn't know for sure who or what that villain was.

When I returned to work, some new policies were in place, including some which dealt with station and truck security and the possibility of crews being called back in to work in the event of a catastrophic occurrence in our region. One other thing changed as well. There was an incredible outpouring of support for firefighters by the public. Everywhere we went, we were appreciated. Strangers thanked us for our service constantly, bought groceries for us at the store and dropped lots of baked goods off at the station; the way neighbors and family do after someone loses a spouse. I remember feeling such a level of sadness that so much life had to be lost in order for people to unite and show support for those around them and come together as a nation.

Our training changed, too. Structure collapse had been glossed over a bit in the TRT calendar in prior years, but suddenly became a hot topic. And different training on explosives incidents and terrorist attacks of all types came to the forefront of our attention for several years to follow. "WMD" or weapons of mass destruction suddenly took the stage in our training also.

Shocking news came in 2002 when the final count for FDNY fatalities at 9/11 was released. 343 firefighters, nearly 100 more than the total number of firefighters working in Scottsdale at the time, had lost their lives when the towers fell. It's a number I still can't wrap my head around when I imagine numbers in excess of my entire department being wiped out at a single emergency scene. The effect on America and the world would be lasting, and instantly brought one simple fact of a firefighter's life to the front of everyone's mind: It's entirely possible that I could die in the line of duty, protecting the lives and property of perfect strangers because if I weren't willing to do the job, who was? The nobility of the profession had a light shining on it, if only for a time.

I wish 911 had never happened. And I know that many lives more than the 343 firefighters lost that day were affected by the tragedy. Lung cancer, PTSD and other ailments would continue causing harm for far more people than the firefighters who died at the scene. I wish we could learn lessons and somehow benefit from the lives lost that day, and perhaps we can. One thing is for sure; America united is much stronger than an America divided. Too many people these days seem to have lost sight of that fact. We can only hope that it doesn't take another 9/11 to reunite our country.

Chapter 12
"From Rescuer to Rescued"

———

THEN THERE WAS THE day I broke my back. I started rock climbing in 1987 soon after my family had relocated to Arizona from Ft. Worth, Texas. I was inspired after being invited to do something called bouldering[18] with some neighborhood friends. Soon thereafter, I had sticky rubber climbing shoes and a chalk bag that I'd ridden my bike 30 miles to purchase at a shop called Desert Mountain Sports, in downtown Phoenix. My mom drove me to Echo Canyon on Camelback Mountain, smack dab in the middle of town, and waited in the parking lot while I hiked five minutes up the trail to a 40' tall boulder. Known as "Practice Rock", the base of the boulder allows a climber to traverse from one end to the other without getting higher off the ground than one would want to fall. I was hooked. The feeling of making my feet stick to unlikely rock surfaces and moving over the stone was exhilarating, and it wasn't long before I'd gone back to DMS to pick up a harness so I could climb with friends who had the required rope and gear to tackle taller heights. I made friends with local climbers I'd run into at Camelback and over time had introduced the current friends I was racing bikes with to the sport of climbing. During my high school years, I climbed thousands of vertical feet of rock and acquired my own rope and gear with money earned at the bike shop, freeing me to climb wherever and with whomever I chose.

I'd been a rock climber for 15 years when a prominent Scottsdale landmark, Pinnacle Peak, was reopened to the public and in turn, to rock climbers. The area had been one of my favorites growing up, with great climbs on granite, which is a much more solid rock than that of Camelback Mountain. The area had been closed when high-dollar homes were built at the base of the mountain and was now being reopened as a city park. Anxious to get back up there, my climbing partner and I headed out on the first Monday that the park was open. I was about 12' up an arching crack in the vertical face of one of the rocks when my foot slipped and I took a big fall. I had my harness on and was tied into a rope for safety, but hadn't placed any gear yet because I simply didn't have anything big enough for a crack that wide. I'd looked higher up, where the crack narrowed, and had a plan for where to stop and get the rope clipped into something and decided to go for it when the slip happened. I fell the full 12' and landed in a seated position on a rock at the base of the wall. When people break their neck, it's said that it feels like their head is going to fall off of their body. However when I stood up, it felt as though my upper body was going to fall off of my hips. I'd fractured two vertebrae in my lumbar spine. I sat, and then laid down on the gravel next to the wall in my beloved climbing area, feeling forsaken by the trust I'd put in the rock's ability to hold my foot. I felt betrayed by my 15 years of climbing experience, feeling as though that much time and mileage should have somehow magically protected me from making such a mistake. The climb itself was of a difficulty level well below my capability and I'd let my guard down just long enough for my life to take a very big turn in direction without me knowing it at the time.

There was no way I was going to be able to walk down off the mountain that day, and the climb I was on actually required some steep climbing to even get to the base of. The normal Stokes basket and big wheel used by crews for trail rescues wasn't going to cut it here. My evacuation was going to be complicated. My climbing partner, also a Firefighter/Paramedic with Scottsdale Fire, called 911 and got the ball rolling. Soon thereafter, the truck I'd been running calls on just the day before pulled into the parking lot about 500' in elevation below. Around fifteen minutes later, Ian arrived at my side. A respected and experienced medic from the other shift, he knelt down, put a hand on my shoulder and asked, "Hey bro, how bad is it?"

"It's pretty bad. We're gonna have to fly, and my legs are starting to go numb."

"Okay, I'll get things started."

Ian began to work on the logistics of getting me off the mountain as Shelly arrived with medical equipment. She was a medic also and started an IV on me through which Morphine could be administered for my now growing levels of pain. Aggressive pain relief was in vogue at the time, and Morphine was what we carried back then. After a dose or two hadn't helped much, I think a third and even larger dose was given and that knocked out my pain. But Morphine's wretched side affect had made an appearance too, causing me to struggle to breathe. It was similar to the sensation I'd felt of not being able to breathe at the Rio Fire years earlier, but without the panic. This time it just felt like I was falling asleep and had no drive to stay awake or alive. Knowing I'd only have time to get a few words out before I lost consciousness due to hypoxia, I looked up at Shelly and said, "Bag me."

She looked at my climbing partner and said, "I think he wants us to bag him." Moments later, a bag-valve-mask was being squeezed to ventilate my lazy lungs with oxygen while we waited for my flight to arrive. It was a very strange sensation to have a friend breathing for me while my legs went numb and I fought to stay conscious at the base of a rock climb I'd done at least three or four times in the past without anywhere near this kind of drama. Fortunately I was too injured to feel embarrassment.

Having been involved in technical rescue for the prior seven years or so, I'd run plenty of mountain rescue calls, which were both a blessing and a curse in the given situation. On the one hand, I knew exactly what was going to happen. But on the other hand, I knew EXACTLY what was going to happen. Crews would have to perform a helicopter operation known as a "long line", where a 70' rope hanging from the bottom of a hovering helicopter is used to carry a patient (me this time) in a metal mesh basket from the site of the accident down to a crew waiting at the bottom of the mountain on pavement.

I could hear the helicopter coming. I could feel the rotor wash when it arrived, blowing down on me as if to try and assist the efforts in progress to make me breathe. The sun flashed rapidly through the rotor blades like a strobe light as it hovered above me and I remember thinking how beautiful it looked, almost like an angel reaching a hand out to lift me to the heavens. Morphine's a hell of a drug! My friend Marc, the third paramedic on the crew, flew with me down to the parking lot, attached next to the Stokes basket and ready to manage my airway should a problem arise. It couldn't have taken more than a minute or two to fly from the base of the climb to the parking lot, but it felt like an eternity. I was gaining a very real appreciation of what my patients felt like when I was rescuing them, and I always remembered what it was like years later any time I flew with someone or packaged them in a Stokes basket.

Normally, an ambulance is used for the remaining transport to a hospital after a flight off of the mountain. But I had sustained a great enough fall to require treatment at a trauma facility and Scottsdale Memorial Osborn was over 20 miles away. The helicopter doing the long line operation was DPS Ranger 41[19], which was not configured for transporting a patient inside the cabin. A second helicopter was the answer, and a unit from Air Evac responded. Two landing zones had to be established; one for DPS and one for Air Evac. An ambulance would be waiting for me at the first LZ and would transport me a couple blocks to the other LZ, where I'd be transferred over to Air Evac for the flight to Osborn. That whole plan materialized down in the parking lot and several news stations also arrived while the crews were treating me up on the mountain.

The whole thing, as complex as it was, went off without a hitch. Before I knew it I was being wheeled into the trauma bay at Osborn and treated for fractures of L3 and L4 vertebrae in my lumbar spine. I remember lots of people being there in the hospital when I arrived. Word of what had happened travelled fast, and many of my firefighter friends had shown up. I vaguely remember the trauma surgeon asking me if I wanted a priest. I said no, and then they asked if there was anyone else I wanted there. I asked for the fire chief and he was there minutes later. It felt like ten people were all touching me at the same time and before I knew it I was naked on the table, free of all the straps and tape, which had been used to stabilize my spine during transport. I was the patient in what had arguably been one of the most complex rescue operations yet undertaken in the city and I owe the use of my lower extremities in large part to the careful packaging and care that so many people gave me on that April day in 2002.

During my hospital stay, which consisted of a few days in the ICU followed by the remainder of a week in a regular room, hundreds of people came by to show their support. My good friend David, who was the Member Services Director for our union local, organized all the visits. Firefighters, bike racers, friends and family all showed up. But it was the act of one man named Johnny, which still remains fresh in my mind. You see, I'd met Johnny at Bartlett Lake one evening a month or so prior when I was out riding the new sport bike I'd had for several months on the twisty canyon road next to the water. He was sitting at a picnic table out at the end of Rattlesnake Cove, with his sportbike parked nearby. I parked and introduced myself. We chatted for a few minutes, rode out of the canyon together and I'd never seen him again. But I remember being amazed at how hard it was to keep up with him at dusk on that twisty road. It was one of those chance, pleasant encounters that you kind of forget about after a while. A few days into my hospital stay, someone I didn't immediately recognize walked in with a shopping bag full of magazines. It was Johnny. He'd seen the news coverage on TV and bought every different sport bike magazine on the rack at a bookstore and dropped them off to me. It was an incredibly kind and thoughtful act and I still think of that once in a long while.

Just over eight weeks into my recovery at home and with a heavy dose of cabin fever setting in, I decided to go out into the garage to see if I could get a leg over my motorcycle. I sat there for a while, thinking that I may just be able to pull off a ride if I were careful. The Internet was still relatively new at that point, and I'd been looking up groups or clubs to four-wheel with or ride motorcycles with. I happened upon something called the Phoenix Sportbike Club. They had a website describing what the club was all about and a message board, which was private and locked until approval was gained by showing up in-person at a local car/bike show night at the Scottsdale Pavilions, a shopping center about ten miles away from my place. When Saturday night rolled around, I checked to see if my riding jacket would fit over my TLSO[20] brace, which was a hard plastic shell that encased my torso from shoulders to pelvis. It did, barely, and I fired up the engine of my Superhawk for the first time in months. The freedom you feel on two wheels is amplified greatly after a long break, and riding again was complete bliss. Arriving at the show, I found a group of sportbikers hanging around one section of the parking lot, and backed into a spot nearby. I noticed "PSC" stickers on several of the dozen or so bikes and knew I was in the right place. As I walked over to the group, I extended a hand to a friendly looking guy who was smoking a cigarette and looking at my bike. I said, "Hey, I'm Rick. Is this the PSC crew?"

He replied, "I'm Bill, this is the crew and what is that?"

As he pointed with his cigarette between two fingers, I realized he'd seen my blue turtle shell.

"Oh yeah, uh, that. Well I broke my back a couple months ago and it's kind of like a splint. I thought it was about time to get out and ride, so I came here to find you guys."

Bill, the then president of PSC said, "That's awesome. What's your email, 'cause you're IN!"

Bill and I would be best friends for years after a short time riding and going to events together until he and his family moved across the country to Maine. I miss him and our times together greatly. I remained involved in PSC for the next six years and took over as president when Bill left. During the days with PSC, I started riding open track days at local circuits, got my racing license, and had a ton of success and eventually started teaching racing on the track. Overall, my involvement in the club had a very positive impact on my life and I'm happy to have had so many opportunities for friendship, charity, competition and great experiences. If there was some reason for breaking my back; if there was some purpose for that pain and suffering, I think it was to put me on a path to something entirely different in my life. It sounds odd even to me, but in some small way, I'm glad it happened. I'd been through a trauma room, ICU bed, got transported by my friends in an ambulance back home, spent a few weeks there in a hospital bed, had a blood clot in my leg, broke a dependence on Morphine and eventually made my way back to work with one hell of a story to tell. My back does ache once in a while after heavy exertion, but I have no lasting physical deficits from the fall, and made a relatively rapid recovery. The neurologist said I'd be out for six months, but I made it back in three with hard work during physical therapy.

When I returned to full duty, I had a renewed interest in work and a new appreciation for those around me. Things looked different to me after being critically injured and unable to do my job. I really missed it while I was gone and getting back to work was the motivating factor in quitting my use of pain medicine. I didn't have to stop those meds in order to return, but wanted to be free of that influence and any impairment it could cause. I gradually reduced the dosage and quit comfortably, but my back did require healthy doses of physical therapy and Ibuprofen. Staying active was vital to my full and complete recovery, which took a few years, but did happen.

Getting back to rock climbing was challenging. I lacked confidence for a long time, but started slowly and eventually got back on the climb I'd fallen off of at Pinnacle Peak, called "Varicose". I stood on top of that climb after successfully leading it almost a year to the day later and cried like a baby. It felt like an insurmountable mental obstacle, but I'd conquered my fear and done it. I had a new appreciation for my climbing ability and realized that sometimes we can't truly appreciate our abilities or special things in our lives until they're gone.

Chapter 13
"Tight Squeeze"

PARADISE VALLEY IS a high-dollar residential community that lies between the cities of Scottsdale and Phoenix. Its population is only a fraction of the other two, but the average wealth of its residents eclipses the other cities by a large margin. And the houses there stand as monumental reflections of that wealth. Being a small town, fire protection was provided through a contract with Rural/Metro, and this was a reflection of a different sort. If there's one thing rich people like doing with their money, it's saving it. And Rural saved the town of Paradise Valley lots of money over what it would cost to form their own municipal fire department. But the town only had one Rural/Metro fire engine to protect an area of just over 15 square miles that are crisscrossed by mountains, making rapid responses to emergencies inconsistent at best. That's where we came in, and the Rural fire stations in Scottsdale regularly responded into Paradise Valley for large fires.

At the time, station 19 ran as a truck company. We had a 75' steel aerial ladder on top of our truck, which was a refurbished pile of junk with an updated, enclosed cab instead of the old, open rear cab it used to have when I learned how to drive it as a reserve firefighter several years prior. What they didn't do to match the updated cab was any engine work or ladder updating whatsoever. So it was a really S-L-O-W truck. When I drove it to calls, nine times out of ten I wouldn't even turn on the lights and siren because it wouldn't go fast enough to pass traffic that was going the speed limit!

Early one winter morning, there was a fire in a huge house in Paradise Valley. We responded because they needed an elevated master stream to apply water from above the house, which had been written off due to the extent of fire involvement. When we arrived, fire was blowing out of every window and door of a 6,000 square foot mansion and interior firefighting crews had been pulled out of the structure for their safety due to the risk of structure collapse. It was one of those fires that put off an uncomfortable amount of heat from over 100' away, standing in the street. We positioned our truck for the best access to the house and "put up the stick", or raised the ladder. Being old and outdated, the controls for nozzle movement were located up at the top of the ladder, which had two sections. The "bed" section was the base of the ladder, and was as long as the truck from front to back. The "fly" section was the same length, but extended out from the bed section via an assembly of hydraulics, steel cables and pulleys. Up the aerial rose above the house and the flames consuming it. Being a single-story house, it appeared to our engineer that we wouldn't need to extend the fly section to reach the fire. In my turnout gear and SCBA, with my facemask on and fresh air flowing, I climbed the near-vertical ladder and attached myself to the top rung with a ladder safety belt. This is no mean feat, considering I was carrying not only my 6'2" 180 lb. frame, but also another 75 lbs. in protective gear. When I reached the top of the aerial I was struck by the beauty of the scene below. As unfortunate as the obvious loss of the home and property was, I couldn't help but take a moment to calmly observe what was happening. As the desert sun rose behind me, orange, yellow and red flames consumed everything below. Walls and portions of the roof structure were barely discernable in the inferno. I looked for firefighters on the ground because I wanted to keep from hitting anyone with the freight-train force of 1,000 gallons per minute (GPM) of water, which would soon erupt from the 2" diameter smoothbore nozzle sitting near waist height in front of me.

With the small toggle switch control panel, I aimed the nozzle toward the main body of fire and called over the intercom for water. "Water coming!" said my partner on the ground. When that much water is flowing, there's a tremendous amount of force pushing backward in the form of something called nozzle reaction. It's the same type of force one experiences when shooting a shotgun. There's a "kick" to it. On the ground, a firefighter must brace himself quite a bit with just 170 GPM flowing from a hand-held fog nozzle. Now put almost six times that amount up on the end of an elevated ladder and imagine what it feels like to sway forward and back on a rickety old perch above a roaring inferno. In a word, it's AWESOME! Here I was, with the best view of the scene, essentially putting out a huge house fire by myself. But the sheer size of the house was presenting a problem. I wasn't able to reach the far end of the house, where the fire was still burning pretty aggressively. We needed more height to reach that far, and I called for the ladder to be extended. One of the things that our old truck company lacked was foot steps on the top of the aerial, which meant having to stand directly on the round, rubber-covered rungs of the ladder itself. When the ladder is extended, those rungs pass close by one another through their path of travel. As the top few rungs moved, my feet were in their path. They caught my feet as the ladder extended and it very much felt as though my feet were being torn in half by the force. My turnout boots did have steel toes, but they didn't protect my mid-foot or arch and I suffered crushing injuries. Had it not been for the ladder belt around my waist, I'm sure I would've fallen down the ladder to the ground. I felt my knees go weak under me as I agonized and tried to figure out a way down as I was still being raised up above the fire on a ride I no longer wanted to be on. When the aerial reached maximum height, I set the nozzle on the largest body of fire and started my slow climb down 75' of ladder to the ground. Once I got there, I sat down and when asked if I was okay, said, "No, my feet just got crushed in the ladder rungs."

An ambulance took me to the hospital and I had x-rays in the ER. There's something about being wheeled into the hospital, still in my fire gear, smelling like a house fire and drenched in sweat that feels like being a soldier brought into a field hospital during a war. Everyone wonders what happened and if the person they'd seen delivering patients to the ER day in and day out was okay. But there was another, more surprising feeling that I had that morning; in a way I felt ashamed of myself for getting hurt in the first place. After all, firefighters are the ones who solve people's problems. Getting hurt in the process isn't supposed to be part of the deal and I found my head hanging low with disappointment. Thankfully I hadn't broken any bones in my feet, but they still hurt like hell for a few days and I walked with a limp for a week or so. I had a few shifts off to recover and came back to find a new set of fold-down foot steps atop Truck 19's aerial, which would prevent such an injury in the future.

As interesting, exciting and heroic as getting one's feet crushed in an aerial ladder at a fire might sound, it was psychologically traumatic. There was a very real chance that I could've fallen the equivalent of seven stories as I unclipped and somehow made my way down the ladder that day. I didn't address it or recognize it at the time, but I felt helpless and powerless, incapable of keeping the incident from happening in the first place. For the second and sadly not the last time, the job I loved would hurt me, and on some level and in some strange way I felt as though I'd been betrayed by it the same way I felt after my climbing accident. Being more careful is only one part of a possible solution, and that alone can't prevent all accidents, which is what this was. But again, we're meant to be the ones responding to accidents, not getting into them.

A firefight is a dangerous place.

Chapter 14
"Unhappy Holidays"

FLASH BACK TO MY DAYS as a reserve in Scottsdale, before I'd been hired full-time. Thanksgiving was always a contentious holiday for me ever since I'd moved out of my parents house, and I annually dreaded having to sit with my dysfunctional family and act as though everything was fine amongst us during the holidays, or worse still, answer all of the "How's the fire department, have you run any good calls?" questions. One year, we were just about to sit down with full plates of food when my radio pager went off. "Scottsdale Reserves to respond, commercial structure fire at 5th Avenue and Brown."

"Well, I've gotta go. Happy Thanksgiving, everybody!"

I think I laughed all the way to that fire in old town Scottsdale, and headed home afterward instead of going back to dinner hours later. Being a reserve wasn't all that bad on that day, for sure and on that day I found respite in my trade.

But a few weeks later, I'd have a different opinion when I was paged to respond to a house fire. It was mostly out when I got there, but there'd been an "Oh shit" moment when the first engine arrived and couldn't establish a water supply to their truck. The hydrant they'd set up on had a 4" cap that was rusted solidly closed and couldn't be opened. The firefighter who was assigned to hook up to the hydrant was a monster of a man named Ron. In trying to open the cap, Ron actually bent the hydrant wrench, a 5 ½lb., 1" diameter, 2' long, steel handled tool with his bare hands. Such is the level of adrenaline involved when the alarm goes off and there's smoke showing from someone's house. The second engine to arrive at the scene laid supply line from the next closest hydrant down the street and the fire was knocked down quickly.[21] I was assigned to assist with the "extensive salvage" operations and made my way to the company officer in charge of interior operations. He pointed to the soot-covered living room where the charred trunk of a seven-foot tall evergreen tree stood limbless above a huge quantity of unopened Christmas gifts. A salvage cover[22] was laid out on the garage floor and I joined the other firefighters in solemnly moving a family's surprises out of a huge puddle of water that came from that secondary hydrant down the street. It was one of the saddest moments I'd had at that point, and I instantly regretted having run out on my family during that Thanksgiving dinner the month before. The job had taught me a lesson that I'd not acknowledge or recognize until many years later.

Thanksgiving and Christmas are also house fire season in Arizona. Lots of people crank up their fireplaces during the holidays, but not all of them remember to open the chimney flue because they use their fireplace so infrequently. I actually had to explain what the flue was a few times over my career after a first-time fireplace user ruined their living room with a huge dose of smoke. After they light their cozy fire, the smoke fills the house and the fire department gets involved. Normally, this situation is easily handled with a large scoop shovel. My style was to go in, scoop up the burning wood or waxy fire log in the shovel and carry it outside for extinguishment on the driveway. You see, when you hit a fire indoors with water, you create a special steam/smoke combination that permeates everything in the person's house, especially in the case of one of those damned wax logs you buy at a grocery store. Those put off a special kind of stink that just doesn't go away. Taking the fire outside prevents that from happening and gives the homeowner a little less of a headache when it's time to clean up. It also makes it easier to forcefully ventilate the house, as smoke blows out much faster than dirty steam.

The holidays also bring out an increase in domestic violence incidents, which makes sense to me in light of my own family's tense relations. You take a bunch of people who come into town to visit family, perhaps after not seeing one another for an extended time and add a holiday celebration that often includes alcohol and get a situation that's primed for confrontations. It's also really sad to see.

Firefighters are responsible for protecting the lives and property of the communities in which they work. But the job of being a firefighter is about people, not things. It's about bringing order out of chaos. It's about trying to make things normal for people when everything's upside down. It's about walking out of a burnt house and handing over an aquarium full of still-living pet turtles to a young girl. It's finding and protecting a family photo album during a firefight. It's about searching for and saving a beloved dog or cat. Sometimes it's even about unclenching death's grip around a person and miraculously arriving at an ER with a previously pulseless patient who now has a blood pressure and respirations thanks to your crew's skills. But far, far too often it's about witnessing unimaginable loss over and over again, and feeling as though you're a failure despite heroic outward appearances. And for many firefighters, it eventually turns into lying awake at night in a twin bed at a station far from the comforts of their own home, hoping that the lights never come on again with the alarm of another call and more loss, especially not during the holidays.

Birthdays are another source of sad calls. I know this seems like a total mystery and you may be thinking it has something to do with a cake and candles, and I wish it were that simple. Arizona, and the

Phoenix area in particular, is the land of swimming pools. Looked at from above, I'd say more than 90% of the houses in Scottsdale have a little blue oasis in the backyard, and children's summer birthday parties often see a group of kids gather for a pool party at the birthday house. More than once, I ran drowning calls at houses full of parents and kids who were there to celebrate a birthday, only to lose sight of one of the guests for a few seconds as they slipped silently and helplessly beneath the surface.

It was a hot summer day and I was working overtime at one of the stations in far-north Scottsdale when the tones dropped[23] for a drowning. The call was miles away from the station in Phoenix, and the first-due unit must have been on another call at the time, so we were dispatched to cover for them. Having a long response meant that we had a bit of extra time to talk about who would do what on the scene. We discussed launching a helicopter for transport, who would run the cardiac monitor, prepare drugs, start an IO or intraosseous line, and who would handle the patient's airway. Before the parking brake had even been set, the four of us jumped out of the engine ready for action. The adrenaline was flowing heavily and I remember the street being lined with cars as we pulled the medical gear from the side compartment of our engine.

"We're gonna have a big audience on this one." With the front door open and a few people feverishly waving us in, we made our way through about 20 people in the main part of the house and out to the backyard. A bystander was giving chest compressions to a toddler on the cool deck next to the pool. I put my hand on his shoulder, then scooped the little boy up off the hot deck in one arm and carried him inside like a football, clearing off the kitchen island like an angry employee sweeping off their boss's desktop. A workspace was made and we set about our business, with access to all sides of the patient.

"Launch that helicopter; we're too far away from Phoenix Children's for an ambulance."

I opened our orange trauma box and set up an IV bag and tubing, then loaded the IO drill with a pink, pediatric-sized needle while one crew member did chest compressions and the other set up a bag-valve mask or BVM to artificially breathe for the patient. As I pulled the trigger and the drill set off spinning, the effort required to push through the front of his tibia seemed peculiar and so much easier than doing this on the adult patient's I'd worked on recently. I also noted how limp he felt. After confirming that I got the IO in the right spot, I plugged in the infusion and we now had a route for resuscitative drugs. Next was getting the cardiac monitor and defibrillator hooked up. Simple enough, one pad goes on the chest and the other on the upper back for a patient this small. Now we had a picture of his heart rhythm. My partner who was dealing with the airway was having a bit of trouble with it, so I took over and set up to intubate, or place a breathing tube into the patient's trachea. He was so small that I'd have to use one of the uncuffed tubes in our kit and hope for a good enough seal against the narrowing portion of his trachea. As I passed the tube to the right of the short, straight laryngoscope[24] blade, I realized that my hands weren't shaking during this incredibly stressful encounter. Everything seemed to slow down. I could hear the mother gasping and sobbing as I worked to save her son. I also heard silence from a living room full of people who had begun to leave the house. And then I heard, "Rick, what can I get you?"

I snapped back to reality and said, "Epi, please." I needed to get a first dose of Epinephrine into this patient quickly if he was going to have any chance at survival. Through the IO it went, but I never felt pulses return in the boy's arm, despite seeing an organized rhythm on the small screen of our monitor. Nice QRS complexes with no pulse to go along with them. From that point on, we followed our pediatric cardiac arrest protocols for the next several minutes until the faint, then loud thumping of a helicopter's rotor blades circled, then passed over the roof of the house. They were sound of salvation. We prepared the patient to be moved from the kitchen island out to the helicopter crew who made their way to the front door. I gave the flight nurse the patient's information and a synopsis of our treatments thus far. She signed my paperwork as I carried the boy toward the helicopter, tossing my hat to someone in the yard along the way between providing chest compressions with only a few fingers. He was that small. It's a real rookie move to have your hat blown off by rotor wash, and even worse for everyone involved if that hat winds up where it doesn't belong in something spinning. After the patient was secured, I walked out to the side of the helicopter so as to avoid the dipping front rotor blades and headed back to the house, where our captain was explaining where the patient was going and how to get there while confirming that someone other than the mother or father would be driving. Back in the kitchen, the rest of the crew had nearly finished cleaning up the mess of medical supply wrappers and disposable equipment we'd used. Most of the bystanders had left the house by this point and we were largely alone.

It was a heartbreaking scene that I have an emotional time even describing. The pain and loss that those parents surely still feel to this day is unimaginable. And what about that "no shaking" thing that happened? The best explanation I have for that is the fact that I don't have any kids of my own, so when we stepped into that scene I didn't have thoughts of my own family and what it would be like to lose a son or daughter. Make no mistake; I was affected by the call, but in a more distant way, as more of an observer, or a witness to the whole thing. My training and experience had taken over and

I'd operated largely through muscle memory, completing dozens of tasks and working through the fast-paced chess game that working a cardiac arrest can be. But this wasn't a game.

Someone from the hospital called the station hours later with the bad news. Despite our efforts, the boy had perished. No critical incident team came to meet with us. No battalion chief stopped by to see how we were doing. No one even called. We were left, like so many crews in the past, to deal with the aftermath of the call on our own. It feels like a loss to firefighters when they lose a patient and it doesn't go down easily. It stings and burns and makes us cry and punch a wall and exercise hard and isolate ourselves and drink and do anything we can to avoid seeing, thinking or feeling things that remind us of not being able to save a child's life on that hot summer day in Phoenix.

Chapter 15
"Forming a Family"

———

ONE OF THE STRONGEST crews I ever worked with at station 19 was made up of Captain Jim Loper, Firefighter/Paramedic Mack Vega, Firefighters Benny Olson and Gil Red and myself, the other Firefighter/Paramedic on the crew. Back then, there were only three people assigned to each fire truck in Scottsdale, with rescues (ambulances) staffed with two people. I rotated with Mack between the truck and the rescue, while Gil and Benny rotated in the same manner. Remember, there were only two shifts in the city: A&B, and they rotated perpetually. We worked every other day for six shifts, and then had three days off. Our next rotation was every other day for five shifts, then five days off. Then the process would repeat itself. I had a Tuesday "Kelly Day" with a Thursday "Kicker". What that meant was I never worked on Tuesdays and only worked every other Thursday. The thing I liked best about the schedule was having every other Monday through Friday off, which allowed me to enjoy outdoor activities like skiing, hiking, cycling or just living life while everyone else in the world was at work. The worst part of the schedule was working that period of six shifts on and off in a row, with only one day to recover in between. By the time the sixth day came around, we were so fatigued that it was hard to function. Luckily we were young. How Jim did it is beyond me. He was in his 50's by that time and had been in the fire service since 1974, when I was just two years old.

Jim stood about 5'10" and was in really great shape for a guy with so much fire service mileage. He'd grown up practicing karate and had a studio of his own where he taught prior to being hired on with the fire department. When we worked out, he hit the weights pretty heavy and hated doing any form of cardio conditioning, which was what I always seemed most interested in because I was almost constantly racing bicycles. When rock-climbing season came around in the summer though, I'd transition to a better-rounded routine of half cardio and half weights. He and I had many arguments about which workout theory was best. Hell, we had many arguments about lots of things over the years and I'm pretty sure we each felt like we were part of an old married couple toward the end of our time together in 2016. Jim's downfall was that he liked to micromanage. He'd tell someone what to do, but then watch and tell them how to do it. As a worker who needed independence and autonomy as a reflection of trust and respect, he and I were a bad match that became worse as I gained experience of my own. It took years to evolve, but Jim eventually did change his leadership style toward me quite a bit and at times I even felt as though I was running the show from the back seat of the truck. But I did get better at giving more to the relationship from my end as well over time. I think what infuriated me the most from time to time was the fact that I respected him, yet felt little in the way of expressed respect in return. The feeling served me well later in my career when it was my turn in the front seat as a company officer, because I always treated those on my crew and their opinions with respect and dignity. I came to adjust my expectations from leaders over the years and tempered my behavior in the process. I believe that just as much can be learned from a bad example as can be taken from a good one. Over the years, many people asked why I didn't just transfer out to another station in order to promote through the ranks and the answer was always TRT. I knew that if I left special operations that the odds of ever getting back there were somewhere between slim and none. The action outweighed the price. And that speaks volumes about how much I loved TRT. But my relationship with Jim became strained when he started favoring Gil, much the same way my relationship with my dad went south when it became clear that he and my mom were favoring my sister. The two things Jim needed from me were my TRT experience and my medic cert. When a TRT assignment involving just one rescuer came up, nine times out of ten, I'd be the one to handle it. I was the one to climb up and get the guy, crawl in and rescue the animal or quite frequently, fly in and evacuate the hiker or climber. Station 19 was now the TRT station, in the special operations division of the fire department. And I got to do more of the technical rescue work than anyone else on my truck. Sorry, but I'm not sorry. It's a very unfair system in which those who already have it usually continue to gain even more experience. I suppose that as far as medics went, I had become Jim's top guy after Leif left us for another station. But I always felt as though the "favorite" role was handed down begrudgingly.

Mack and I had a very odd relationship. We could be friends one shift and be at each other's throat the next. He'd been a medic for a few years longer than me, but started as a reserve at about the same time. We were within two years in age. Mack was thin as a rail when we started in the fire service, but through working out and some supplements, rapidly bulked up into the consummate shape of a typical firefighter. He'd also secured a full-time position before me in no small part because of his medic cert, so he had a little bit of seniority. Mack was a partier. He and his wife Angie had a rock-n-roll lifestyle the likes of which were legendary around the department, and didn't care what people though about him. He had a boat, which he'd take to the local lakes nearly every weekend during the summer and would occasionally share pictures of the onboard debauchery that nearly always ensued. For the most part, few other firefighters joined him, but many ridiculed him for his ways, myself included. Perhaps what people couldn't understand about Mack was how he could live such a lifestyle and have a young daughter and son at home. But for his interesting life choices, Mack was a trustworthy person with a heart that was probably a little bigger than his head. On calls, I always knew I could count on him to watch my back as the other medic and he knew I always had his as well. I suppose we grew up together in the fire department, as so many did back then and still do. It seems like a very large number of us all started together as kids, then slowly began getting married and having kids and houses and money and divorces and everything else a normal life throws your way over time. There just seemed to be a cycle of life we were all going through and evolving into together, most of the time not even realizing what was happening.

Benny Olson was one of the most amazingly kind-hearted and hilarious people I'd ever met. His quick wit and sarcasm brought comedy to some of the most tragic scenes I've experienced. He was also one of the first Mormons I've ever spent a considerable amount of time around. Benny was a hard working EMT and was always able to anticipate what the paramedics were going to do on EMS scenes, which are both hallmarks of EMT excellence. He had a wife, son and daughter who he was deeply devoted to and was involved as an elder in his church. He also had a penchant for flatulence. A little heavier than the rest of the crew, Benny frequently worked passing gas into conversations and situations that would have the crew in stitches. Once while leaving a scene, Benny let loose in the cab of the truck for a good five or six seconds straight. He must've been saving it up for a while, and the stench was so bad that the engineer had to park the truck in the middle of an apartment complex while we all opened the doors and windows and stood outside. It was one time of many that Benny had me laughing to the point of tears. When we climbed back into the truck and put our headsets back on, the first thing I heard was Benny saying, "Lord, I apologize." I have a picture of the two of us standing on the balcony of a burning apartment complex in the late 90's. In it, we look like a couple of young kids wearing their dad's fire gear. We were that young. He and I worked many rescue shifts together and he was always that partner who made the long hours pass effortlessly. And he always had my back the same as I had his. That goes a long way toward feeling safe and secure while on the job. I'll never forget the amount of empathy he could display, and the fact that I was one of the reasons he made the decision to go to paramedic school while stationed with us at 19.

That brings us to Gil Red, the same Gil I'd gone through the full-time fire academy with. Gil and I seemingly had very different ideas about the fire service and what working meant. Obsessive about cleanliness, Gil polished the fire truck so much that I'm surprised there was any paint left on it. We didn't have an official engineer rank at the time, but Jim was very particular about who drove for him. This was mostly because he didn't like being scared by poor or fast driving and Gill catered to that. He also happened to be a good engineer and Jim knew that was one less thing he'd have to worry about when Gil's skills were called into action on a fire or other emergency scene. Gil and Jim became friends and frequently went to movies or lunch together off-duty and spent more time with each other than most in a captain/firefighter relationship. That fact played against both of them within our crew at station 19, as Jim was known to play favorites and Gil was perceived as a kiss-ass. Both of those perceptions played out as truth over the years, but I had one very large advantage over Gil at TRT calls and that was the medic patch on my right shoulder. As long as I was a medic and he was an EMT, I'd always be called on to do more at the scenes that mattered most to me. Following the trend of growing up in the fire service, Gil married a cute girl named Mary and they had a son of their own later. We had a delicate relationship over the years, and did spend some time riding motorcycles together for a while, but gradually lost touch when a more senior engineer replaced him in a future year.

Like most brothers, we fought, worked together, laughed at each other and despite outward appearances really cared for one another. We played relentless practical jokes on each other, but when push came to shove, I felt more like this crew would stick together tighter than any other during my days in the fire department. I wish we'd have been older and more mature when we worked on the same crew, but I guess you can't have everything. It's just that when I think of some of the days I really miss, it's this crew that comes to mind the most. We ran some of the craziest calls together and worked together seamlessly. We were one of those crews that the battalion chiefs never focused on because we got the job done without drama or hang-ups. And we were led by one of the most senior captains in the department, which went a long way toward keeping us not only safe, but also respected.

I asked Benny what he remembers most from the days at station 19 and he said this:

"A couple of thoughts about the 19 days for me. That was during a time in my career when I finally figured out what being a firefighter was all about. When you're brand new you don't know a damn thing. Take some time to run some calls and be around guys that know more than you to figure things out. That's even if you take the time to look and even care to know. When I got to 19 I had a few years under my belt and I was working with some salty dogs that knew a hell of a lot more than me. I guess for me, that's when brotherhood really meant something. I finally understood it. We always had each other's backs no matter what. Thinking back even with somebody like Mack or Robert or fill in the blank we still had their back regardless of whatever circumstance. You don't always see that in the moment but I see it pretty clearly now.

Benny's absolutely right about brotherhood and what it meant to all of us. We may have had different off-duty lifestyles, political persuasions and religious beliefs, but when it came down to it, we were fiercely loyal to each other in a special way that I've rarely experienced since that time.

For all the good about the conditions, rescue shifts were a royal pain in the ass at station 19 because of those Fountain Hills move-ups. But those shifts also afforded an amount of freedom, which I regularly abused in sometimes-legendary ways. I'd been assigned to EMS supply ordering for the north half of the city when I got to station 19. There was a supply room at our station, which held every durable and disposable piece of EMS equipment carried on a fire truck or rescue in Scottsdale. This was another royal pain in the ass because I had to keep the supplies stocked and place orders with our warehouse regularly, keep an inventory and confirm receipt of anything that was ordered when it arrived. Having several vacant rooms since fire prevention moved out of station 19, but some leftover office equipment, it wasn't long after I'd been handed the shit sandwich of EMS ordering that I'd turned the current supply room into my own private office complete with a desk, chair and shelving for durable/expensive EMS supplies and taken over the room next door for all of the disposable supplies that crews would come to the station to restock on a regular basis. I added a stereo and a TV to the office and ended up having a place for the firefighters on my shift to hang out in whenever the door was open. Turning such shit into sunshine is a talent shared by firefighters the world over, and that office was arguably better equipped than the captain's office down the hall.

I used our supply program as an excuse to travel citywide and have fun and freedom during rescue shifts by seeing crews at every other station. Want pizza for lunch? There's a great place over by station

14. Let's drop off some IV supplies to those guys. Need to pick up paint for a project at home? Well then, station 10 needs some winter blankets because the paint shop is right down the street. The project had its privileges. But what on the surface appeared to be a benefit was becoming a way of isolating myself, and my EMS office was detaching me from my surroundings. The year was 2004 and I was already showing signs of something that wouldn't fully be diagnosed or understood until 15 years later. Isolation was not only a symptom of the problem, but was also my unhealthy coping mechanism.

Chapter 16
"Crashed and Burned"

———

"ALERT 3" IS THE FIRE department dispatch code for a plane crash. On a sunny summer weekend day, we were assigned to a TRT Alert 3 in the desert east of Fountain Hills. We pulled into a large dirt area about a mile away from a huge column of grey and black smoke coming from a brushy hillside off in the distance, with flames visible from our position. Smoke color, quantity and speed of travel all provide valuable clues to firefighters regarding what's burning and this particular column meant that not only was a crashed plane burning and putting off billowy black smoke, but the surrounding brush in the desert was also ablaze, sending wispy grey smoke skyward. Fortunately, the smoke was heading straight up into the air, meaning the fire was most likely not making an aggressive run in any one direction. But there sure was a lot of smoke rising very quickly; meaning that the fire was quite hot, considering the ambient temperature was probably near 100 degrees.

There's perhaps a little more art than science involved in making the decision to fly instead of walk to a scene. Things like the condition of any patients, terrain, weather and equipment required are all taken into careful but rapid consideration before flight. Knowing that time was of the essence, it was decided that we'd need a helicopter to access the crash site and Jim called for Maricopa County Sherriff's Office (MCSO) Fox 1. The brown and gold Bell 407 helicopter arrived quicker than normal after dispatch, as they'd been alerted to the call through the airport at which they were based and were ready to go when our call came for their help. When they landed, the crew took the side doors off the back of the aircraft. Doing so prevented damage to the doors during rescue operations and made it a hell of a lot easier for us to manage equipment and patients. We loaded our two yellow and black EMS backpacks into the ship as per usual, but this time we had a fire to deal with as well. Mack and I had suited up in our Nomex flight suits and class-3 rescue harnesses, but this time we added initial attack wildland fire packs that carried drinking water and a fire shelter, which resembles a one-man foil tent that firefighters can deploy as an absolute last resort in the event of an approaching flame front that can't be avoided by other means. You may remember that I didn't have time to deploy it at the Rio Fire years earlier. In addition, we loaded two 5-gallon water bladder bags, a shovel and McLeod (a two-faceted rake/scraper) with which to fight the brush fire. In short, we were loaded HEAVY. In fact, I'm amazed that we were allowed by the pilot to carry that much weight, and having sharp tools with us in the cabin of a helicopter probably wasn't the safest idea. In order to regain some lifting capability, the co-pilot or "observer" stayed back at the LZ (landing zone) and we lifted off, headed into a pretty serious situation. We arrived overhead in about one minute, and orbited the crash site once or twice to get an idea of what we were dealing with. From 300' above, it looked like a movie scene. I could see the remains of a crashed yellow airplane in the middle of about an acre of burning brush. Only the ends of the wings and part of the tail were still distinguishable as yellow, as the rest was burned black. It appeared to be an old two-seat open cockpit plane, with one seat in front of the other. And it was clear from above that those two seats were in fact occupied. A remarkably symmetrical, 200' circle of two to six foot tall flames appeared in a ring around the plane, with a black center portion. Inside the circle, the remains of several Palo Verde or mesquite trees already smoldered grey amongst the wreckage. One thing stood out about the scene. It looked like the plane had just dropped straight down out of the sky instead of skidding in. There wasn't a long debris field or any obvious scrapes or damage to the ground behind the aircraft. The smell of smoke entered the helicopter cabin as we decided on a path of least resistance to enter the burning circle on foot.

We set down about 100 yards from the base of the 50' tall hill atop which the plane was located because landing within the body of the burning brush would present obvious problems due to rotor wash. One thing about fires in the Sonoran Desert is that the large vegetation and associated flames are usually spaced out a bit. Picture 20' tall trees with grass, rocks, cactus and shrubs between and you've got a pretty good idea of what it's like. Now light it all on fire and decide which flames you want to run through in order to get to the downed plane with two more than likely dead bodies in it. We aimed for the burning grass, which only puts up flames about a foot or two tall, an easy jump if you're not carrying 45 lbs. of water, 30 lbs. of EMS gear and a hand tool.

Adrenaline and training really do take over in situations like this. But all of the training and experience in the world can't adequately prepare one for these conditions. Dealing with one dead patient, or a plane crash or a brushfire each on it's own is tough enough. Now add all three together, plus helicopter work and you're in a war zone minus the gunfire. It was definitely an ICBIDT (I can't believe I'm doing this) moment.

Mack and I unloaded more gear from the helicopter than we could carry in one trip, and keeping our top priority in mind, each carried an EMS pack and hand tool, leaving the water bladders for the next crew to manage. As FOX 1 lifted off and returned to the LZ to pick up two more people, the loud turbine whine was replaced by the familiar campfire-like crackle of burning desert. Charging through the shortest flames we'd scoped out from above, we entered the brush fire and crash site at a near running pace, causing us to cough and choke in unison when we hit the smoke. Undeterred, moments later we stood next to the burning wreckage of a pre-WW2 era plane, its two occupants still seated inside. The front seat had the flight controls in it and an adult male. The back seat had an adolescent male in it. Both bodies were burned beyond recognition and looked like dark grey mannequins with patches of burned flesh draped over them. Any hope I'd had for saving lives on this day evaporated into thin air just like the smoke from what was left of these people's fun day out flying. There was no pulse-check, no shake and shout and no check for breathing. They were gone.

The radio traffic:

"Rescue to command..."

"Command, go..."

"We have two 901H[25] in the aircraft and a one acre bush fire in light to medium fuels, backing downhill at a slow rate. We're conducting fire attack and need additional manpower. Two bladder bags are located south of the fire."

"Copy that. You have two 901H and one acre burning. Manpower is on the way in FOX1."

In order to make a desert brush fire go out without any water, you must dig down through grass and other vegetation until mineral soil is reached. This effectively takes away the fuel from the approaching flames. Mack and I set out doing just that, digging and scraping a line about 1' wide, snaking around trees and bushes along a path a little longer than the entire perimeter of a football field. Jim and I think Gil arrived with the bladder bags and began mopping up hot spots near our fire line and within an hour or so, the fire was declared under control. That time passed remarkably fast, as I think I just zoned out and went into wildland fire mode while I dug line, kept an eye on the flame front and tried unsuccessfully to put what I had seen earlier out of my mind. And then the questions started. Who were they? What kind of plane was that? Why did it crash? But the absolute worst question of all came later that afternoon when one of the Sherriff's Deputies on scene asked if we could help get the victims out of the plane and into body bags.

With a body bag resting on what was left of the right wing, we positioned ourselves to lift the backseat passenger from the vintage plane. I was at the head and per normal procedure for a living patient, would make the call for four of us to begin the move. When my count reached three, I went to lift and support the victim's skull, which collapsed in my hands, exposing his brain matter. It almost didn't seem real. I did my best to keep not only myself together, but also what was left of his skull and brain as we moved him into the first body bag and then his father's body into the second. It was later reported that the plane had been seen doing aerial acrobatic moves, including loops, just before the crash. As in the past, none of us spoke much about that call ever again. I wish we had. Over twenty years later, remembering it still has an effect on me that I can't seem to shake. It doesn't stay on my mind for extended periods, but it's just... there.

Here's the odd thing about "career" calls like this. Somehow the triumph outweighs the tragedy at the time. All the excitement of flying into scenes like that, making decisions about what to do and the four of us putting out a brush fire on our own initially covers up the fact that a father and son had died. It's not until sometimes weeks or months later, when that adrenaline rush is long gone, that it hits you. You think about their lives and what affect their loss will have on their loved ones, family and friends. Then you start to think of your own life and your own loved ones. But as much as you want to and as natural as it would in fact be, you keep yourself from breaking down. You don't cry. You don't express emotion. You put up the strong appearance expected of you not only by those around you but also by you yourself. All this may be to prove your strength and unshakable courage to those around you, but it's probably got more to do with proving those things to yourself. But the reality of the situation is that the more calls like this you run as a firefighter, the better you become at your craft and the more confident you become in your skills, especially when they go "well". How could it ever be said that something so tragic went "well"?

Chapter 17
"Out With The Old"

RURAL/METRO HAD A LONG history in Scottsdale, which was actually the first community Lou Weitzman ever protected with a single fire truck in 1948. Back then Scottsdale had a population of just 2,000 people, and was more of a farming and ranching community than the sprawling resort city it is today, with cattle and cotton fields spread out to the east of Phoenix. In 2005, Scottsdale had a population of over 200,000 and was outgrowing the private fire department model. In short, Lou's concept for providing protection for a small community was out of date and inadequate for a city of nearly a quarter million people. As a private fire and EMS protection provider, the bottom line often came to the forefront in our operation with Rural. This became clear with regard to equipment, staffing, and numbers of apparatus, pay and benefits. We had three firefighters on trucks and in some stations only two. Equipment was in some cases outdated and pay was consistently behind the average of other area cities. A 401k plan was available, as was a stock purchase plan, since "Rurl" was publicly traded on the stock market. At a point after the new millennium, several firefighters banded together and talk of forming a union began. It got ugly for a long period of time and the tension between admin, politicians and firefighters built to a boiling point. The city hired an outside specialist to do a study regarding the efficiency of Rural in Scottsdale, and it was revealed that increased staffing, training, stations and apparatus were needed in order to increase service levels and decrease response times to emergencies.

The ultimate outcome was a fight to oust Rural/Metro, forcing Scottsdale to take over its own municipal fire protection by forming the Scottsdale Fire Department a few years after Rural employees formed IAFF Local 3878. Despite having a collective bargaining contract with Rural, the local membership still felt as though we'd be better off working for a municipality rather than a private corporation, and I agreed wholeheartedly with this. A measure was put on a ballot and it went to a vote before the citizens. The yes/no issue was unclear to voters in that many of them believed that a municipal department would mean that all of the current staff would go away and they'd lose their beloved firefighters who'd served them for years. There was a massive campaign launched by Rural to steer voters toward a no vote because Scottsdale was their largest and highest paying contract; losing Scottsdale would have a massive affect on stock prices and it would clearly open the door for other communities protected by Rural to take over their own services as well. The local wanted a yes vote and knew that a municipal department would be better in every way, with better pay, four-person staffing on every truck and one of the most important things: participation in the state of Arizona's Public Safety Personnel Retirement System, or PSPRS.

Election day came. Leading up to that day, union members from Scottsdale and every Valley department had gone door to door in an attempt to educate voters on the issue and get "yes" votes. Our local did a massive amount of work with mailers, signs and all the usual behind the scenes political work involved in trying to get such a large ballot measure to pass. Rural's main argument was the added cost of running a municipal department, which struck a chord with Scottsdale's affluent population. There was even a committee called the "Know Enough To Vote No Committee", co-chaired by a city council member.

Firefighters assembled at every polling location, conducting informal exit polls. I personally heard nearly every voter I asked about their vote tell me, "I voted for you guys, I voted no." What they didn't understand was that we'd have hiring preference over outside personnel if a new department were formed. And for that to happen, we needed them to vote "yes". To say we were uncertain about how this was going to turn out is a massive understatement. There was a big gathering put on by the union at a local hotel conference room with cocktails and dinner. Harold Shaitberger, President of the IAFF, flew into town and was present. Supportive members of the City Council were there as well. The atmosphere was one of high anticipation, along with a bit of confidence that the vote would go our way. Late in the evening, the 10 o'clock news came on with the results. In the May 20, 2003 Scottsdale Special Election, 29% of the cities residents voted and propositions 200 and 201 failed to gain a majority of the votes. We'd lost. The voters' answer to our plea to form a municipal department was no.

You could have heard the proverbial pin drop in that room with well over 300 people in it. Everyone there was devastated. We'd all had hope that our dreams of having better working conditions, a real retirement and a brighter, safer future would come true. We'd all had hope that there'd be new and better equipment to do our jobs with. We'd all hoped that our local would take a massive step forward in our community with regard to respect in the eyes of other firefighters. But I think in that moment, many of us lost hope.

Morale took a nosedive. We were pissed. The voters didn't understand what they'd done. I actually remember a woman patting me on the back in the Safeway produce section days after the vote, saying, "We voted no so we could keep all you wonderful firefighters!" We had come to hate the people we served now, and felt betrayed by their incompetence. I remember things like engine and rescue crews responding to quiet neighborhoods in the middle of the night for medical calls with sirens and air horns blasting as if at the busiest of intersections. "Wakey, wakey, no-voters", said a crewmember on an overtime shift I was working one night. Work became a seriously toxic environment for some time. Then something very curious happened. Something we didn't expect or think was possible. The tide turned, and in a very big way. At the end of 2003, Rural/Metro announced that it would not pursue another contract with Scottsdale after the current one closed on July 1, 2005. Their Chief Executive Officer cited the company refocusing on their subscription-based services, but I can't help thinking that there were some behind the scenes dealings between Rural and the City that brought about the change.

One would think that this would be cause for massive celebration amongst the ranks, but consider this. There were many, many questions about how this transition would happen, who would be hired, what the process would entail and at least a dozen other things we didn't think of at the time but which surfaced later on. In all, I'd say it was the most stressful time of the entire workforce's lives. But there was a pale glimmer of something so badly needed by everyone then: Hope.

Chapter 18
"The Transition"

TO THIS DAY, WHEN YOU mention "the transition" to anyone who worked for Rural/Metro in Scottsdale in 2004, it means the 18-month process of removing the private company that had provided fire protection to the city for over 50 years and replacing it with a municipal department. The sting of having the citizens vote to keep Rural just a few months earlier was seemingly erased by the proposition of such a huge change in working environment for everyone, but there was some seemingly bad news. We'd all have to test and interview for our jobs with the city. The process would even include a firefighter-specific physical agility course. It was the sort of thing that 20-year old kids took when they were first getting into the service. But we had men in their 50's who would have to do the same test, for time, in order to keep working in the same place they'd been for in some cases, several decades. I'd been on for just over ten years, was very fit and healthy (despite the rock climbing and aerial ladder accidents) and it was still very stressful for me. Kind of like Eminem's song, "Lose Yourself", this was our one shot, our one opportunity to seize everything we'd ever wanted. Would we capture it, or just let it slip?

Chandler, a city about 14 miles south of Scottsdale, would host the physical agility portion of the testing process and would supply the proctors for the event as well. It was probably a good move, because I'd venture to guess that not a single person in Chandler knew anyone from our department and they'd therefore be impartial. There had been much debate about alleged conjecture regarding the timing of each event in the test, but the city did it's best to see that there was research behind every decision they'd made and things moved forward. Over the course of a week, every "Phase 1" applicant for Scottsdale Fire went through the testing process in Chandler, which included a 200' charged 1 ¾" hose drag, a hydrant connection, an extension ladder raise, a sledge hammer sled obstacle and a 150 lb. dummy drag. When my time came, I floored it and passed by a supposedly large margin. Whatever the time, it was generous. I believe it was pass/fail, with no documented time recorded. And I don't remember hearing about anyone failing. Furthermore, we were allowed to take the test in our PT gear, helmets and gloves, forgoing the full turnouts and SCBA commonly worn during such tests today.

The next phase of the process was to be a one-on-one interview with the incoming Fire Chief, Billie McDowell. During the transition, there was much cooperation between Billie, the existing fire department command structure and union officials. This was an attempt by the incoming staff at seeing what characteristics of our fire department culture allowed us to have a current public approval rating just shy of 100%. But there was an overarching feeling within the ranks of firefighters that what Billie really wanted to be was different. That idea did more to stir discontent than to motivate, as it was unclear as to what he really wanted out of the incoming personnel.

Stu Sommers was the president of IAFF Local 3878 throughout this time and was a friend I'd known since I started with Rural. He rubbed certain people the wrong way, but we always seemed to have a relationship based on mutual respect. And anyone who didn't like or trust him probably had just heard the abrupt, truthful way in which he was notorious for communicating. He was an old-school paramedic, but had a caring bedside manner that defied his outward appearance most of the time. In a nutshell, he was tough when he needed to be and compassionate the rest of the time. He was actually one of the first paramedics I'd modeled my own practice after, and I very much valued his opinion.

Also during this time, brain, lung and testicular cancer survivor Lance Armstrong was laying waste to the entire professional cycling world on an annual basis at the Tour de France, a 21-day road bike stage race. His ubiquitous yellow cancer awareness "Livestrong" bracelets were absolutely everywhere and I'd started wearing one for the first time two days earlier. One morning, when we ran a call on Rescue 19 for an "Ill Person", I showed up with my partner Benny on rescue 819 to find Stu and his engine crew treating a frail looking woman for nausea and vomiting. The scarf wrapped around her head was a clue as to her underlying condition. Because she was too weak to walk, we lifted her small, almost weightless frame gingerly to the gurney for transport to the ER. Stu climbed into the back of the ambulance to give me a report on our patient and when he said that she had terminal cancer, I focused my gaze on her and asked if she knew who Lance Armstrong was. As she shook her head "no", I took the yellow rubber bracelet off of my left wrist, put it on hers and said, "They'll tell you all about him and this bracelet at the hospital." We were then ready to leave the scene with her and headed out.

Knowing that Stu may have some valuable interview information for me (You know that I sure did like my interview prep!), I hopped out of the rescue for a moment with him.

"Hey Stu, what do you think Billie will be looking for when he's hiring people? What should I expect on the interview?" Without missing a beat he replied, "The kind of people who'd give their Livestrong bracelet to a woman with cancer." Patting me on the shoulder, he turned and walked to his truck. Although they have all but disappeared now, I still remember that day, that call, that woman and what it felt like to truly care for a stranger when I see someone still wearing one of those yellow bracelets now. And it was out of homage to that woman and that small act of kindness that I never replaced the yellow band I'd given her that day.

My "Billie Interview" day finally came and, dressed in business casual attire, I went to his new office at fire headquarters. The interview was quite forgettable really, with some pretty easy situation-based questions and one about diversity, which was fitting, as Billie was African-American and to my knowledge, only the second black man other than my buddy Ron Benly to ever work for the fire department in Scottsdale. We hit it off and I liked him immediately, and although certain people held him in poor regard, I didn't mind working for him. What I did very much mind later were his uniform policy and choice of recruit personnel for an academy a couple years later.

For all of time leading up to the transition to Scottsdale Fire, our uniform had consisted of the typical navy blue t-shirt and navy pants or shorts, depending upon the weather. When Billie took over, we were no longer permitted to wear shorts and had to wear a "Class B" shirt over a short sleeve duty shirt during business hours of the day. The Class B was a dressy collared shirt to which our metal badge and nametag were pinned. This one poor decision on Willie's part would forever cost him the trust and respect of every firefighter in Scottsdale, including me. I know it sounds petty, but it felt like he was taking away the comfort of our hard-working group for the sake of making some kind of statement to those close around him. It felt like he was trying to give us a good old-fashioned dose of discipline by sharpening up our look.

Billie made another very foolish mistake when he selected people for Scottsdale's first municipal fire department academy. He hired a couple of good guys in that group, but clearly wanted to make a statement about diversity and not quality. Every race was represented and they were nice people, but overall their skills were deplorable. I'm not stating anything that nearly everyone in the Scottsdale Fire Department doesn't and didn't agree on. When one particular candidate was struggling in every way, multiple instructors and firefighters came forward with their concerns to Billie. He reportedly said, "Everyone passes this academy." Clearly performance mattered less than variety of skin color and age. And after several years, many from this first academy were gone due to poor on and off-duty decision-making and injuries. That did, by the way, include several white guys. It's a shame that the brave and skillful men and women in Scottsdale had to work with these people, and they weakened our department. It's also a shame that the residents and visitors of the city had to count on them for service. I hold no ill will toward any of my brother and sister firefighters, regardless of race, age or any lifestyle choices they make. Such characteristics mean nothing to me. But what's inexcusable in any fire department is chronic tolerance of poor performance, dishonesty and downright cowardice.

As part of the transition, there was a rebid of all positions in the department based on seniority within Rural Metro. Everyone would lose their current station assignment and have to rebid from scratch. One other big change was that we'd no longer have rescues to man. That service would be taken over by a private company called "PMT", which meant the hellish shifts spent on move ups and transporting people to the hospital long into the night were over. (Ironically, Rural bought PMT about six years later.) It also meant changes to our crew and shift structure. We'd be getting a "C-shift", and would work a "3-4 shift"; 24 hours on/24 hours off for three shifts, then have four days in a row off. It was a far cry better than anything we'd had in the past with Rural. My Captain was still Jim and my EMT firefighter partner would still be Benny, but an engineer rank was added and would be filled by a paramedic with a good amount of time on by the name of Don Hadley. He'd worked TRT at 19 on B shift for a few years prior to the transition, but was still a bit wet behind the ears when it came to rescue work. What he lacked in that area he more than made up for with paramedic experience. He'd been a medic for several years before I even started, and had experience working ski patrol at Sunrise, a ski area in eastern Arizona.

Working out the kinks is part of such a large shakeup in manpower, equipment, scheduling and everything else that was new at the time and it was decided a few weeks after the formation of the new department that we'd put on a palm tree rescue drill for some of the new senior command staff to see. We loaded up the crew in our trucks and went to a recently abandoned hotel parking lot, which had lots of tall trees to choose from. Palm tree rescue is one of the disciplines practiced by TRT crews in the Valley. With an abundance of the towering trees present in the area, landscape workers occasionally get into trouble while working high above the ground, with either an equipment malfunction or a medical emergency to blame. The fastest and safest means of rescuing an arborist in one of these swaying giants is the use of a ladder truck with its aerial bucket, which was what our first training evolution entailed. But there are times when a regular ground ladder or aerial truck doesn't have access. In this case, the only option is for a rescue tech to strap on gaffs (instep spikes which dig into the tree trunk) and a harness with a flip rope around the tree and start climbing up to the patient. There's a fair amount of rope rigging involved with the operation, and a high level of fitness combined with a low body weight help considerably. I had a fair amount of palm experience both on-duty while training and off-duty trimming several of my own palm trees each year in my yard at home and with several of the new senior staff and battalion chiefs present at the drill site, I was called into action to show how it's done. I climbed to the top of a 60' high palm in the parking lot to act as the arborist "victim" while another tech got ready to come up and rescue me. In a nutshell, a rope is rigged from the victim to a pulley placed above and out to an anchor away from the tree, which allows a crew to lower the victim to the ground with a lowering device called a brake rack. A common complication is when the arborist's gaffs are firmly planted into the tree trunk, not hanging free from the tree. To overcome this and free the gaffs, crews perform a "vector angle" by pulling the rope at an angle down toward the ground, which in turn lifts the victim a few feet, freeing the spikes from their hold on the tree. Once everything was set up, my partner called for the vector. I felt the rope pull snug against my harness and I was lifted enough for my gaffs to pull free from their purchase, about three feet. Then the ground crew made a big mistake. Instead of walking the vector angle back out of the rope smoothly and gently, they let it go all at once. The 1/2" static rope snapped taught as a bowstring and I dropped about four feet, caught by my harness and the rigging. Being static rope, there is essentially no stretch during an impact and this violent shock load hit my back only a year and a half after my rock climbing accident. My back felt fine for about 30 minutes after the drop, and then began getting more and more painful to the point that I couldn't function at work. I took a few shifts off to recover from that one, and our TRT crew looked foolish in front of new chiefs who'd been hired from other departments. But worse, my own faith in my partners at work took as equally strong of a shock as my back had. I'd sustained yet another physical and psychological trauma, but shook it off as "part of the job". If there's one thing I've always hated, it's that feeling of falling. Go skydiving? No. How about bungee jumping? Hell no!

Soon, the stresses of having all these new things in place with our "new department" really started to show. The new uniforms, new chiefs and unclear expectations were all hard to deal with. Everyone seemed to be operating at a heightened state of stress and pressure to perform flawlessly. And for the most part we did just that. But now instead of doing it out of our sense of duty and valor, it felt like everyone was being told to be "World Class". And yes, staff actually used those words.

All while this transition was going on, there was another one going on in my family. When I was growing up, I can remember one of my mom's sisters having something called Alzheimer's disease. Age 9 or so was the first time I'd heard the term and at the time, it was just explained to me that my aunt Anita didn't recognize the people around her any more and that her memory had gone. Later, as an adult, I'd been running calls in the same Scottsdale neighborhood area for almost 13 years. During that time, I'd seen several people's mental health decline due to this insidious disease and the affect it had on the family members standing by their sides.

And here is how I knew something was wrong in my own family. My mom had made a coconut cream pie for my birthday ever since I could remember, so I knew something was off the year she showed up at my house with a banana cream pie instead. Yes, something that simple was the first clue I saw in my own mother that something was off. I wish I could forget talking to my dad in my backyard that very same night, having pointed out my observation of her apparent mental decline and possible difficult decisions in the future regarding her extended care. Enraged, he told me that it was none of my business and that he would take care of her forever. He and I had an on-again, off-again relationship since I moved out, when he had said, "You won't have a pot to piss in if you move out now." What he couldn't have known then was that saying those words to me did nothing but motivate me to excel at every pursuit I'd ever engage in, partly for my own reasons, but also to prove him wrong. Unfortunately, motivating me wasn't his intent. It was to continue to belittle me the way he had for a long time prior and it made leaving home all the easier. After a tense birthday dinner the night of our backyard talk, they left the house and I made no attempt to speak to him for a period of time.

Months later, while on shift at station 606, my dad broke the silence and called my cell phone. Shaken, he said that his wife of nearly 40 years didn't recognize him and kept telling him that he'd have to leave the house because her husband was going to be home soon. He wanted me to come up to the house and help calm her down. Looking past my feelings about him, I turned my focus to her. Mind you, I'd been commuting to work via bicycle for years at this point and had no quick way to get to my parent's house, ten miles north of my station. I told Jim about the situation and he immediately said that I could take his personal vehicle and handle what I had to. There's a certain "family first" mindset within the fire service under which family emergencies take precedent over work and I'm glad that Jim supported me in that way. The backstage really just involved Jim calling our battalion chief and advising him that I'd be gone for a few hours taking care of my mom and that they'd be "running light" during that time, with my position not filled. If I needed to, I could take the rest of the shift off, with a firefighter called in to finish my shift on overtime.

When I got to their house, my mom answered the door and let me in after recognizing my face. I saw my dad behind her in the living room, pacing back and fourth with his hand on his forehead. My mom shuttled me into the front room and said that she was trying to get this other man to leave before her husband came home.

"Mom, the man in the living room *is* dad. THAT'S your husband."

"Oh my gosh, are you sure?"

"Yeah mom, look at this picture of the two of you."

Picking up a framed picture of the two of them on a golf course together, I pointed to them, then to my dad in the other room. Perplexed, she thanked me for coming over to clear things up for her. To confirm that she understood, I brought her into the living room and the three of us talked for a few minutes. It seemed like all was fine for now, so I headed to the door to leave. My mom walked me out, told me she loved me and I didn't hear from my dad again after that for several more months. I did however visit my mom on occasion, which was complicated by trying to avoid further contentious encounters with my dad. My heart was gradually being broken in multiple ways.

My transition to Scottsdale Fire may have been in full swing, but my mom's transition to Alzheimer's disease had only begun to show itself. And I knew there would be no going back.

Chapter 19
"Family Matters"

———

JAY AND LORETTA BUCHER adopted me when I was four days old in a small town south of Chicago. My adoption was arranged through a friend of a friend, whom was a nurse working in an Illinois hospital. She had a patient who was also Catholic and needed to give her baby up for adoption after he was born. That baby happened to be me. My parents took me home to Georgia with them and promptly (accidentally?) had a daughter of their own nearly nine months to the day after I was born. Unfortunately, Heather and I never had any sort of real fraternal bond and I felt a constant need to fight for the attention of my parents. I rarely got into any real trouble during my formative years. My means of getting attention were never really trouble, but instead leaned toward overachieving. With the exception of getting good grades, I tried very hard at whatever presented itself to me. I'd say the environment at home was more one of neglect than abuse, but it was otherwise a typical middle-classed upbringing. My parents, and my dad in particular, just never seemed very available to me. I played every team sport in and out of school, golfed, shot archery, raced BMX, flew model rockets, built model airplanes with incredible detail and played saxophone. I was a jack-of-all-trades. Or actually a Jason, since I'd gone by my middle name until age 14, when my family moved to Scottsdale, AZ from Ft. Worth, TX. When we moved, I insisted I be called by my first name because I felt more like a Rick than a Jason. It was tough sledding, because we'd relocated in the middle of my freshman year of high school. I didn't seem to fit in with any one group in particular, and mostly spent time with adults I'd met through my newest passion:

road cycling. With a thick Texas accent lingering, my nickname in high school was "Tex". I was pretty much a B/C student, had steady girlfriends and made sure to ditch classes at school the three maximum allowable days each semester more out of principle than purpose. Scottsdale stood in stark contrast to Ft. Worth, what with its palm trees, golf courses and resorts and lots of pretty people. It really did feel like I was on some sort of a vacation for at least the first year, with a swimming pool at home and beautiful weather. During the first four years in my new home state, I also discovered mountain biking, skiing, rock climbing, motorcycling, fly fishing and I'm sure multiple other things I'm forgetting. My parents supported my decisions and I paid for them with money earned working those bike shop jobs over the years. Apparently I've always been blessed with a very healthy sense of curiosity and the ability to almost surreptitiously ask myself, "I wonder if I can..." To my amazement, far more often than not, the answer was always, "Yes. Yes you can." Realizing that answer to be true seemed to drive me to keep asking the question.

Prideful, private and stubborn are all words that depict the character of my dad. He grew up in Kansas City, Missouri in the 40's and 50's and had a poor relationship with his father also. I'd actually seen them in a full-on fistfight at our house in Texas when I was around ten years old, after which I never saw my grandmother or grandfather on his side of the family again. It was with great confusion that I grew up seeing how that relationship came to be when I was too young to understand the dynamics between fathers and sons. He was a self-proclaimed "jock" in high school, playing basketball, football and baseball. He went on to play minor-league baseball with the Washington Senators, but never made the majors. When I was old enough, he pushed me into all of those same team sports he'd been involved in, adding soccer and golf to the mix and coaching a few of the teams I played on. Tall, thin and somewhat uncoordinated,

I struggled in all four of those sports, but my physical attributes weren't the limiting factor that I remember the most. I remember not having a clue as to what I was doing on the field of play most of the time. As good as my dad may have been at playing sports, his ability to teach technique and strategy was dismal at best. It felt as though he believed that I should have intrinsically known as a pre-teen boy how to throw a football, where to be on a basketball court or how to follow through with a baseball bat at the plate. I don't remember him ever looking me in the eye and saying anything like, "Looks like you're struggling with this a bit, let me show you how to do it better." Or, "I love you son, and I'm proud of what you've done with your life." As an adult, the first real time I ever heard him express such feelings to me was a "We luv ya." and a pat on the back as I left their house one day, many years after I'd started with the fire department. He really struggled with that communication, and it formed a boundary between the two of us that was never overcome. Couple that with all of the baggage of being adopted and you have an incredibly complicated situation. In the end, it proved too much for either of us to get past and I just consciously decided as an adult to love myself enough to hopefully make up the deficit and move on without worrying unnecessarily about our relationship. It was simply drowning me and I had to get out of the frigid water before it was too late.

When we travelled together as a family in Texas, Heather and I were always allowed to pick out one souvenir from the destination. A trip to the Alamo in San Antonio got me a leather fringe-covered Davey Crocket canteen. A commemorative coin came home with me from Colorado. And at a trip to Six Flags one year, we were standing in front of a table of trinkets when my sister picked out a 14" long paddle with the six flags logo on it. I forget what I picked, but I'll never forget both of us getting punished with that paddle for years afterward when my dad saw fit to spank us for acting up. Later, my dad told me not to leave water in my Alamo canteen because it would turn into "poison". At one point growing up, I intentionally drank months old water from that canteen, hoping that it'd bring an end to the pain, confusion and anguish I was feeling. I couldn't have been more than about ten years old at the time. I struggle to call it a suicide attempt, but it really was, since it was premeditated and I knew what I was trying to do. Imagine my dad's surprise a couple years after that when he found the Six Flags paddle sitting on his garage workbench with the handle cut off after he paid a particularly painful sounding visit to my sister with it the night before. Every grain of sawdust sitting in a neat little pile I made on the bench shouted, "Fuck you" and I was feeling more and more like I didn't belong, like I had to escape, like I had to never come back. So I ran to my saxophone. And I ran to my BMX bike. Practicing for hours and riding for hours more each gave me an escape, mentally and physically. All that practice got me first chair in the Ft. Worth, TX All-City band on alto sax in 1985. Keep in mind that I was probably up against a few hundred other kids playing alto that year. Neither my mom nor my dad ever asked me to play at home for them. Not for special occasions, not for friends, not even "Happy Birthday". Playing music wasn't "cool" in their eyes. Imagine the confusion you'd experience playing the horn that they had rented so you could be in the band under these circumstances! My sister, by the way was a second-rate flute player in school and, fair enough, they didn't ask her to play either. I went on to play baritone sax in the jazz band at school and can remember playing a solo during a concert that brought the house to its feet. Days later during practice in the auditorium, I set down my sax at the beginning of a song and asked the prettiest girl in the seats to dance. And while we did, right there in the front of the middle school jazz band as I danced with her, I asked her to go to the upcoming school dance with me. We were a little couple from that point on until I moved away to Arizona a year later. I guess I've always been a hopeless romantic. "I wonder if I can…"

My mom, in contrast to my dad, had always been very affectionate and at least somewhat supportive. A first-generation Italian-American, she was the youngest of twelve kids born to full-blooded Italian immigrants in Youngstown, Ohio. Family and food are two huge items in the Italian culture and when I'd visit home as an adult, she always asked if I'd eaten and would comment on how thin I looked, with a caring hug to follow. My 6'2" frame dwarfed her some 5'2" height. She was a good cook and there were always leftovers available in the fridge. She worked as a secretary at General Motors in Lordstown, Ohio in the late 60's about two hours from Columbus, where she grew up. This is where she met my dad, who also worked for GM at the time. They were now each on their second marriage, a fact that I wouldn't learn about my mom until I was in my late 30's.

Heather was heavily involved in dance while growing up and went on to become a Phoenix Suns dancer. Curiously, I never went to a single Suns game over the years, partly because I didn't care about basketball, but mostly because I wasn't invited but perhaps once or twice. She went to NAU in Flagstaff with support from our parents then became an elementary school teacher. Also with support from my parents, she and her husband got pregnant with twins. I've met Carlton and Keegan exactly one time, the day after they were born. Later on, I'd be invited to holiday events here and there at her house, but my parents and most importantly my dad were always on the guest list and that was a deal-breaker for me that she never came to understand. Looking back now, she was simply caught in the middle of the conflict between my dad and I and although they did favor her in most ways during our formative years and later, she carried on blissfully ignorant of what it's like to carry the kind of baggage I was loaded down with over time. What she also doesn't know is that our parents later said that they knew I'd be fine on my own without their support, whether financial or moral. It reminds me of those parting words they had for me when I moved out and how I went on to prove them wrong, and makes me wonder what direction my life would have taken if they'd instead said, "We want the best for you and will always be here for you if you need us." Probably the biggest wedge between my sister and I is the fact that we just don't have a damn thing in common, other than being raised by the same parents. And unfortunately for her, what I see the most in her is a reflection of the qualities I disliked most in my dad.

When I was 16, my parents wanted me to go to classes at church to be confirmed as a Catholic. I objected on the grounds that I couldn't be involved with an organization that had such a dubious sex scandal going on at the time. Furthermore, my bicycle races were held on Tuesday nights and Sundays, which presented a scheduling conflict. Cycling had become my church and the people I was spending my time with there were my congregation. What I didn't tell them was that I was leaning toward Atheism. Resisting religion was probably the first factor in separating from my family as a young man. My preference for older girlfriends was probably another one.

Here's how I wound up leaving home. When I was 19, my sister and I had been sharing a 1983 Honda Accord for the previous two years, which was extremely restrictive for me. I commuted everywhere I could on a bike, but needed the car to get to bike races or for dates. I'd gone to Tucson for a race one weekend in the Honda and was driving back home when it suddenly stopped running about 60 miles south of Phoenix on I-10. I called my dad and asked him what he thought we should do. With no idea or mechanical help to offer, I asked him to grab my rock climbing gear bag and drive down. He towed the Honda home after I rigged up a section of some webbing from inside my climbing pack that was up to the task. A tow truck showed up at the house the next day to take the Honda to a shop for repair. A day or so after that was when my dad came to me with the estimate. The timing belt had failed and the shop wanted over $2,000 for the repairs. I'd been working in bicycle shops for about four years at this point and had just enough money saved up to fix it. I told my dad that I'd pay for the repairs, but that I wanted the title in return, since the car wasn't worth much more than the repair bill. His eyes widened and his jaw cocked forward the way they did when he was angry and he said, "No, you'll pay for the repairs and then we'll talk about how much you're going to pay for the car!" and walked out of the room. Having thought silently about moving in with my girlfriend for some time, I knew that there was an open door for me with her if I wanted it. I took the Honda key off of the ring in my room, walked into my parents bedroom where my dad was, set the key on the dresser and told him the car was all his and that I'd be moving out that week. Further infuriated, he started toward me. My mom yelled, "Jay, don't." I was an inch taller, forty years younger and plenty fit. Looking him up and down, I said, "Pffft! Let's not do that" and left the room. I'm pretty sure that stuck in his craw for the rest of his days. This is where his "...pot to piss in" line came in, not the, "I love you, son. Let's work this out." that I needed.

After I'd moved out, about six months passed before I spoke to my parents again. My mom called to see how I was doing and I was shocked to hear that my dad had moved out of the house also! He cited an inability to handle my mom and sister "ganging up on him". I'm guessing it had more to do with his drinking habit, but the reality is that it could've been anything, since my parents were each fiercely private about their relationship with one another. He moved back in around the time my sister went off to college, and I never got anything I'd consider a truthful story about the situation from any of those involved.

So that makes me the "black sheep" of the family, an outsider or maybe more accurately, an outcast by choice, but mostly by necessity. I didn't do the things they did, I didn't go to the places they went to and I didn't value the same things they held as important. A week after I moved out, I bought my first motorcycle and went to that first aforementioned riding school. Just weeks later, I had my job waiting tables and had enough money to keep a nice bicycle under me, buy my first pair of skis and start travelling a little to use them both. Within a couple of years, my life was heading in the fire department direction.

Back at station 606, occasionally over the next year or two, I'd be called into action by my dad for help with my mom and eventually she became too much to handle at home. It was then that she'd go to live at an in-patient Alzheimer's care facility. I'd visit her occasionally, which was difficult to do because I knew that her decline was irreversible and I'd seen it before in my own patients over time. I was notorious for not remembering birthdays and anniversaries, but always brought her flowers and an all-important card for her birthday and mother's day.

Tension mounted between my dad and I during this time, as he refused to acknowledge the frequency of my visits as anything more than unsatisfactory. He and I were oil and water and there was never going to be anything that would change that. When my mom succumbed to breast cancer years later, my dad stood on the stairway of the nursing home and said, "If I ever see you again, I'll knock you on your ass" as I left the facility, having paid my mom one last visit before she died. It was because of him that I didn't go to the funeral.

It was also because of him that I didn't go to his funeral a couple years later when he died of bone cancer. I haven't kept in touch with my sister at all, with one exception, for years now and I'm at peace with that.

As disjointed, fragmented and dysfunctional as my family life was as a youth, I always had clothes on my back, food in my stomach and school to attend. I also had extracurricular activities to pursue. It wasn't a "bad" upbringing, but I definitely felt neglected with regard to having loving, quality time with my parents. There just wasn't a connection there, and I think that not being blood relatives played a key part in the equation. It boils down to nature vs. nurture. More confusing was the existence of my stepbrothers, Steve and Jack. They were products of my dad's first marriage, and were about six and eight years older respectively. I only remember seeing them a couple times when I was growing up, still back in Ft. Worth. But they were more accessible when we moved to Scottsdale because they each lived in the Phoenix area. Jack had a tumultuous relationship with our dad over the years and regularly stayed out of the picture for years at a time. He had two sons, who my dad clung to and consequently after their divorce, Jack's ex-wife became a fixture because she was dad's gateway to his grandsons. Steve on the other hand was a more present figure. He and his wife had five kids over the years before they too finally divorced.

Several awkward holidays spent with relatives who lived in the same metro area, but never visited during the rest of the year sealed the deal for me when I was around 19 years old. I had absolutely nothing in common with these people, who despite being fine folks, were of no blood relation to me and I felt like a stranger in a strange land any time we were together. I felt like a stray dog that'd been rescued and I didn't belong. So I drifted steadily away from the family, and as if being towed in a dinghy behind a sailboat, I unwrapped the towrope and allowed it to slip away, trailing behind a circus of humanity that I was no longer interested in traveling with. I'd decided to sail my own ship moving forward, and despite the unknown waters ahead, knew in my heart that I had what it took to hold the rudder straight no matter how big the waves would get.

Chapter 20
"My Heart Is Racing"

THROUGHOUT MY LIFE, I've been involved in one form of competition or another almost constantly. It could be said that attention from my parents was the first thing I competed for, but a track and field day in fourth grade is the first actual race I can remember competing in. That track and field day at Eastern Hills Elementary School in Ft. Worth, TX consisted of several simple events held out on the two-acre or so recess field. The event I'd signed up for was the 40-yard dash. There were eight of us in the first heat, then four in the second and at the end just two in the final, third race. I can't remember where I placed in the first two races, but I know that the final would see me line up against a fast black kid named Trayvon.

I landed in Eastern Hills partly as a result of the 1967 desegregation of public schools in Texas. In 1981, I was bussed three and a half miles there from my Woodhaven home in an effort by the school board to blend black and white kids in schools. For the first time in my life, I'd come to understand what race even was, and what it was like to be in the minority, which I most definitely was. I'd seen fights between black and white kids and heard all manner of racial slurs, yet had close friends with black, white Vietnamese and Hispanic backgrounds. At an early age, I'd come to appreciate people for whom they were and what they did vs. jumping to conclusions based solely upon skin color.

Back to the other race I was telling you about. By the time our final rolled around, several of the other events had concluded, leaving lots of kids lining the course, spectating on both sides. It'd be like running through a tunnel when Trayvon and I were given the start. Black kids outnumbered white at the time by about ten to one, and to some extent, the two groups were separated along our 40-yard run. When we lined up, I thought I didn't have a chance, as Trayvon had won both of the two elimination heat races by wide margins. But on that day, with that cheering group of kids waiting for this race, something came alive in me. Whether it was adrenaline, fear, excitement or something else is not clear to me, but when we were given the go, I ran faster than I ever had in my life. And I won. Breathlessly walking back to the start line, cheers and applause erupted from everyone there, regardless of race. "You smoked Tray, you smoked Tray!" yelled one group of black kids, who I walked over to and celebrated with. When Trayvon came back to the line, we shook hands, and then hugged. There was only one race that day for me and I'd won it. The spirit of competition on that field unified us all if only for a short time, and it felt magical to me. I'd experienced a sensation on that day in fourth grade that I would go on to experience over and over, perhaps more than a thousand times during my life. The unifying power of competition goes unseen quite often, blurred by the fog of "war", but a true teammate or athlete will always see it quite clearly. Racing, unbeknownst to me at the time, had literally been bred into me. I was a racer on a cellular level and I'd just had the curtain pulled back on this fact.

As impactful as the 40-yard dash victory was, I didn't pursue running for competition. I did continue to play defensive end on the football team and alto and baritone saxophones in the band through middle school, but there was something new making an appearance in my life: BMX racing.

BMX started in southern California in the late 60's and early 70's, when dirt tracks with jumps started popping up as venues for kids to race their Schwinn Stingray 20" bikes. My first exposure to it was in a movie called "BMX Bandits" in 1983. You've gotta love that new thing called cable television! I was eleven years old and was amazed by the kids on screen lined up on the start gate, then jumping seemingly impossible heights into the air on the track on their way to the finish line and the glory of trophies for the top three racers. Pair that with the BMX Plus and BMX Action magazines I found on the grocery store shelf and a new passion was born. I wanted to be a BMX racer.

I already had a 20" BMX bike, and after begging my parents to take a trip to the local track to watch some races, I found myself begging them again to buy me a helmet so I could give it a try myself. And yes, back then all you had to have was a bike and a helmet to get out on track! A visit to the local bike shop later, I had a license application to the American Bicycle Association, or ABA. Enclosing the check my mom had written, I mailed it off to their headquarters and had my first racing license in the mail a few weeks later. I lined up as a 12 year old beginner on a 20" Murray BMX bike for the first time, had a hard time understanding the start gate and felt remarkably uncomfortable over the jumps, but fell irrevocably in love with the challenge and excitement immediately.

One weekend at the Lake Worth BMX track, I'd been working up the nerve to "double" a set of 2' tall jumps spaced about seven feet apart, which is faster than hitting them one after the other. I stood next to the track and watched the fast kids launch over them seemingly effortlessly, keeping their bodies low over the bike to maintain speed and forward momentum. When the gate dropped for my next practice run, I was determined to give it a try. I accelerated off of the left-hand berm in front of the jumps faster than

I had before and pulled on my handlebars as the front tire hit the first jump. Suddenly I was airborne and weightless. A seeming lifetime later, my rear tire met the dirt perfectly on the back of the second jump. I'd done it; I'd jumped my first set of doubles! What I failed to do however was prepare for the second set of doubles about 20' after the jumps I'd just cleared. I hadn't kept my speed up enough by pedaling, and realized this at the last moment as my front tire hit the front of the next jump. This time I instinctively pulled extra hard on the bars, hoping I could get enough air to somehow clear the second jump. It wasn't even close, and my front tire dove right into the face of the second jump, causing my bike to stop dead in its tracks. My body kept moving though, and I took the top of my handlebars right in the gut, then flew over the bars and landed flat on my back in the middle of the track. I couldn't move. I couldn't breathe. Several people gathered around, including my dad in that funny circle of faces looking down at you from above. As I struggled to catch some semblance of normal breathing, my dad said, "Ha, you just got the wind knocked out of you, pardner!" Adding insult to injury, I'd broken my poor bike's frame with that hard impact. The department store bike I'd started on wasn't up to the task of hard landings under a beginner rider. It was a long ride home in the car that night, what with a broken bike and my shattered confidence.

My next bike was a "proper" BMX bike, a Schwinn Predator. Paid for mostly with my lawn mowing income, I remember coveting it's shiny chrome frame and lighter weight than what I'd started with. I also remember taking off the front brake, reflectors and chain guard, and attaching a number plate to the handlebars, all common modifications to BMX race bikes. That bike served me well and before long, I had some success and upgraded to the Intermediate ranks, then started racing against some faster kids. But that bike also gave me something very much more important than race results. It afforded me the freedom to get out of the house and explore the neighborhood, seeking adventure further from home than I'd ever been. Mind you, three miles feels like the other side of the planet to a twelve year old kid. That ability to escape my family was something I clung to for years thereafter in the sometimes sweltering hot, sometimes freezing cold climate of north-central Texas.

The next upgrade was to my racing kit. I had a red full-faced helmet and goggles, but that's where the "cool" ended. The fast kids all had "leathers", which unlike their motorcycle-racing equivalents were made of vented nylon with padded knees and shins. They had jerseys and gloves that matched the pants and all looked very professional. My first BMX racing kit consisted of the aforementioned helmet and goggles, a baseball jersey, work gloves and, wait for it, blue parachute pants. It's what I had at the time and I made do for a while until Christmas of 1984. I'd asked for a set of leathers and had tried on several sets at the local bike shop. That racing gear was the best Christmas gift I ever got as a kid, but I doubt my parents understood that. No matter, I now felt like a "real" BMX racer!

This was about the time that my dad got laid off from his job at Boeing Electronics in Texas, setting him off on a nationwide job search that lasted months. After months of mailing résumés all over the country, the tension in the house was palpable, with regular shouting matches between him and my mom, seasoned here and there with paddling punishments for my sister and I. By this time, he'd stopped using his belt for the task and was hitting us with the Six Flags paddle my sister had so unwisely chosen as a souvenir exclusively. Most of the time, it was clear what I'd done wrong, like the time I accidentally scratched his car door with my bike, but there were times that it wasn't clear what rule I'd broken or what I'd done wrong. Two other things made permanent appearances around the house: green bottles of J&B scotch whiskey and white cans of Miller Light beer. He endlessly had a red Solo cup in his hand before it was cool or featured in a popular country song. Later in life, as a new EMT, I can remember running on the first extremely drunk person I'd ever seen. Odd, drunken behavior and slurred speech aside, that person smelled EXACTLY the way my dad had smelled for years when I was growing up. The necessity for a bike as an escape vehicle should now be even clearer.

After months in the job market, my dad took a position with Motorola in Scottsdale, AZ in late 1986 as a manager of material and production control. Our house in Ft. Worth took about six months to sell and during that time, I'd been charged with taking care of the yard and being the "man of the house". In return for those services, my dad told me that when we moved to Scottsdale, he'd buy me a "moped", or motorized scooter like the one our neighbor in Texas had. He turned back on his word when we moved, saying that it was too dangerous to ride on the streets of Scottsdale. I was devastated, and trusted my dad even less than I had before the move.

I raced BMX for two years in Texas, until we moved to Scottsdale. After the move, I went to the track in Old Town once or twice, but at age 14, realized that I was starting to outgrow the sport. What I noticed was a number of people riding ten speed road bikes out on the streets and bike paths. The added range of a road bike would mean I could explore even further away from home than ever before. Sensing a deal when I showed interest, my dad offered to buy me a road bike instead of a scooter and we were off to another local bike shop to find one. The irony of this "deal" was that instead of riding a motorized scooter on the roads of Scottsdale, I'd soon be pedaling a bicycle in the very same traffic he'd been so concerned about turning me loose in! Let the exploration begin.

My first road bike was a blue Schwinn Traveler with twelve speeds. I didn't even have a helmet to wear while riding it for the first six months or so, until I'd happened upon something called a "race announcement" one day at the same shop my dad had bought the bike from. The "Desert Cycling Classic" was a 50-mile race on the south end of the valley, and I signed up. Turns out helmets were required for the event, so I got my first one, in blue to match my bike. A pair of black, padded cycling shorts and some fingerless gloves were added to the ensemble and off I went.

My dad drove me to the race, with my bike sticking out of the trunk of his 1979 Cadillac Coupe de Ville. It's the exact same type of car Ray Liotta's character drove in the 1990 movie "Goodfellas". I finished somewhere deep in the field of riders, but had experienced my first taste of road racing, including a small crash in a corner after others had gotten tangled with one another in front of me, leaving me with no escape route. I had just some minor scrapes, but still finished. That's all it took. I was in, hooked deeply by a sport that would play a pivotal role for the rest of my life. Weeks later, I had my first United States Cycling Federation or USCF racing license and began racing in the 14-15 age category with the Phoenix Consumers Cycling Club. I'd acquired my second racing license.

I had no idea who Greg LeMond was before I swung a leg over my first road bike, but quickly learned one Saturday morning when "Wide World of Sports" came on TV. There was this big race called the Tour de France, and LeMond had become the first American in history to win it in July of 1986. Watching the television coverage and seeing the pros duke it out over the roads of France sparked my imagination, and much the same way Lance Armstrong had done a decade later, LeMond's success drove a national interest in the sport. I got my feet wet in 1987, but then I entered nearly every race offered in the entire state in 1988. I raced on most Saturdays and Sundays and again on every Tuesday night, when a criterium[26] series was held in a large parking lot at the base of South Mountain Park in Phoenix. Many events were road races held out on the quiet back roads of Arizona, with the junior categories covering perhaps 40 or 50 miles. But criteriums suited my bike handling skills, acquired from BMX, and my ability to sprint at the finish, with racers riding in very close proximity and commonly bumping into each other over the course of the race. My sprint would become somewhat notorious, and I won seven races in my first year, along with a slew of "primes" or races within the race on certain laps. Primes could be merchandise, gift certificates or my favorite: cash. I was 16 years old at the end of my first full season of racing, and had developed wicked tendinitis in both knees after putting them through thousands of miles of racing and training before they were ready for it. But I continued on.

Another type of race was the stage race. Like the Tour de France, the stage races held in Arizona at the time took place over multiple days, but never as long as the three week affair in France. Stage races nearly always include an individual time trial, which is a solo event against the clock, at least one road race and many times, a criterium. Overall time determines the winner, with time bonuses awarded at certain points in each stage. One of the biggest stage races I did was the Tour Of The Future, held in the southern Arizona towns of Bisbee, Sierra Vista and Tombstone. The race was for juniors only and after five days of racing, the finale was held in Bisbee. And for the first time in my racing career, there would be a team time trial. I was racing for Team Strada, sponsored by Domenic's bike shop in Tempe. Domenic was an Italian immigrant who raced on the Italian national team in the 70's and early 80's. Before Team Strada, I had raced for the Phoenix Consumer's Cycling Club and was coached by Susan Bookspan, a national-level coach and official. She'd taught me how to put together and follow a training schedule, which was actually based on Greg LeMond's, and the basics of racing. Domenic, on the other hand taught me tactics and strategy, which won me more races than my fitness ever did. The man not only knew what to do during a bike race, but more importantly, *when* to do it. Domenic had a team van that was painted to match the team's jerseys and it had a plush and very Italian red interior, ideally suited to the purpose of carrying a team of five guys, their bags and bikes, which were mounted to the roof rack in several rows. When we hit the road for southern Arizona, there were ten bikes on the roof and a dozen spare wheels. We looked and felt just like the pros featured on TV that I used to watch and wonder, "What would that be like?"

The first stage of our tour was a road race. Over 100 of us rolled out onto the course, which consisted of a few laps of nearly 20 miles each. As a sprint specialist, I liked the idea that I'd get to preview the finish a couple times before the real thing. There were guys from all over the country at the race; from teams I'd never before heard of, riding bicycle brands I'd never seen. And they were fast. Faster than most of the guys I was used to racing against. My teammates Will Philson, Adam Dash and I stuck together pretty well in the pack, as we had experience racing together. Our other two guys had a tough time, partly due to fitness, but mostly because of aggression. It takes a certain amount of aggressive riding to maintain forward position in a field of riders that big. And if you're not toward the front, you're not really racing.

Rolling into the final five miles of the first stage, the road steadily sloped downhill, allowing us to roll along at about 45 miles per hour. Elbows and hips bumping off of each other, the squeal of brake pads and the constant whirring noise made by chains on sprockets and rubber on the road are all part and parcel of the buildup to a final sprint and it's one of the most energizing, rewarding and terrifying experiences you can have on a road bike. I felt like an absolute monster, and sitting pretty in about the sixth row of riders with just over a mile to go, I was positioned perfectly to go for the stage win and a nice time bonus. Then it happened. When riders are this close together, one of the most dangerous things is overlapping wheels with the rider in front of you. When this happens, there's a chance your front wheel will get turned by the leading rider's rear wheel, causing an unrecoverable fall. That's exactly what happened two rows in front of me, and there was nowhere to go but down at over 40 miles per hour. It's like being thrown into clothes dryer made of asphalt when you fall at that speed. And as I tumbled, I was being slammed into by the other riders and bikes falling behind and on top of me. In the end, it was a dog pile of racers and bikes with me near the bottom, sliding along and eventually coming to a stop about ½ mile from the finish line. As the pile came apart and guys got their bikes untangled, the weight pressing me down onto the pavement lessened and I was finally able to get up. Taking stock of my condition, I found wounds on every extremity, with particularly deep ones on both hips. My right forearm had "road rash" abrasions from elbow to wrist, and the watch I was wearing on my left wrist had been ground down from the outer crystal to the face, completely removing the hands. I was able to ride my bike the remaining distance to the finish line, ensuring I'd be allowed to start the next stage, a team time trial scheduled to begin just a few hours later that afternoon.

As painful as a fall like that is, the scrubbing involved in the shower afterward is way worse. But it's what must be done to prevent infection and speed the healing process. This is one of the reasons cyclists shave their legs. This allows bandages to stick better and makes changing them pain-free. Walking into the hotel room from the shower to find my teammates wide-eyed and slack-jawed after hearing my groaning, I got bandaged up and tried to get my head back in the game for the next challenge.

In anticipation of the team time trial stage, the five of us had trained twice weekly on our time trial bikes. They had solid carbon fiber disk rear wheels, smaller front wheels and aero bars, or clip-on type bars with elbow pads and extensions, which allow racers to get into a low, aerodynamic position, leaning far forward over the front wheel. The key to a fast team time trial is trying to keep the whole team together until late in the race. At the finish, the clock stops when the third member of the five-rider team crosses the line. So there are essentially two "disposable" members on each team. In the case of this five-man race, each team starts at a one-minute interval, spacing the teams out away from each other on the road. The five of us lined up side by side across the road, feet fastened into our clipless pedals, held up by officials from under our saddles. The clock ticking down to our start time, I felt like I was a bull, barging against its pen at a rodeo, waiting to buck the rider off. My heart was beating out of my chest and I felt a focus like none other I'd felt in my life up to that point. The energy was amazing. When we started together and settled into our rotational order taking turns at the front of the group, I realized just how painful this stage was going to be. The road rash on my right arm sat squarely on the handlebar pad and was excruciating. Adrenaline was taking over, and I started pushing. A team of five riders on time trial bikes, all taking turns at the front and rotating in a line is a beautiful sight to behold, and we were killing it. We had about 30 miles to cover as fast as we could, and at about 20 miles, our weakest rider was having trouble, unable to take his turn at the front. A short time later, we dropped him, followed later by our fourth rider. So it was left to me, Will and Adam to cover the last five or six miles on our own. The three of us dug in deep, each taking longer pulls at the front to allow the other two to recover, then rotating again. Our team van pulled up next to us in the oncoming lane of traffic, Domenic leaning out of the passenger side window, maniacally banging his hand on the door and yelling, "Go, go, go!" We crossed the finish line with only three guys and set a time that was in the top 10 teams and best of all seven Arizona teams entered.

The rest of the stages were fairly anticlimactic. I was so sore and beat up from the stage one crash and digging so deep during the team time trial that I felt like I was just riding to survive. I'd traveled with my teammates from hotel to hotel until the last day, when my family came down from Scottsdale to see the last two stages of racing. My 16th birthday was coming up at the end of the summer and I had my learner's permit to drive. My family surprised me when they arrived in a grey 1983 Honda Accord. It would be mine until my sister turned 16, 9 months after me, at which time we'd have to share it. I ordered a Yakima roof rack at the shop I worked at and soon had a perfect car for getting to and from races, not to mention to work, school and dates! I also sprang for a set of tires and some maintenance items here and there, keeping the car washed and waxed. But nine months later, I had a colossal problem when Heather wanted her share of time with the car I'd been spending time driving and money maintaining. We worked it out, but only temporarily as the fuse was lit on a powder keg waiting to explode.

When I raced as a junior, virtually all of my income went toward gas, car insurance, bike parts, race entry fees and hotel stays. My world revolved around racing and I was good at it. I lost track at some point of how many races I won over the years, but I know the number is well into three digits. Back when I moved out of my parents' house, I had been racing for about five years, and I had also added mountain bike racing to my repertoire, but never won a race in that discipline. I really enjoyed the training on dirt much more than that on the road, though. It reminded me of the fun of BMX, but was much faster. There was a mountain bike racing series put on by the Mountain Bike Association of Arizona, or MBAA and over the course of the season, the organization sanctioned about six races, each in a different part of the state. The leader in points at the end of the season was crowned state champion. The National Off Road Bicycle Association (NORBA) held mountain bike races all over the country, as well as the national championship races. More prize money was available at the NORBA races for those willing to travel and compete against the best racers the country had to offer. More fun was available at the MBAA races though, which took on the feel of a camping trip with racing as a side attraction since most people camped out at the race venues, nearly always on public land. A mountain bike race is like a time trial on dirt. The entire field starts together, but seldom do more than a few riders wind up even close to one another at the finish. A solitary race by nature, I didn't care much for it. The team tactics and strategy of road racing always appealed much more to me, so for most of my racing career mountain biking was used more as a fun training tool than anything else. The experience I gained in both road and mountain bike racing served me well later in my fire service career for many reasons.

I rolled up to the start line at bicycle races somewhere around 1,000 times in the thirty-four years when I did it. It became as natural to me as breathing and I loved almost everything about it. Considering a nearly one in ten success rate over those years, I drew an obvious amount of self-confidence through participating in the sport. And I also made many lifelong friends in the process. It's a very special thing, winning a bike race. One special enough to have still brought me to tears after the finish line nearly every time, well into my 40's. There's just so much suffering, pain, risk, time and money invested in training sometimes more than 20 hours per week that strong emotions are natural when all of the sacrifice yields results. Often it's as much a feeling of relief as it is joy.

Oddly, my involvement in motorcycle racing began with an injury and ended with another. It was a broken back that eventually led me to my sportbike club and then a racing license with the national level Championship Cup Series (CCS). A close friend named Fred Jackson ran the local CCS affiliate, Roadrace Southwest (RRSW) and also taught for TEAM AZ, the local riding school backed by the Motorcycle Safety Foundation. I'd gone to their classes when I got my first motorcycle after moving out of my parents' house, and had been invited back to teach their basic rider course. Fred, a well spoken and intelligent, British expat, was incredibly influential in our community and was loved by all those around him who weren't "twats" or "cunts", as he referred to them. Above all, Fred provided unwavering support to the friends he made. I wish he'd gotten that support in return from everyone, but can say that he absolutely got that from me. His exuberant "What's up buddaaaay!" still echoes in my memory today.

Being too busy with getting hired onto the fire department in the past, a second opportunity had presented itself with the company years later when I had my girlfriend at the time take the basic riding course. The offer to teach still stood, so I went to their Rider Coach Prep class for a month and had started my apprenticeship with them when I broke my back rock climbing. Unable to stand on my feet all day to teach, the street instruction spot evaporated before my eyes. But about a year later when I started doing track days, John, the owner of TEAM AZ, approached me. He said that he needed an instructor and wanted me to ride with the beginners, watching for safe riding and offering coaching where I thought it could help out in exchange for free track time. Turns out John and a few of his instructors had been watching me ride and thought I'd be a good fit. I couldn't say yes fast enough, and when I showed up the next month, I was handed an orange traffic vest with "Instructor" on the back. In addition to riding with the beginners, I was allowed to ride in the intermediate and expert groups as I wished. This effectively more than doubled the amount of time I could previously spend on track, and caused a rapid increase in my skills because in addition to giving riding advice to beginners, I'd begun actively seeking guidance from the fastest experts, all of who had number plates on their bikes indicating that they were racers. At that point all I wanted to do with this track thing was have a great time getting everything I could out of my old 1998 Honda Superhawk, wearing my tires out all the way to the sides of the tread, and being part of the best sportbike club in Arizona. As you may predict, one thing quickly lead to another.

A custom motorcycle leather manufacturer called Vanson Leathers offered a discount for MSF rider coaches, so I requested a measuring kit and ordered a custom set in black perforated leather. I upgraded my helmet to Arai, a top manufacturer. Next was my motorcycle. I loved Hondas, so I shopped around for their top sportbike at the time, the RC51. A big, powerful bike, the RC51 was Honda's racing platform in both AMA and World Superbike classes, piloted by Nicky Hayden and Colin Edwards, who became my heroes of the day. Just months into this, people started asking me about racing. Fred approached me at a TEAM AZ track day at Firebird International Raceway one day.

"Dude, why don't you start racing? I mean, you're riding in the expert group and are faster than a lot of the guys who are racing. You could kick some major ass and make some money!"

"Aww, c'mon Fred. I'm getting all the track time I want right now and it's totally free!"

"Okay, buddy. But you should really think about it. You can make some cash with as fast as you are."

Not much more than two months later, I'd crashed my RC on the track, requiring new bodywork and paint. I'm very much a do-it-yourself kind of guy. For most of my life it's been out of necessity because it costs a lot of money to replace things with new ones instead of repairing the old, or paying someone to do work that you don't have the tools for. Paint kind of went that way for me. I went to the local PPG auto paint store, asked tons of questions and did lots of research and when the new fiberglass bodywork for my RC showed up, I painted it myself. That first job was more of a 50/ 50 job than anything else, looking great from 50' away at 50 mph! But I did it, though, and now had all the equipment required to do professional level paintwork.

A thought turned into plans and plans turned into action. Through the online club message board, I solicited PSC interest in getting a group together to take the new racer's clinic and the next month about ten of us filed into the class trailer first thing on a Saturday morning. By noon, we'd learned everything amateur racers need to know and had certificates to prove it. The next day I lined up on the grid for my first motorcycle race on a used track bike I'd bought from a friend. And I won the Heavyweight Superbike race that day. The sensation I'd felt while bicycle racing was back. And the emotion of winning was there too as I entered the paddock area with a helmet full of tears of joy. I was again hooked so deep that there was no turning back. I was still racing criteriums on my road bike on Tuesday nights, but motorcycle racing would now take the top spot on my list of passion projects. I came up with a stunning paint scheme for my race bike and actually won the CCS Heavyweight Superbike Championship that first year. Now, instead of running the yellow number plates required in the amateur class, I could run the white number plates of the expert class. Along with the new plates came a different bike. I needed a 600cc bike so that I could race in multiple different classes, so I sold my first steed and bought a friend's 2003 Honda CBR 600rr race bike. My third paint project, it came out looking very sharp and I was able to do up to seven different races on Sundays because it met the equipment requirements for the different classes. It was that racing season when I was approached to act as assistant instructor for the RRSW New Racer's Clinic (NRC). I was running the clinic on my own the following season. And the season after that, I rewrote the curriculum. Teaching new racers was almost more fun than racing, and I had a steady stream of people coming through the clinic sourced from my ties with PSC, which I was now running as well with the help of a fantastically loyal core group of moderators. Years earlier, attendance at the clinic was an average of three or four people each month. After I took over, RRSW had to buy a bigger trailer for the clinic, which regularly had at least a dozen people. And the variety was amazing. Men, women, young, old, fast and slow all turned up to get into racing and it was pure magic to see the excitement on their faces when they came back into the class after their first "mock race". I put my heart and soul into teaching those riders and I was able to pass on one of the most important things one can take away from racing; the lessons you learn through racing can be applied everywhere else in your life in one way or another. Whether it's a job interview, a promotion or a first date, the ability to stay calm when you're scared or nervous on the start line applies to those other situations too. Taking care of your equipment, helping someone else in need, practicing good sportsmanship and not only being a gracious victor but studious in defeat apply elsewhere in life. It's these principles that guided the rest of my racing career and I'm so very grateful to have played a part in the lives of the few hundred people I taught over the years.

It was summer in 2008 when something changed inside of me. I'd had some success during the racing season, but wanted more. I wanted an AMA Pro racing license, and the opportunity to compete against the fastest racers in the United States. I'd been teaching the NRC for three years and had an idea for putting on my own high performance riding clinic using the new GoPro action sports cameras, the first generation of which had just been introduced, along with on-board and trackside video feedback. These changes were happening off-track, but there was something changing when I was on the track. I wanted to find out how fast I could go. I wanted my lap times to drop. I was ready to really explore the limit and expand what I was capable of on two wheels. "I wonder if..."

There are generally two types of people who race motorcycles. One is the aggressive rider who tries very hard, but falls down often. The other is the timid rider who never gets up to speed and lacks the confidence required to push hard and ride at the fastest level. Then there was me. I was quick but conservative, knowing that any injury sustained at the track would probably be bad enough to keep me out of work for a while. I eased up to the limit, but never really stepped over it very often. After the summer break in 2008, I started pushing. I started exploring the limits of traction and lean angle, never jumping over the limit with both feet, but regularly going there with one foot and coming back just to test the water. I repeated the process over and over, and maximized the quality of my riding time on track by hitting it hard 100% of the time, right from the pit lane every time I went out for a session. It wasn't so much that I was trying to crash as much as it was that I didn't mind anymore if I did. I didn't crash, but I started winning again, and in the fall of 2008 started sending sponsorship proposals to everyone from Red Bull to Coca-Cola and my favorite local restaurants. I also asked for the required letter of recommendation from the CCS administrative staff and included it with my racing résumé in my request for an AMA Pro road-racing license. A month later I was a professionally licensed motorcycle racer, #531. In the winter of 2008, I secured a Dunlop tire sponsorship, VP race fuel support and had deals with five different motorcycle parts companies and two local motorcycle shops for everything from oil to clothing. But the crown jewel was my Yamaha factory deal for a 2009 Yamaha R6. I was doing it. I was chasing my dream and it was coming true!

I had done custom paint on around ten or more bikes at this point, and painted a great looking set of race bodywork for the R6, made to look just like the stock street bodywork in an effort to show that Yamaha's "Win on Sunday, sell on Monday" theory could hold true. Off-season development went great and I had some very good settings for the suspension to handle the rough surfaces of my local tracks when the season started. The bike was a rocket ship, and with my new attitude toward speed, the bike's capability and the support of a great crew of people in the paddock, I was able to win 28 straight races in early 2009, going undefeated for the first four months of the year. My heart most certainly was racing, and it was going faster than ever.

Chapter 21

"Near Miss"

————

IN MAY OF 2009, I ALMOST died again.

The morning started off warm, but beautiful as I watched the sun rise over Interstate 10, just 1000' from the quiet paddock at Firebird East. I'd taught another New Racer Clinic the day before and saw a few of the excited students walking here and there around the paddock, giving me a wave, a thumbs up or just a kind nod when I saw each of them. My Yamaha R6 was up on front and rear stands, with tire warmers bringing my tires up to operating temperature while I added just one gallon, or roughly eight pounds of race fuel to the tank. I had started bringing my bicycle with me to the track, partly for transportation around the paddock, but also for warming up before races on my stationary trainer. I was mentally ready for the seven races I was signed up for and had leads in all seven class championships, along with the overall points lead for rider champion with RRSW after four months of racing so far this season. If this streak continued, I would win seven number one plates for each class at the end of the season and the overall championship. And the way would most certainly be paved toward AMA professional racing, bigger sponsorships and a new way of life. But that's only if the streak were to continue.

I got a poor start in one of my first races of the day, and was behind my friend Jeremy for the first several laps. This was one of the Superbike races, and I was keeping up with his 1,000cc Suzuki on my 600cc machine. Nearing halfway through the race, I'd studied his weaknesses enough to make a passing plan and decided it was time to execute it. I took a run at Jeremy entering a sweeping right hand corner called the "Lake Turn" at about 80 mph when he fell directly in front of me. There was nowhere to go and nothing I could do. My right knee slider was dragging on the ground when he fell and I stood the bike up to try and avoid him. I ran over his body as he slid helplessly in front of me, fracturing his pelvis and sending my bike and me skyward as if I were back racing BMX. Saving the bike from a crash was hopeless. I landed hard on my head and shoulder, and then slid for a long way with my left leg trapped under my motorcycle. Coming to a stop in the gravel trap next to the track, I sat up and took stock of my situation as the cloud of dust settled and the smell of race gas and burnt rubber came up all around me. I'd struck my head hard enough to deeply gouge my helmet and break the visor off, and something felt wet in my left boot. I looked for Jeremy at this point, but my view of him was obstructed by the crash truck that had arrived on the scene and was parked between the two of us in the gravel. I was able to walk on my own (with a considerable limp) and got a ride off the track in the crash truck. Back in the paddock, after taking off my leathers, I realized that I'd ground completely through the leather and underlying plastic armor protecting my left knee, and had taken off the skin next to my knee cap, deep enough to see bright white bone below. And what about that wet feeling I had earlier? That was my boot partially filled with blood from my knee injury. As I heard the helicopter lift off with Jeremy on the way to the trauma center, I wished I had a spare pair of socks with me and distracted myself from thinking of the underlying possibility of crashing that every racer is haunted by on some level, whether they admit it or not. I had more racing to do and had to look forward rather than focusing on the incident. It was time to try and put Humpty Dumpty back together.

Using my extensive first aid kit and medic knowledge, I quickly and privately bandaged my knee and then joined my pit crew in looking over the R6. It had sustained heavy body and handlebar damage, and the foot pegs were broken off of both sides of the bike. Having spare parts and friends paid off, and about an hour later, after the lunch break, my bike was back up and running. I had a spare set of leathers, as well as a spare helmet, gloves and boots. In short, my bike and I were put back together before the lunch break was over and I was ready to go out in my next race.

My friend and race organizer, Fred, had visited my pit to see how I was and checked to see if I needed anything. Here's where the mentality of a racer comes into play. Under normal conditions, if a racer crashed and damaged their helmet in any way, their weekend at the track was over. My main helmet was heavily damaged and sitting inside a storage bin in my trailer, but my undamaged spare was sitting on the table next to Fred when he walked up. When it came time for someone to inspect my helmet, it was passed because I had moved the inspection sticker over from the crashed one and I was consequently deemed ready to roll. When a racer, and I mean a true racer, suffers a setback, the first thing they start thinking of is how to get back on the track, how to get back into the race. But it goes further than that. We always want one thing: More. More speed, more victories, more points, more sponsors and more fans cheering in the stands and wishing you good luck in the paddock. The finish line and crossing it first is all that matters. It's both the beauty and the curse of racing, which provides laser-sharp focus and renders you incapable of worrying about anything else in your life at the moment. You could be bankrupt, in the middle of a divorce and unemployed, yet when you're heading into turn one with twenty other lunatics behind and beside you battling for the same small piece of tarmac, it all just melts away. I've never felt more centered and present in a moment, and it's a very special thing. But it's also highly addictive. When success comes in racing, one of the first things that go through your mind on the cool-down lap is the next race and the next opportunity to win again. It's like a kid getting off of an amusement park ride and getting right back in line to do it all over again. And after lunch that Sunday, I was back in line to do it all over again.

I was on pole position again for the next race because I was the season points leader, and got a little slower start than normal. I decided to sit in the pack, a few positions out of first, but with the leader in sight, while I took it somewhat easy to make sure the bike and my brain were working right. Around four laps into the race and with everything but my knee feeling fine, I decided to go to the front. Over the preceding laps, I'd been twisting the throttle hard to the stop out of every corner, which rotated the throttle housing on the right clip-on handlebar enough to inhibit the travel of my front brake lever and when I went for the brakes heading into the slowest corner of the track, I had about half the normal braking power required to slow from about 90 mph to just 35 for the corner. Knowing I wouldn't make the corner and still traveling at least 50 mph, I ran off into the gravel trap, and headed straight at a tire barrier, turned hard left and managed to make it a glancing blow when I ran into the four-foot tall wall of hard rubber. But now I had an injury to my right lower leg where the bike had pinned it against the tire barrier. Yes, now both of my legs were injured. I didn't tell anyone that and the process of putting Humpty Dumpty together started all over again.

This time was less involved than the first, for sure, but I'd hit my head again in the fall. My buddy James' helmet appeared on the table this time, but this time no one came around to inspect it and my crew adapted the handlebar so that the throttle housing wouldn't rotate again this time. I was ready to go again for the next race, and lined up on the grid on pole position again. In this race, I went much easier at first, running fourth behind three buddies of mine who were lined up essentially nose to tail as we circulated the track at racing speed for the first three laps. The pace was fast, but nothing I wasn't completely comfortable running. In fact, it was entertaining to see three of my friends dicing it up with one another right in front of me, all the while making another passing plan that I would soon put into motion. With my bike, if not my body, feeling good, I decided that it was time to go for it again heading into that slow corner because I knew I had lots more speed available than my friends there. I allowed a small gap to open in front of me during the next lap to get set up, and then with a great amount of closing speed, made a strong run at the inside line of the lake turn at around 100 mph with my right knee slider firmly planted on the asphalt. This was it, and I was fully committed to an aggressive pass. When I stood the bike up and went for the front brake lever, it came all the way to the handlebar, building no brake pressure whatsoever. The following events took place over the course of about four seconds. I pumped the front brake lever to try and build pressure, but there was none there. Knowing that if I maintained my current line into the corner, I'd take out all three of my friends like a bunch of bowling pins, I quickly headed left, to the outside of the corner and away from their path while getting all over the rear brake to try and slow down, missing the rear end of the third place rider's bike by about two feet. What you should know is that Firebird isn't the safest track for motorcycles, and the only impact protection provided on the outer walls of the property is afforded by barriers of used tires, stacked about four to five feet high and bolted together. These tire barriers are meant for stopping the weight of a car, not a motorcycle, and they're pretty solid. As an ironic aside, I had written to an organization just months earlier with a proposal for air fence, a safety barrier specifically designed for motorcycles. My proposal had been denied. With my rear brake locked and my bike fishtailing through the gravel trap at about 90 mph, I knew I was going to hit the tire barrier head-on, and that this was going to be a very hard impact. The last evasive measure I tried was another turning maneuver in order to keep from going head-on into the wall. It didn't work, and the lights went out for me as soon as I made impact. What happened next was something I'm glad I don't remember. There's a 10-foot tall chain link fence surrounding the track property, with steel vertical I-beam girders holding it up. My body and bike hit the tire barrier and flew up over the fence and landed outside the track. When I went back to visit the site a year later, about two feet of the fence were still bent over at the top, immediately adjacent to a steel I-beam upright that, if I'd hit it, would've certainly cut through whatever it contacted at that speed. It took some time for the crash crew to even find me, as they had responded to the *inside* of the track in the corner where I had crashed. They had to actually drive *out* of the track's front gate and around to where I lay, next to the smoking wreckage of a once beautiful Yamaha R6, with the entire front end torn completely off of the rest of the frame. My friend Casey said that I was screaming the whole time I was being treated by the ambulance crew, who launched a helicopter for transport to Scottsdale Osborn. After loading the wreckage onto the crash trailer and looking it over, one of the guys wanted to cover it up with a tarp because it looked pretty serious. Casey said, "We can't do that, everybody will think he's dead when we get back to the paddock!" My other friend James, who was also by my side at the crash site, said that it was one of the worst moments of his life and was told by the flight crew that they didn't think I would survive as I was being loaded for transport.

The first memory I have from after the accident was sitting up on the bed for about thirty seconds while I was being wheeled to surgery. The trauma surgeon was confirming with me that he'd be operating on my left femur. I remember looking down at my grossly swollen, twice-it's-normal-size leg and seeing what looked like sharpie pen marks all around my knee. The surgeon had marked all of the upcoming incisions he'd soon be making in the operating room. In no condition to respond, I put my head back, collapsed flat and passed out again. About a day later, I regained consciousness upstairs in the ICU and got the news. I had fractured my left femur, left ankle and neck in two places. I had a cervical collar around my neck and my left leg felt like it was swollen to a point that the skin seemed more like a sausage casing, wrapped up in a bulky dressing that hid the carnage from view. They'd screwed my ankle back together and placed a titanium rod inside the full length of my femur, with screws through each end to hold it in place. I was on a pain pump for the second time in my life, and the familiar warm sensation of a million poppies flowing through my veins as though drifting along on a summer breeze only just barely masked the pain that I was experiencing. This was a bad one.

Fortunately for me again, I was in extremely good physical condition for this accident and more than one doctor told me that had I not been, the chances of me walking again would've been poor. The prognosis was a probable return to work in six months or so with extensive physical therapy involved. I made it back in three. Again. The racer inside of me approaches injuries, even catastrophic ones, as temporary setbacks. But this one was different and would require some serious work. It also came at a bad time in my life, when my first marriage had been failing for a while. Adding insult to injury, I vividly remember my parents walking through the door of my ICU room, shaking their heads at me in disappointment. They didn't rush in, saying they were concerned for me or were glad I was still alive. They just looked disgusted and disappointed. And, Morphine or not, I found that disgusting. It couldn't have been clearer that I'd be on my own to recover this time and despite the number of visits from friends and coworkers, I was beginning to feel an irrevocable sense of loneliness and sorrow. I also knew that my professional motorcycle-racing dream had come to a violent end. I was descending further and further down into a tunnel of darkness and despair, with not only shattered dreams, but also a broken body to go along for the ride.

After a week in the ICU, I got an ambulance ride home, where a hospital bed was set up in the living room. I had to stay off of my leg for a few weeks, and then got around with a walker, then crutches and eventually a cane. During my recovery I developed blood clots in my legs, requiring painful abdominal injections of a blood thinning medication to prevent a stroke, heart attack or pulmonary embolism, which could be caused by a dislodged clot. To compound the problem at hand, my wife at the time and I had just purchased a new home, thinking it would be a good way to somehow salvage our failing relationship. So that purchase went on while I was still on a walker, less than two weeks after my crash. The whole thing was a colossal shit show.

The new house was a fixer-upper, but was livable. It was also very large for just two people to live in. The plan was for us to renovate it and sell it as an investment a few years later. The crew from my station and several friends helped move everything into the new place and I was left to recover and make plans for the upcoming renovation. I had plenty of sick and vacation time, but still required some donated time from other members of the department toward the end of my recovery in order to have enough time off until I was cleared for a light duty assignment. Eventually, I made it back to the truck and got my work life back to normal. And yes, my heart was still in racing, but it was broken because I knew that I'd never go back to my motorcycle racing family. I'd had an accident that came close to not only ending my fire career but may have ended my life, had I not been able to change course just a few feet like I had, unknowingly avoiding that post at the track. It's a harsh, but probably inevitable outcome when you enter the motorsports world. The fact is that sooner or later, you're going to crash. You're going to destroy expensive equipment. You're going to have some physical scars to remind you of things years down the road, long after the scabs and bandages are gone. And you're going to have some mental scars, which may never heal completely no matter how hard you try. Perhaps the hardest thing for me was this. Motorcycle racing had become my identity. It's what I loved and who I was. I put my heart and soul into it and it burned me. I had survived another catastrophic injury, but in that four seconds going into turn 10 at Firebird East, I lost who and what I was to some extent. I didn't think of myself as a firefighter who raced motorcycles. For six years, I had felt like a motorcycle racer who fought fire and rescued people as a side job for money and benefits. My world was upside down, but like a snow globe, when things settled, my vision was clearer than it ever had been before. As had happened before, I was going through an even bigger reset of sorts for nearly every significant factor in my life.

Chapter 22
"Bitch Slaps"

———

NOTHING ACTS AS A BIGGER bitch slap than a near-death experience. It forces one to reevaluate not only what caused the brush with death, but also causes a more global scrutinizing of one's life in general. Or at least I think it should. And for the second time in my life, I was re-evaluating things.

I hadn't been happy in my marriage for a few years, and had turned to motorcycle racing to fill the vacuum left by a relationship gone cold. With racing now gone, the discontent I had been successfully coping with grew to an unbelievable level and it only took one more factor to tip me over the edge. Beginning about a month after my motorcycle racing accident, every night just as I fell asleep something horrific started happening. Thoughts swirling in my head, my mind would begin riding Firebird East again. This mental visualization training was something I had used with great success while I was still racing, but now it was different. I could smell the sweet fumes of burned race fuel coming from the three bikes in front of me. I could feel my body climbing from one side of the bike to the other as I negotiated the corners of the track with a knee dragging on the ground as motorcycle racers do. I could hear the wonderful shriek of power coming from my beloved R6's engine as it revved to the 16,000 rpm redline. And very vividly, I could feel the front brake lever come all the way to the handlebar in my right fingers as my brakes failed. I could feel the bike straighten up as I avoided colliding with my friends and the rear end fishtailing violently left and right with the rear brake desperately locked up and doing virtually nothing to scrub speed. And even more vivid was the sensation of striking a tire barrier at 90 mph, which caused me to jump violently in bed before sitting up, breathless and sweating. I couldn't understand why this was happening every night, but knew that I needed help to get through it. My then wife provided no such help, and no sympathy when I explained what I was going through. She actually wanted me to sleep in another room so as not to disturb her. I felt like she may have had a "That's what you get for racing" sort of attitude about it. Even after I started going to a therapist to work through what was happening, she didn't want anything to do with talking about my feelings or for that matter, her own. I was having flashbacks from the accident and needed serious help to start healing my mental wounds.

And that was it, the last straw. I couldn't be with this person for the rest of my life, which I had a newfound value for, if this was the best support on offer. I knew that I'd be better off alone than with her, and a few weeks after my flashbacks had begun, I told her that I wanted a divorce. The next period of time was spent going to physical therapy, managing pain with Oxycontin and waiting for a light duty assignment to materialize at work. All of it was painful, and I feared that I'd be assigned to review patient care reports at a desk for months before I could make it back to the truck because this seemed to be where every injured firefighter was being sent at the time while they recovered.

I knew that at some point I'd have to stop the pain meds so that I could get back to work and when I went in for an appointment with my pain control specialist, I asked about stopping the Oxy. She said that she could gradually reduce my dosage and over the next two months, stop altogether. I asked if I could just stop on my own now, to which she replied, "Well, I can think of a lot more humane ways to do it." I left with a slightly reduced Oxy dose prescription and a plan. What I didn't know at the time was that no one would ever ask whether or not I was still on pain meds when I returned to work. I could have kept taking opiates forever and no one would ever have been the wiser. But it was still my goal to never run a call at work under the influence of narcotic pain meds.

It was a Friday morning when I decided to skip the morning Oxy pill. I was now out of my neck brace and had been walking with a cane for a few weeks, attending physical therapy three times per week and still having flashbacks each night before falling asleep in a narcotic-laden fog. I occupied myself that morning without incident, but at around noon, I felt a chill as though it was freezing in the house. I got up to check the thermostat and saw that it was at 78 as per usual, with an Arizona summer outdoor temp nearing 100 already. I though nothing of it until a few minutes later, when I realized that I was sweating profusely. "Fucking thermostat", I thought as I went back to check the temp again. Huh, 78 again. It then dawned on me that I was going through common symptoms related to narcotic withdrawal. I made it another hour, alternately sweating, then freezing and was reduced to crawling on the floor to get to the thermostat as I obsessively watched it for a change that never came. I couldn't take it any more and took an Oxycontin at around 1:00 and another that night. The next day, I made it until around 2:00 before I took my first Oxy of the day, with sharp pain stabbing through my left knee, ankle and neck and more withdrawal signs and symptoms showing themselves.

Something terrible happened next. As I was ridding my system of narcotics, I fell into a deep depression. Here's how deep. I had these things on my plate: A failed marriage, shattered racing plans, a broken body, an uncertain professional future, a narcotic addiction, a non-existent and unsupportive family and nightly flashbacks from a nearly fatal accident. One afternoon I found myself ruminating on these undeniable facts on the downstairs floor in the basement of my house, with a loaded .357 magnum in my mouth, thinking of how to get the angle of the shot lined up to ensure that I'd take out the brain stem at the base of my brain, guaranteeing death. While I did this for a few minutes, I gazed across the room at my mountain bike sitting in a stand next to the wall. I hadn't ridden anything with two wheels for months, but there it sat. Staring intently at it now, I thought about how good it felt to ride. I thought about what the freedom of cycling meant to me, and started to feel that bike speaking to me, begging me to get out on a beautiful single-track trail again. I thought about the first memory in Texas I have of looking back over my shoulder, pedaling away from my mom's safe support, riding a bike for the first time without training wheels. I remembered the joy of crossing so many finish lines on a bicycle with my arms outstretched overhead in victory. I thought about the relationships I had built over the years with so many teammates, coaches and training partners. And as I slowly pulled the gun from my mouth and safely lowered the hammer, I had the strongest urge I've ever had to go for a ride. And just as my passion for two wheels had very nearly cost me my life a short time earlier on that racetrack, the desire to go for a ride had just saved me. That's how powerful a force something can be in a person's life, and that's how powerful riding and racing have been in mine. What doesn't kill you truly can make you stronger.

Knowing that I wanted to kick the drugs in order to get back to full duty at work, I made a plan. Over the next week, I switched over to Percocet, a weaker medicine for pain and stretched the time between doses as much as possible. The following week I switched to Vicodin, the weakest of the pain relievers I'd been prescribed and then was able to control my pain with just Ibuprofen shortly thereafter.

I had done it. I'd kicked a physical and mental narcotic addiction for the second time in my life and gained an intimate knowledge of what's required to do so: determination. I felt like I had dealt addiction a bitch slap of my own and it felt great to be dealing one out instead of repeatedly being on the receiving end. I was going to turn this thing around for myself. I was determined to turn my entire life around.

The remains of my R6 sat in the garage, useless to me. I got a call one night from a racing friend who asked if I'd be interested in selling it for parts and I agreed. My old engine went on to race at the AMA national series without me for the rest of the season. I threw what didn't get sold into the recycle bin. I sold my race trailer to another friend, who used it to transport equipment for his band. For some sentimental reason, I held onto a set of my tire warmers, but finally tossed those as well a few years later. And so with the exception of tons of scars and lots of photos, motorcycle racing was dismissed from my life forever. But the mental impact of my accident would remain.

The fire department had hired a new wellness coordinator named Stefan. His heart was in the right place, but his delivery of the importance of fitness was in a completely different language than that appreciated by firefighters. Small in stature, Stefan had the idea that instead of lifting weights and running the way we all had done all our lives up to that point, firefighters should do workouts with bouncy stability balls and rubber resistance bands. And he had taken over a group of peer fitness counselors on staff to help him deliver the message. I was one of them, and had joined the program before he came on with the hope that I could have a positive impact on firefighter fitness. When he came on and delivered his new message I was about to distance myself from the program when my accident happened. It dawned on me that I may be able to leverage my situation in order to create a light-duty assignment of my own design and I called Stefan to pitch it. I leveled with him and told him that the majority of the firefighters in the field hated him, his program and his bands and balls, finding no value in it. Where I came in was as an example of how fitness can be a strong ally in recovery from a catastrophic injury such as mine and how without the level of fitness I had at the time of my accident, my outcome may very well have ended my fire career. After a few minutes laying out the situation and the fact that I could help him get this idea out to the membership, he said he'd call me back. Minutes later, after presumably consulting with senior staff, my phone rang.

"What do you need and what do you want to do?" asked Stefan.

"I'll need a department vehicle and enough time to visit every station on every shift in order to reach out to the whole department."

"Okay, your assignment starts on Monday."

For the first time in months, I put on navy blue and reported for duty. I had no expectations and no real plan, other than to sit down with every crew individually at their stations and have a conversation about the importance of fitness in my life and how it had helped me recover from two big accidents, allowing me to get back to normal. Stefan shadowed me once or twice to see what it was all about and then turned me loose to run the program and schedule as I saw fit. I visited up to three stations per day, Monday thru Thursday for a month. I got to see everyone in the department, which was energizing to me because with our new shift schedule and station assignments, there were firefighters in the city that I hadn't actually seen in years. And somewhat to my surprise, everyone was very supportive and happy to see me. It felt great and I felt like part of a very cohesive family, a sensation I had never experienced before in my life.

My final appointment with the neurologist went well later that month, and I was released for full duty. I had plenty of time to reevaluate my life and my priorities while I was recovering this time and knew that as brokenhearted as I was to have lost motorcycle racing, I was left with the power to manage how I felt and the feelings I had toward it. I decided to look at motorcycle racing with fondness and to focus on the positive experiences that I had over those years and to feel thankful that I had the opportunity to do what I had done instead of regretting the loss. I also came up with a new analogy for life. I now thought of life as being absorbed in a towel, and it was my job now to squeeze as much out of life as I possibly could, living every day as if it could be my last because eventually there will come a day for all of us that will indeed be our last.

And yes, at around this time and with tears of joy streaming down my face, I did get to enjoy the feeling of undeniable freedom I'd been missing so badly when I finally went for that mountain bike ride.

Chapter 23
"Not A Perfect 10"

THE NEXT PORTION OF my life was full of highs and lows, with little normalcy in between, and was quite a rocky road indeed. I had gotten back to full duty at work after my motorcycle crash, and soon thereafter the technical rescue team was relocated from station 606 to station 610[27]. This was another tactical decision, this time made by the city after a study had been conducted to evaluate the best locations for all units, including special operations. What it meant to us was a nearly threefold increase in TRT calls and a slight increase in other, "normal" calls like fires and EMS. Located at the base of the McDowell Mountains in Scottsdale, station 610 is tucked into an otherwise useless piece of land behind a grocery store at the end of a strip mall. Within its "first due" area lie two world-renowned landmarks used to host massive events in Scottsdale. One venue, the Tournament Players Club or TPC Scottsdale, hosts one of the largest golf tournaments in the world, the Phoenix Open. Known for years as the rowdiest stop on the PGA tour, the place is more like a party with a golf tournament going on somewhere behind the scenes. Look up a video of Tiger Woods on the 16th hole and you'll have an idea of what I'm talking about. The single-day attendance record is over 216,000 people. Ironically, that's within a few thousand of the total population of Scottsdale, all tucked in an area of less than a quarter of a square mile. It's a nightmare during the day and even worse at night when concerts are hosted at a makeshift venue under an industrial tent called "The Bird's Nest". The sport of golf largely takes a back seat to the sport of drinking, which generates a massive strain on EMS resources during the event. Over the years, I ran lots of interesting calls at the Open, including people jumping into the golf course lakes (technically a water rescue call), a guy who fell 20' from the top of a fence after trying to sneak in without a ticket and even a drunken spectator who stumbled and fell into a massive cholla cactus. The other venue is something called West World, which hosts a load of equestrian events (always good for a few EMS calls for falls from horses), a polo tournament, a motorcycle rally and most famously, the Barrett Jackson Auto Auction. While fun to check out while on shift for an hour or two, these huge events quickly get old as many of the calls are for minor things like heat exposure or ground-level falls. But over the years, there were lots of crazy things that happened at the site, including the entire vendor and expo tent for the Arabian horse show burning down early one morning.

Also over the years, between the Open, Bike Week and Barrett Jackson, I got to see bands like ZZ Top, Joan Jett, Snoop Dogg, The Goo Goo Dolls and Poison perform on stage, sometimes standing just feet away from the performers. I also got to see the original Batmobile and Ghostbusters wagon go across the auction block at Barrett. It was on one hand a unique privilege and on the other a complete nightmare of drunken, high and otherwise completely inebriated humanity. I'd be lying if I didn't admit that it really was fun most of the time.

Event season ran from roughly January through March, making station 610 a hub of activity. The events were always staffed with extra manpower and equipment, but we always had to pick up the slack when things inevitably got out of hand and had to run calls at the events. On either shoulder of event season were the two seasons of mountain rescue calls, when people would most commonly get injured or heat affected on the trails of the McDowell Sonoran Preserve and other local trails throughout the Valley, including

Camelback Mountain, where I had learned to climb as a kid. And we went on tons of them. At some point I lost count of how many TRT calls I had run and started counting only the helicopter missions. Eventually I lost count of those also. My Captain, Jim, wasn't a paramedic, so either my partner Don or I were almost always the ones to fly helicopter mountain rescues. Remember, this was part of the reason I went to medic school in the first place! And because I was about fifty pounds lighter than Don, the crew chiefs always chose me because the helicopter needed the extra lifting capacity, particularly during the hotter summer months when engine performance suffered. Couple that with the fact that I was the strongest hiker on the crew and it quickly made sense that I often had first patient contact on many mountain rescue calls for several years, whether we made access via air or ground. What that means is I was the one who evaluated how sick or injured or dead the patient was and in most cases, decided how to get them out of the backcountry before the rest of my crew arrived, minutes later. I knew the preserve like the back of my hand because I had been rock climbing, hiking and mountain biking our local peaks and trails since I was a teenager. This gave my patients the advantage of getting the most rapid evacuation possible based on the severity of their injuries and the resources available.

Years earlier that respected battalion chief by the name of Fred Lighte I mentioned earlier wrote a document called the "3 and 1 Playbook" in which the appropriate actions for a first arriving company officer at a structure fire were laid out. It included things such as fire attack, search and rescue, water supply and structure protection and what to assign each arriving fire unit. This playbook was the go-to document for fire captains for years and it did a lot to clarify expectations on fire calls. There'd been confusion on many mountain rescue calls over the years regarding how decisions were being made around gaining access to patients, treating them and getting them out of the backcountry. It seemed no one above the rank of TRT captain had any concept about how to handle a mountain rescue and on more than one occasion, battalion chiefs made poor and overly conservative decisions regarding our tactics. Most of these chiefs were old-school TRT guys who were part of the team back when I started with the department and before they promoted. Years after being out of the game, these chiefs sometimes still thought they knew what was best for the patient and for the crews treating them.

Here's an example of the lunacy involved in a poorly run TRT call. An old-school TRT chief shows up and takes over command on a mountain rescue. The patient has a broken ankle, is located three miles away on a single-track trail and it'll be dark in two hours. The chief assigns two TRT companies totaling eight people to hike in with the Stokes basket and big wheel to package the patient and wheel them back out. The Stokes basket is a metal stretcher used to carry a patient, and the big wheel attaches underneath, using an ATV tire to support the Stokes and patient above. This rig takes at least four people to manage and if loaded with gear, can weigh in excess of 120 lbs. Oh and by the way, that patient's location is 1,200' higher in elevation than the trailhead and it's 100 degrees out. In this scenario, nine people are going to suffer. It's a nightmare for those eight people to manage the Stokes, climbing and then descending 1,200' in the heat, and even worse for the person with the broken ankle as they bounce along the trail. Access will take just under two hours and egress will be about the same. That's a four-hour ordeal, finishing after sundown. Here's what makes more sense. Launch our rescue helicopter, Firebird 10; have them land at the trailhead to pick up EMS gear and one paramedic, fly them out to the patient and lower them to the ground on the hoist cable to make patient contact. That first part would take less than 30 minutes, allowing us to get the patient's ankle splinted and to start an IV with pain meds if appropriate almost an hour and a half sooner than the ground crew could do it. If the medic needed more hands, they could call for them on the radio. The medic would get the patient packaged in a big sling called a screamer suit and call Firebird back to hoist the patient up into the helicopter and transport them to a waiting ambulance at the trailhead. Then, depending on their fuel situation, Firebird would return to hoist the medic back up and return to the trailhead one last time. Easy, and the whole thing took about a quarter of the time ground access would have taken, and only exposes one rescuer to a lot less work than the eight-person crew would have to do.

Narrow-minded incident commanders chose the slow way too many times and this motivated me to write the Mountain Rescue Playbook, which outlined the who, what, when, where, how and why of making decisions regarding how to get to patients in the backcountry and how to get them out. When I presented the document to Jim for review, he actually asked me, "Did you write this by yourself?" "Fuck me, yes I actually have some experience with this shit." is what I wanted to scream, but just shook my head at him in equal parts disbelief and disgust. It met resistance at higher levels too, as the training chief didn't want to add it to the department's online documents and balked when it was recommended that I teach the material to the entire department over the course of the next quarterly training sessions because I wasn't a captain. This is when Jim made up for his earlier comment by telling the chief in question that I should be the one to present it because I had "written the book" on mountain rescue and was a subject matter expert. Never mind the fact that I was a can-act-captain, capable of filling the right front seat on any truck in the city, including most importantly, our TRT stations! For the next three months, I again got to see every face in the department, but this time I was presenting guidance on how mountain rescue worked. It proved very empowering and bred a new level of confidence and competence, and reminded me that there's not much better way to get really good at something than to teach it. What progressively happened next was a deeper involvement in work through teaching. What I was subconsciously doing was trying to somehow reverse all the bad experiences I'd had on complicated, unsuccessful TRT calls over the years. I was trying to make myself and my co-workers masters of the trade, thinking that this would somehow prevent bad things from happening in the future. It quite simply couldn't have done that. And it didn't. But I had to try.

What all that extra time teaching did for me was give me a ton of overtime hours and some extra money. It also gave me some notoriety and street cred in the TRT community of southern Arizona. Over the years at 610, I taught most of the various disciplines covered by regional training and arranged year-end evolutions that were attended by all of the valley fire department TRT companies. At the end of the day, it was fun, but it did make me a better rescue tech than I'd ever been before. I was flying high (sometimes literally) and felt like I was mastering being a firefighter, paramedic and rescue tech all at once.

The feeling was amazing, but I didn't advertise. I grew my hair long, had no fire department stickers on my truck, wore nothing fire-related like hats or t-shirts emblazoned with a Maltese cross on my days off and had no fire memorabilia in my house, except for the old fire and TRT helmets hanging in the garage with a couple of pictures. When I was off duty, I wanted to forget that I was a firefighter altogether. I wasn't interested in talking about calls I'd run the day before and wanted nothing to do with lights and sirens still ringing in my ears and flashing when I closed my eyes. I just wanted to enjoy some semblance of peace and quiet in my personal life and didn't even keep in touch with anyone at work during my days off. There was a wall present, and I kept adding bricks to it, one by one.

Having given up on motorcycle racing, I absorbed myself with bicycle racing again, doing long road bike and mountain bike training rides during the week and racing on the weekends and most Tuesday nights. Teaching even spilled over into that for once, and I formed a company as a cycling coach. But it turned out people were more interested in buying new bikes and gear than spending money on coaching, so the doors were closed after just a single year. I was a category 1 mountain bike racer and category 2 road racer at the time, which meant that I was mixing it up with the fastest guys in the country and racing at the highest of levels, but it wasn't making me as happy as it used to. Was it the sport changing or was it something in me? Most likely it was both, but at this point it would have been helpful to realize that loss of interest in once-pleasurable activities is a symptom of PTSD. Isolation is too, and I loved my time away from people in the form of all those long training rides.

Things were changing, but I didn't see them. In fact, this five-year period of my life is actually pretty hard to remember. It just seems foggy to me, with certain highs and lows punctuating an otherwise nondescript paragraph. If anything, this paragraph was punctuated by bicycle racing. And I mean a LOT of bicycle racing, with even more training hours backing it up, typically around 20 per week in the months leading up to racing season, and "only" around 12 hours per week during the season which lasted nine months and sometimes longer. For reference, a 20-hour week of training on the road means covering well over 300 miles, or nearly the distance from Los Angeles to San Francisco, California.

Encouraging this return to cycling was Anne, who I had met in physical therapy and who would become my second wife four years later. She raced bikes also and we frequently competed as a team in endurance mountain bike races, which could run for up to 12 hours. Our relationship was built completely around riding and she rarely wanted to do anything else during our spare time together. When she was at work, I'd train on my own in a more structured program, with sprints, intervals and strength training on specific days of the week. On top of all this, I was busy renovating my 4,500 square foot house in Carefree, Arizona. Bought as an investment, it was far too much square footage for just two people to live in, but would make a great home for a family in a few years, when the plan was to sell it and downsize into something else. I poured my time and unwisely, my retirement funds into the place in a gamble that I'd come out ahead in the end, since I was doing all the work myself. It took five years to complete, but came out incredibly well. Unfortunately, I'd be splitting the proceeds from the sale just two years later when Anne and I split up after she refused to address a personal problem that I had grown unwilling to tolerate any further. I felt like a failure, and when things got to their worst, I actually said to Anne that if things didn't change, I was either going to leave her or kill myself. Weeks later, I told her that I had news. I wasn't going to kill myself and would instead exercise the other option I'd laid out. Threats and ultimatums had fallen on seemingly deaf ears for the three years that we were married, and for the second time in my life, I had to say the dreaded words, "I want a divorce." Here we go again...

Chapter 24
"Larry The Crow"

FOR YEARS, I COMMUTED to and from work on my road bike, covering nearly 40 miles round trip on my way to and from station 610. My therapist had encouraged me to do so, as part of a plan to mentally prepare for my shift on the way in and mentally decompress from my shift on the way home. I thought of it as mentally putting on, then taking off my "cape", or going into then coming out of the superhuman mindset required to get me through working in dangerous conditions with actual life and death consequences. When most people think of that situation, they consider their own mortality. But in my game of life and death, the stakes were also the lives of the people I was entrusted to serve. I used my one-hour commutes to reshape how I thought of myself, to think about the day ahead and prepare for the both rewarding and costly experience of being a firefighter/paramedic/rescue tech who could also be called into the position of engineer or captain at literally a moment's notice. I used to actually practice on-scene radio reports aloud as I pedaled along, simulating what I'd say as the first-arriving unit on a variety of emergencies, or would mentally review paramedic treatment modalities and algorithms. To call climbing in and out of these roles stressful certainly doesn't do it justice. But the meditative rhythm of pedaling through the Sonoran desert in the early morning did a lot to calm me. I did it in light and dark, wind and rain, hot and cold every shift unless I needed to drive for some reason, like teaching a regional TRT drill session the day after work.

The tones dropped one Saturday on a mountain rescue at the Gateway Trailhead in Scottsdale, just two blocks from our station. The additional information on follow-up revealed a male patient who had fallen from a mountain bike, which was normal enough. But this time the alarm room said these words: "CPR in progress." I knew the logistics and probable outcome of working a cardiac arrest or a "code" in the preserve, and they weren't good. You see, there are treatments like chest compressions and oxygenated artificial ventilation, which have to essentially be carried out continuously throughout the encounter. And while not moving, a crew can do these things and much more just about anywhere. It's when the patient has to be physically moved a significant distance that things get complicated. We had no way to continue providing CPR during patient movement from this scene in the mountains to an ambulance. Our patient was about two miles from the trailhead, but only a quarter mile from a neighborhood. It was akin to the feeling of crawling through the desert, desperate for water, only to see it constantly just out of reach. We prepared for a helicopter evac, and sent the next arriving unit to make access from the nearby neighborhood. They made patient contact and started Advanced Cardiac Life Support (ACLS) just a few minutes before we lifted off in Firebird 10. Jim was with me this time and we talked with the crew chief about how to handle the situation of not being able to perform compressions or ventilate during the two-minute flight from the accident site to the landing zone (LZ), where ACLS could be resumed. It was decided that they'd just have to fly fast. We concluded that flying would limit the time without compressions better than trying to evacuate with a ground crew. The other obvious option would have been to do a shorter flight with the patient from the site to the neighborhood, but our hoist wasn't rated for forward flight with the cable extended, meaning that we'd have to have air rescue techs in the neighborhood waiting to receive the patient. And that would've taken an extended period to set up. We were going to have to do the best we could with what we had at the time.

As we entered the air space above the scene, I could see the typical flurry of action going on for a code, but instead of it taking place inside someone's house as per normal, it was happening in the middle of a single track trail in the desert. Wrappers and packaging for all the used medical supplies were strewn about and the ground crew was apparently doing a good job with their efforts. One person was running the cardiac monitor and controlling defibrillation shocks. Another was pulling cardiac drugs like Epinephrine out of the drug box. Another was performing chest compressions, and the fourth was attaching an Oxygen mask to a green and silver O2 cylinder, placing the mask over the patient's nose and mouth as he involuntarily and rhythmically nodded up and down in reaction to the compressive efforts on his chest.

Across the helicopter headset I said, "Put me in about 100' east of 'em, so our rotor wash doesn't hit too hard." knowing that an artificial dust storm would wreak havoc on the ground crew's situation.

"Yeah, roger that." replied the pilot.

After orbiting a couple of times to evaluate wind speed and direction, we came to a hover east of the scene. From above, I could make out three mountain bikes lying on the ground, and the patient's two friends standing on just the other side of the scene from us. A fleeting feeling of sadness for them crossed my mind as the Crew Chief (CC) pulled the hoist control pendant off the wall next to his seat, thumbing the toggle switch to lower the hoist hook and cable down into the cabin before handing the hook to me. Having attached and locked the hook to the front of my harness, I looked the CC in the eyes and nodded.

"Rescuer attached to cable", said the CC.

"Roger that."

The copilot transmitted on the tactical radio channel: "Attention all units, Firebird is conducting a hoist. Hold all unnecessary radio traffic until notified."

Then I heard, "This is my heading and this is my altitude. Begin the hoist" as the pilot essentially handed over control of the aircraft to the CC.

What followed was a sequence of events that I found to be completely normal in the face of total chaos. I had become so comfortable in this situation that a calm would fall over me during the process, and a feeling of being perfectly centered and absorbed in the moment came on like a comforting embrace. It wasn't entirely unlike my emotions during a motorcycle race. How I managed to remain calm during a helicopter rescue, I thought, had to have something to do with that experience. Intense excitement tempered by quiet confidence. I was going to work, and I knew exactly what to do; yet now the screaming engine of my race bike had been replaced by the twin turbine noise of an Agusta helicopter and it's spinning rotor blades.

The CC made a motion to disconnect my seat belt and I did so, refastening it blindly behind my back, careful to not accidentally clip in any of the equipment on my harness, which could snag me when I moved to leave the cabin. Next, the CC pointed to the door. Smoothly and calmly, I reached out to the handle above the door, which was wrapped in red nylon accessory cord to provide a better grip than the original painted metal beneath it. As I climbed out of the door, my head was just three feet below the spinning rotor blades, which provided a strobe affect as the bright sun shone down through them. I felt the hoist cable come tight on my harness and sat down with my weight in it, body dangling in a seated position with my lower legs stabilized at the shins against the bottom of the open side door. I nodded to the CC and he did the same as he thumbed the toggle again to begin lowering me 80' to the ground below. Over the years, I had developed a way to "fly" my body in the hurricane-force rotor wash coming down from the helicopter. By slightly extending my hands out to the sides, I could turn myself left or right by changing the angle of my palms and thereby avoid a dreaded spin that usually can't be stopped until you're on the ground. When I had descended to a height of 10' above the ground, I looked up and extended then retracted my arms out to the sides, indicating to the hoist operator that I was almost down. With knees bent to absorb the shock, one foot forward and the other under me, I set down and immediately unlocked and disconnected the hoist hook from my harness, holding it out to the side to avoid becoming entangled in the cable, which was always one of the biggest hazards upon arrival on the ground. Looking up at the CC, I raised my free arm out to the side and began motioning out, then to my helmet and back, showing the signal to raise the hook. As it passed through 10', I made the signal again out to both sides and refocused my attention to the situation on the ground. I was about to jump in the game and take over running Rescue Sector from the company officer.

I brought something called a Bauman Bag down from the helicopter with me and would use it to package the patient inside for the hoist back up to Firebird. Picture it as a big red and black burrito with straps all around it and a person laid out flat inside. After a 100' walk, I was with four of my buddies who were in the middle of working a code on a man in his fifties who had fallen off of his mountain bike. I thought this was odd because the trail was smooth and had no apparent obstacles in it. How could he have crashed right here? What then became clear was the possibility that he'd had a massive heart attack, and *then* fallen from his bike. The lead medic gave me a report, saying that they had an IV and O2 in place, had given a few rounds of cardiac drugs and had defibrillated the patient twice after his heart had gone into ventricular fibrillation or V-fib. It looked like his heart had a rhythm at the moment, but there was no pulse, so chest compressions were still in progress. The crew was providing an artificial pulse for him with their efforts. I took over the scene and had the guys disconnect the monitor but leave the O2 mask on and tucked the cylinder between the patient's legs. Strapped to a backboard and with a rigid collar around his neck to protect a potential spinal injury caused by the fall, our patient was lifted over onto the now unrolled Bauman Bag. I tucked the IV bag and the paper patient care report under the patient's arm and began fastening the straps on the bag and finally attached a trail line to the end of the it to control a possible spin during the upcoming hoist. As I did so, I had the crew evacuate the area, but left one person behind to continue chest compressions. This entire process took no more than two minutes.

"Rescue to Firebird", I said into the radio mic attached to the front of my harness.

"Firebird, go."

"I have a 200 lb. male patient in cardiac arrest packaged in the Bauman Bag. He's oriented head to tail and the trail line is in place. Confirm Firebird will put angle in the trail line. Ready to hoist."

"Firebird copies you have the patient packaged with trail line in place. Affirmative, Firebird will put angle in the trail line. Ground units, hold your radio traffic."

That bit about "head to tail" refers to the orientation of the patient's head relative to the tail of the aircraft, and sets the patient up with their head next to the cabin for flight. That would also allow the crew to reach out and provide airway management, if not chest compressions.

As the hook began to lower from Firebird and the ship started moving sideways toward us, I patted my partner on the shoulder and motioned for him to get out of the area and over to his crew. During a hoist operation, one of the biggest hazards to crews on the ground is getting tangled up in the hoist cable if there's an excessive amount of slack on the ground. Another is the trail line, which I'd be using to keep the patient from spinning as he was lifted up into the rotor wash, which can turn a Bauman Bag violently if tension isn't kept on the line during a hoist. Having people in the area who aren't aware of these dangers puts everyone at risk, so I needed to handle this alone. I had one hand on the large metal ring attachment point for the bag and the other signaling Firebird. "RICK!!!" I heard from the group of four behind me. Turning to look, I saw two of the guys motioning for me to do chest compressions. But with both hands busy and a windstorm of dust and medical equipment wrappers about to hit me, there was little I could do but improvise. I positioned my left knee on the patient's chest and began doing compressions with it as best I could while being buffeted by wind and having dirt shoveled into my eyes. Signaling through 10' to the CC, the hook came right to my hand and I attached and locked it to the ring, signaled for the raise, then signaled through 10' again and grabbed the trail line as our patient left the ground. Keeping tension on the trail line, Firebird slowly moved away from directly overhead, which put an angle in the rope and prevented the load from spinning. Once the Bauman Bag reached the door, the CC reached out and disconnected the trail line, which fell to the ground as Firebird flew back to the trailhead with our patient. I retrieved the rope from the desert and loaded it back into its bag.

I'd be hiking out with the ground crew to the cul-de-sac where their truck was staged. There was some disagreement over why we had flown our patient instead of using our "Gator" UTV to evacuate the patient via the ground. This is a small tractor with seating for two up front and room for just a stokes basket or backboard on the back. I explained that the Gator wouldn't make it through the rough single-track section of trail and that there wasn't anywhere to sit and do chest compressions while it was moving. And there certainly was no way to work a code on a patient in a moving stokes basket and big wheel. I was being critiqued and second-guessed by one of the old-guard TRT guys who was now a ladder captain and hadn't been part of TRT in over ten years. I respectfully explained my side, which was the same view held by all of the TRT personnel on the scene, but he wasn't hearing it. Jim had to be the final one to explain our actions to him, and he still disagreed. Despite the fact that this self-righteous ignorant cowboy was wrong, it still had the affect of making me second-guess our decisions that day, which felt even worse when I got a phone call at the station hours later.

"Hey, Larry didn't make it. They had pulses back for a while in the ER, but it didn't last." I thanked the nurse for calling, then told my crew.

That one stuck with me for a while. Here was a guy out riding with his friends when he had the big one. People always point out when someone was "doing what they loved" when they died. The problem I have with that justification is that now they can never do what they loved ever again.

The next morning as I pedaled home up Pima Road in North Scottsdale with tears in my eyes, replaying the call in my head, I noticed a huge black raven flying along with me to the right, about 50' from the road. I had seen ravens and hawks circling in the desert plenty in the past, but never paralleling the road like this. And this one flew there, alongside me, for what seemed like a full minute before banking off to the right and heading back the other direction. It's said that ravens symbolize loss and bad fortune, but they're also know to represent prophecy and insight with their loud voices. I'm not a very spiritual person by nature, but I allowed that to be Larry's spirit, flying free that beautiful cool Arizona desert morning as if to tell me that he was okay after all and also to thank me for doing all I could to save his life.

Fly, Larry. Fly.

Chapter 25

"Lois"

———

AFTER THE STATION TONES dropped for an EMS call, we all loaded into Engine 610 and started toward a girl who was having a seizure at a middle school. The school happened to be almost seven miles from our station, and a closer unit should have handled the call. But the three stations closest to this address were all busy with other calls or training. Naturally, we bitched up a storm during our ten-minute response. But when we pulled up in front of the school, pulled our equipment and were led to a hallway by school staff, it was all business and we went to work. Up on the second floor of the school, a very attractive blonde woman was sitting on the concrete walkway, cradling an adolescent girl who appeared nearly unconscious.

"Lynn?" I asked, confused at who I was seeing.

"Rick?" she replied, looking up at me.

"Whaddaya got?" I asked, wondering what was going on with our patient, but also wondering why the realtor I'd used for a home sale and purchase about eight years earlier was here at this school. She gave Don and I a report on the girl's condition as the crew administered oxygen and prepared for transport. I had the small narcotics pouch with Ativan and Versed ready like a gunslinger waiting for the first sign of another seizure, which never came. As we wheeled the gurney down toward the waiting ambulance, Lynn and I were left behind to catch up for just a moment. It turned out that she had given up on real estate during the market downturn and had gone to nursing school. She had been a nurse for almost five years at that point. And that was about half as long as it had been since I had seen or talked to her. Back in her real estate days, not only had she been my realtor, but she and her husband had become friends with my then wife and I and the four of us spent some time together drinking wine, going out for dinner and enjoying each other's company. The two couples drifted apart figuratively when we each moved to different neighborhoods, too far apart for convenient visits. Through the grapevine, she had heard that I had remarried after my first divorce, and I knew that she had gone through a divorce as well about a year earlier. What she didn't know was that I was going through my second divorce as we spoke at her school that day. She asked if I was on social media, and after a quick thought, I said, "Uh, yeah I think I am." We were communicating days later, and after some small talk, agreed to meet one afternoon for coffee.

The remarkable thing about this chance encounter is how unlikely it was to have even happened. For a second-due truck to respond to a call in another area is fairly normal. Rarely does a third-due truck ever enter the equation, but it does happen occasionally. For a fourth-due truck like us to be called into action is extremely rare. And what were the chances that this call would bring us to this school on this day with this nurse and this patient, and with me on duty? I thought it would be good to catch up with an old friend and looked forward to meeting her after work about a week later.

Our conversation at our first coffee meeting largely revolved around her and her ex husband. I had been in contact with him just a few years earlier, but we had lost touch because he was going through a strange time in his life and I thought better of being involved. I asked Lynn if she had a man in her life, to which she quickly replied, "Yes, but he's a pothead." She made it pretty clear that the days may be numbered on that relationship, but there wasn't much more said about the subject. We spoke only briefly about my second marriage, and not at all of the process of it ending. That would wait until our second coffee outing almost two weeks later.

When we sat down that Saturday, I laid out before her the state of my current relationship, explaining that the opioid abuse epidemic in the United States was real and that my soon-to-be ex had been unwilling to make a change in her life when presented with an ultimatum. It was embarrassing. I also told her about the circumstances of my first divorce, the one that ended my time with her friend who she had also lost touch with before the breakup. I think at that point I told her that I was really upset about wasting the last 20 years in two marriages that didn't work out, but had in the process come up with the three requirements I would put in place in future relationships: She had to take care of herself, had to be honest, including not lying by omission, and she had to treat me right. Essentially, any relationship deal-breaker for me fell into one of these three headings and I would stay true to them moving forward.

There was no hiding the fact that we were attracted to each other now. She had always looked great when we spent time together before, but she looked fitter, healthier and in a way younger that she did back then. And she had stopped smoking, a habit that was a big turn-off, long ago. It was clear that she was taking care of herself. I couldn't help wondering if she was someone who could be honest with me and treat me right. As I walked her to her car that day, I told her that I thought she was beautiful. She replied, "You're crazy."

I quietly thought to myself, "Yeah, maybe so. But you're still beautiful."

Lynn was born and raised in Scottsdale, and we actually went to the same high school, one year apart. She was part of a group of popular girls, and I was a bike racing geek, so our paths never really crossed.

No matter, because we wouldn't have been the people we were as adults had we not gone through our own individual hard knocks over the years.

We went on our first real "date" nearly one month to the day after running into each other on that seizure call at her school. A week later at coffee, she confided in me that there was a lot going on in her life at the time that she was clearly worried about. It seemed as though she really had her hands full, and as we parted this time, I pulled her close in a hug, kissed her on her right ear and whispered, "Everything's gonna be okay" before saying goodbye. A week later, we took a hike together and had our first kiss on a nice outcrop overlooking the Phoenix valley. Everything changed with that kiss, and I knew I was falling in love with her. The timing for a new relationship was admittedly poor, as I was still reeling from the final three years of my second marriage, which were awful, again, on an embarrassing level. But I had reached a point in my life that was remarkably low and dark. Lynn had the power to brighten my dark, and to lift me up from my low, despite never actually knowing just how great an effect she was having on me. I had it bad for this girl, and I was enjoying every minute of it.

We dated all summer that year, and I spent the night at her house for the first time on my birthday in the fall. It wasn't long before I was spending more nights at her house than my own, and when my house sold after being on the market for over a year, I moved in with Lynn. We became partners in adventure, love and life back then. Making plans with her felt so good, whether it was a 16-day road trip in the Western U.S., or just going to the grocery store and running mundane errands. Everything was just better with her by my side and I loved looking forward to our time together. At some point late one night when I was driving back to my house after time with her, I started dwelling on the past again, frustrated at the amount of time I felt was wasted in my prior lives. And right then, I realized something. The view provided by the rearview mirror is quite small compared to the view forward through the windshield. It was time for me to start looking at the future right there in front of me instead of dwelling on things from my past.

Something funny about Lynn was how self-conscious she was about the condition of her garage when we started dating. I'm sure the epoxy floor, nice paint and lighting of mine didn't help matters, but she refused to let me see behind the door for months. One day, I offered to help her straighten it up and she meekly opened the door. Boxes were stacked here and there and there were some things strewn about, but it was nothing I thought she should be ashamed of, although I had a hunch that she'd already put in some work on it recently. So we set about working on it together. Soon, I found a poster board with cutout magazine pictures glued all over it.

"Hey, what's this?"

"Oh, that's a vision board."

"Okay, what's a vision board?"

She went on to explain that she had made the board a few years prior, when she wanted to change her life and take it in new, adventurous directions. The pictures included kayaks, rock climbing gear, mountain bikes, backpacks and a few other things like motivational quotes and phrases. Incredulous, I said that I knew a guy who could take her to do all of those things. She smiled and said, "Yeah, I know that guy too!" Since then, we had kayaked on the Colorado River and several others, rock climbed in a few states, backpacked the John Muir Trail in California and down to the Colorado River in the Grand Canyon, skied in Arizona and California, mountain biked in Park City and Mammoth Lakes, crossed snow fields with crampons and ice axes, explored Yosemite National Park and the high mountain passes of Colorado. We could spend over two weeks at a time on the road, only knowing where we would be sleeping on the first and last nights, making the whole trip up as we went along. We could drive the better part of a day without listening to the radio, effortlessly keeping a perpetual conversation going while we planned, relived and planned again. She gave me hope, made me feel like the most important thing in her world and was the most positive, unstoppable person I knew. She was honest without being cruel. She was compassionate, but would never take in 27 stray cats. She was passionate about not only me, but also other things in her life. She was flexible without being acquiescent. She was true and accountable to herself. She was the best thing that had ever happened to me and I wouldn't be here without her and all that she brought into my life.

On the phone with her one night at station 610, I told her that we had saved someone in cardiac arrest that day, put out a house fire and performed a helicopter mountain rescue all in one shift. It's something my crew and I referred to as a Triple Crown, and it only happened twice during my career. I went on to tell her that I really felt like Superman that day.

"Okay, Clark" was her reply.

"Well, then I guess that makes you Lois" was mine. We stuck with those nicknames ever since that night, and it was Lois that made me feel like and want to be her Superman for as long as we were still together.

Chapter 26
"Down Into The Dark"

CONFINED SPACE RESCUE calls suck. There isn't much more to say to describe them. By definition, a confined space is "...large enough for workers to enter and perform certain jobs. A confined space also has limited or restricted means for entry or exit and is not designed for continuous occupancy. Confined spaces include, but are not limited to, tanks, vessels, silos, storage bins, hoppers, vaults, pits, manholes, tunnels, equipment housings, ductwork, pipelines, etc." One of the disciplines involved with fire department technical rescue operations is confined space rescue, and Scottsdale's TRT crews were some of the best in the business at getting what is the most complex and equipment-intensive rescue evolution set up very quickly. I know this because I trained them and developed some of the timesaving measures that were adopted by other Valley fire departments over the years. In short, if I needed to be rescued from a confined space, I'd want it to be in Scottsdale. We were faster and better than pretty much every department around.

One Tuesday afternoon in late August of 2014, the tones dropped for a confined space rescue just four miles from station 610. Don and Jim were in Engine 610 and I was driving Support 610 with a new crewmember that we'll call "DB". DB had just transferred to 610 from our backup TRT station when a spot opened up. I had campaigned for him to transfer in because he needed some serious help with not only TRT skills, but fire and EMS also. He'd been on the department for about nine years, but had the working capacity of a brand new firefighter. He seemed to have a big heart and dedication, so I thought it would be a good challenge to bring him up to speed. Plus, I was in the groove from teaching regional TRT every Tuesday and having just spent a few months again precepting a new paramedic student.

When we got in the truck for the Con Space call, DB didn't know how to change the radio over to our tactical channel and couldn't work the Mobile Computer Terminal (MCT). I had to handle both of those tasks while driving a 35,000 lb., 39' long truck running code 3 with lights and sirens, weaving through traffic in the most dangerous position: right behind another truck running code 3. Understand, most people see a fire truck go by code 3 and think the show's over and there's no way there could be another one right behind it. They then continue on their way, often right into the path of the following truck. The best thing the second driver can do sometimes is to try to stay close to the first. But Support 610 was severely underpowered for its weight and much slower than Engine 610. I regularly used my motorcycle racing experience to keep up with Don while we hustled to TRT calls, and this one was no exception. I was good at making a slow truck fast by essentially never slowing down once up to speed. And DB just sat in the passenger seat and watched as everything went down. I coached him on the MCT, but we never did get the radio switched over to the correct channel to hear what the alarm room or other incoming units may be sharing or planning. Further, DB didn't read me anything from the dispatch notes available on the MCT, so I knew literally noting about the call we were headed to. When I pulled up behind Don at the scene, we were the first arriving units. We had taken about five minutes to get there. I hopped out and Jim was walking toward me saying that we were in rescue mode. I said that I hadn't gotten any additional info on the radio or MCT because DB couldn't run them, and Jim told me that we had two workers stuck in an underground vault. Don, DB and I set to work preparing our supplied air breathing and communications systems, along with the tripod/

winch system and two sets of rope equipment required to pull this evolution off. Under normal circumstances, the two rescuers each suit up on their own, with a personal gear bag and yellow Pelican storage case in front of them while the third sets up the rest of the equipment. When it happens just right, everything is ready when the rescuers have all their gear on and the crew can pretty much get straight to the work of saving lives. The personal protection ensemble includes normal duty clothes under a Nomex flight suit for flash fire protection, Nomex hood, work gloves and steel-toed boots. Because we were going into a sewer system, we put on white Tyvek chemical resistant suits over all of this, then our class-3 harness which consists of waist, leg and chest support and has an assortment of equipment attached to it such as carabiners, a rappel device and several slings. Atop all of this equipment, we each donned an escape bottle and regulator for the supplied air system. This was another harness that fastened around the waist and across the chest, with a small air cylinder that has about five minutes of pressure in it for use in the event of a catastrophic air supply failure. A TRT helmet, two sources of light, a portable radio and hands-free communication microphone and headset complete the kit. Batman carries less shit than this.

Did I mention the heat? It was monsoon season in Arizona at the time, and the temp was 100 degrees with about 50% humidity. That makes the heat index 118 degrees, a point at which heat exhaustion is virtually guaranteed, with heat stroke possible after prolonged exposure or activity. And I was about to get very active.

Once Don and I had suited up, which took about five minutes, we turned our efforts to getting the rest of the equipment assembled because DB was struggling with it. We'd been coaching him on what to do while we were getting dressed, but little progress had been made. There were two sets of 300' air lines that had to be moved about 50' from the truck to the staging area and DB's small, 5'2" frame wasn't up to the task alone. While heavy, one person commonly moves these unwieldy 45 lb. lines on his or her own. The two air carts were next, then the communications equipment box and rope gear.

We had been on scene for about ten minutes when Jim called out to me and gave me the fingers across the neck sign that we were going to have to transition to recovery mode. We were too late. Our patients were now dead and would from then on be referred to as victims.

We were there because the maintenance crew for the shopping complex we were in had gotten a call to check on an odor of sewer gas in the parking lot. When they arrived, they found that a 25' deep, 4' diameter, round sewer grease trap had filled with water from a recent rainstorm. This trap is usually fairly dry because a pump evacuates any water that accumulates down at the bottom. The pump had failed and the workers used a backup pump to drain the space, which still had water, grease and everything else that went down the drains in the local businesses coming into it. There was a fully extended 24' lightweight aluminum extension ladder in the space, the top of which was about 1' below the entrance, which was a 2' square diamond plate metal hatch, hinged on one side and open. The first worker had climbed down into the space to get the part number from the failed pump. When he became too weak and disoriented to climb back up the ladder, the second worker went down. When he suffered the same fate, the third worker called 911 and climbed down the ladder to help the others. This is a fairly common rescue scenario and the reason that TRT crews often have multiple patients in an industrial rescue setting. As we arrived on the scene, this third and youngest worker was stumbling away from the hatch, covered in grease and sewage. He looked like the 70's cartoon character "Swamp

Thing", and was attended to by the second arriving engine company, just 30 seconds behind us. One of the workers he'd tried to assist down in the sewer that day was his father.

What the workers were overcome by in the space is known as sewer gas, or Hydrogen Sulfide (H2S). H2S has a characteristic rotten-egg odor at low concentrations, is explosive at certain concentrations and can kill if breathed in at high concentrations in just a few minutes. H2S is a byproduct of organic decomposition and is commonly present in every sewer. But the concentration of gas was abnormally high in this one presumably because of the large amount of organic matter down there. The ladder had been left in place in the sewer because the pumps placed down there were failing on a regular basis. What happened when the space filled with water and what we'll call "product" was the ladder got completely submerged. When the water was subsequently drained, the ladder was left coated with sewage and lubricated by restaurant grease, making it difficult to descend even in good conditions and virtually impossible to climb back up, particularly when impaired by exposure to the deadly concentration of gas present. I'm frankly amazed that we didn't have all three workers down there that day.

Once Jim had switched the operation over to recovery mode, I knew that the two workers were dead. But it may not have been the H2S that caused their death. You see, the product was still flowing into the space from the surrounding occupancies and the level of it had covered the workers heads during the time it took for us to prep our gear, meaning that if the gas didn't get them, they ultimately drowned. I was actually clicking the regulator into my face piece and walking toward the hatch to go down there when Jim called off the rescue. He knew there was no chance of having savable lives down there and wasn't going to put me into the space without knowing exactly what was down there and the hazards involved. It remains one of the hardest decisions any firefighter or company officer ever makes, and it sticks with you in a way that can't very easily be explained on an emotional level. As firefighters, we have a sense of being able to solve any problem, to stop any hurt and to stamp out any fire, normalizing the lives of those who called us. As TRT firefighters, we have all that plus the ability to operate in conditions and places where no other firefighter or rescuer can. Above ground, underground and everywhere in between, TRT crews pull off Hollywood movie-level feats of daring do with apparent ease, which does nothing but boost their confidence after doing it for a while. For me, "a while" turned out to be about 21 years at that point, and I had run more rescue calls than I could even remember. If anyone could have saved those workers, it was my crew, even hamstrung by a poor performing member. But it just wasn't to be that hot August afternoon and we settled in for what would certainly be a long recovery effort as TRT and HazMat units from nearly every Valley city arrived on this monumental scene.

With local businesses evacuated, we had our pick as to where to go to cool down and chose a Buffalo Wild Wings restaurant after dropping off most of our gear at the support truck. The restaurant was only about 100' from the space. Don and I were both already overheated from just 15-20 minutes in our gear and began drinking water and snacking on what the restaurant cooks had left behind in the kitchen. Once in a while, someone would come in to let us know the status of the operation and our post quickly became the hangout for unassigned crews when word got out about where we had taken up station. The Hazardous Materials Team (HazMat) was brought in to evaluate the space and take samples of the product within. It was determined that the H2S reading was above the highest level the equipment could measure, and Hydrogen Cyanide, another, even more toxic gas, had been identified in the space. Additionally, there were a few other substances, which could not be identified. The realization then hit us. The Tyvek suit I was going to wear into the space for the rescue attempt would not have afforded ample protection against what was down there, possibly causing exposure to the environment and its contaminants. Trying to save their lives could have cost me dearly, as some amount of risk is normally involved when speed is of utmost importance. In this case, our slower approach during the recovery would mean a larger margin of safety within which to operate.

A new plan was formed for the body recovery. With the surrounding occupancies evacuated, wastewater flow would be minimized and a vacuum truck would be brought in to pump over 2,000 gallons of the product out. I would then be lowered into the space on a tripod winch cable, with a belay rope to catch me if the winch failed. I'd also bring one end of a rope and pulley system down and attach it to the first victim via whatever means I saw fit. I would then be raised out of the space with the winch cable and the first victim would be hauled out with the rope. After I had done my part, Don would do the same for the second victim. But the biggest question was about what I was going to wear to protect me from the hazardous materials present. It was decided that I would be outfitted in something called a "Level B Nonencapsulating Suit", which is basically a big onesie jumpsuit made of heavy material similar to a painter's tarp. It's chemical resistant, waterproof and doesn't breathe. The feet are part of the suit and chemical resistant boots and gloves are worn. I had no experience in such a suit, and that was a concern for the HAZMAT guys. But it was determined that I was the most qualified TRT member to handle the demands of the evolution first, so with the begrudging assistance of the HazMat team, I got suited up and ready to go to work. One of the Haz Techs who was helping get me set up looked at me and said, "Whatever you do, don't tear this suit while you're down there." Unfortunately I had to wait about 15 minutes to actually get started after I was completely dressed and kitted up.

It felt like a sauna in this suit and all I was doing at the time was sitting in a booth inside Buffalo Wild Wings. I had no idea what I'd be facing when asked to work, let alone in the sweltering heat.

When "go time" came, I was escorted out to the entry area of the "hot zone" and attached my regulator to my SCBA face piece. I turned on the headlamp attached to my helmet and the flashlight hanging from my harness, then clipped into the winch cable, tied into the belay rope and attached the end of the rope system to the front of my harness. It was a ton of shit attached to me and as I dangled my feet over the open vault with my weight supported by my harness, I thought, "Well, here we go." Because the hatch was so small, I had to kind of rock my hips to one side, then the other to clear my escape bottle and equipment. And then I felt that sensation you get when you're getting into a cold swimming pool. It's that feeling when your body is trying to tell you not to do something but you're forcing it to anyway. With the Arizona sun setting, my chest, then head passed the level of the hatch and it suddenly got very dark. There were scene lights shining down from above, but in such a narrow space, my body was largely blocking any light from shining down below me. My headlamp and flashlight were essentially the only light sources. It was like being in another dimension; the walls of the space covered with grease and sewage and the still present extension ladder too slippery to stand on or use for support. "No wonder they couldn't get out of here", I thought as I descended toward the two dead bodies and my workspace below. As I got uncomfortably deep into the vertical shaft, my problem-solving mind took over. I realized that there was still some water flowing slowly out of one of several pipes that entered the space right at chest-level, perhaps halfway down the shaft. I called for the team to stop lowering me and asked for one of our bulky blue patient blankets to be sent down. I planned to use it to stop the flow of water long enough for me to work without a sewage shower raining

down on my head. While I waited for the blanket, I had time to look around. The walls of the space were rough concrete and despite being underground, hot monsoon air was being sent down via a ventilation fan with a duct lowered into the space above me. It was like having a thousand hair dryers pointed at me, but was necessary to keep the atmosphere at a less than explosive level. Looking down, I could see the victims at rest about ten feet below my boots. They were laying one on top of the other, with the bottom one facing up and the top one facing down, chest-to-chest. The next image I had is one I wish I could erase forever from my mind. The bottom victim's face was frozen with a horrifying look; eyes and mouth wide open as if he was still gasping, making one last failed effort to breathe. And the steady, slow flow of water coming from the pipe I was about to dam up with a blanket was landing directly in his open mouth. It was hard to keep myself calm right then, but I somehow did as I heard, "Yo!" from above and saw a blue blanket floating in slow motion down toward me. I wadded it up, filled the pipe and called for the crew above to continue the lower. If nothing else, I'd provided some level of dignity to the victim, just a few feet away at this point. This stands in testament to the fact that I always believed in treating my patients with dignity and respect, even with no one to witness such an act down here underground. When I arrived at the bottom, I tried to stand on a rung of the ladder, which rejected my foot immediately with its greasy coating. And with nowhere else to stand in this 4' diameter pipe, now occupied by three people, it dawned on me that I'd be forced to stand on the arms, legs and torsos of the victims' bodies. It was horrifying and involuntary as the winch cable went slack and my boots took the weight of my body on top of theirs. Rigor Mortis had set in and the two bodies were stiff and nearly immovable. Somehow, I had to work. I had a job to do despite the conditions. And I knew that the sooner I did it, the sooner I could get the hell out of here. I had to devise a way to package the top victim so that I could attach the rope lifting mechanical advantage (MA) system for evacuation. The only real way to do this was to wrap a 2" thick cinch strap around his chest just below the arms, with the attachment point on his back. I figured that this would give us the best chance of lifting him straight up and off of his partner. Then the next haunting realization hit. The only way to get this strap around him was to pass it from one side to the other, giving him a big bear hug in the process. As I did so, my SCBA face piece was directly against his back and head, such that when I pulled back away from him, I had to wipe product off of my mask in order to see clearly again. Looking around his body to ensure that he wouldn't get tangled up during the haul, I noticed something odd. There was what looked like a leather cup with a Harley Davidson emblem on it. Looking closer, I realized that this was a protective cover for an amputee stump. The bottom victim was an amputee at the forearm level, and this cover was on the stump of his arm. Now it became even clearer to me as to why he couldn't climb out. What was he thinking going down there in the first place? He had been a very tough man, indeed. With my victim packaged and the rope system attached, I called for a raise and soon felt the winch cable come taught, with my feet leaving their perches and my body seemingly magically levitating up toward the light and the land of the living above. Reaching the hatch, I had to contort myself once more to clear the opening, and then pass through. Standing with either foot straddling the opening, I called for some slack and stepped away, detaching the winch cable and belay line from my harness.

Covered in sewage and grease and still in my complete protective ensemble, I was escorted over to the first of three decontamination pools and a HazMat crew began hosing me down with water and brushing off contaminants. When I lifted a foot for them to get the bottom of my boot, I lost my balance and nearly fell over. I even remember feeling bad about putting my dirty-gloved hand on

someone's shoulder to catch myself. I then stepped into the next pool where a more thorough cleaning was done and nearly fell over again. Now I was beginning to worry. Something just didn't feel right. I was dizzy and my vision was narrowing. Someone brought a step stool for me to sit on in the third and final decon station and when I sat down, I felt a sloshing sensation in my boots. Realizing that my feet were wet, I thought that I'd torn the suit and been exposed to whatever nastiness was present in that sewer. I didn't panic because I couldn't. I was too busy trying to keep from passing out for that. I remember an old friend of mine from Tempe's HazMat team helping clean me off and seeing the genuinely concerned look he had on his face. Taking off the level b suit and my Nomex flight suit beneath, I walked with some assistance over to another crew who were waiting to take a set of vital signs and evaluate me. It was my old buddy John from our backup TRT station ready to check me out. I don't remember my blood pressure, but my heart rate was north of 160 and weak. I felt dizzy, but knew who and where I was. It then occurred to me that I hadn't torn the suit. But what I had done was fill the boots of the suit up to about mid-calf with my own sweat. I was severely dehydrated and had no choice when John started an IV on me and transported me to the ER in an ambulance for evaluation of at a minimum, heat exhaustion and possible HazMat exposure. A couple hours later, Don would get his turn at the fun and recover the second victim from the space in a repeat of the evolution I had done prior. I spent several hours in the ER that night, was tested for various toxins and took on a few liters of IV fluid before being sent home. Don and several other crewmembers found themselves in the very same ER for the same reasons later that evening. Four days after that, I was back on the truck at 610. On the evening of the first shift back, I insisted that we visit our HazMat station and in an act of gratitude, delivered an apple pie and ice cream in exchange for keeping us safe on the scene.

This call gave me some notoriety in the TRT community, and I actually based one of my year-end drills around it. It also stayed with me for a very, very long time afterward. I couldn't get it out of my head and had flashbacks of it. The whole thing would play over and over on a loop. I also avoided manhole covers and any chance of smelling sewer gas. Again, in retrospect, these are all signs of PTSD. But I denied that I could have it, thinking that my years of experience were there to protect me not only physically, but mentally as well. If only it worked that way. I rethought that call again and again, trying to draw some conclusion or closure by figuring out where we had gone wrong. But even if we'd been ready five minutes earlier, pulling off the rescue would have been a pretty tall order, particularly with the space refilling with product and inadequate protective clothing. But there was absolutely, positively a chance that we could've gotten at least one of the patients out while they could still be considered patients.

With DB's performance being the only real weakness, I decided to address it. After dinner that first night back, I sat out at the table in front of the station with him and said that I never wanted to have to explain to his wife why he didn't come home from work one day. I also explained that I never wanted him to have to do the same thing for me. After that, I explained that I was willing to teach him everything I knew, and only asked for his performance in return. He agreed and told me that he'd heard that I was the best TRT instructor in the Valley and that he had transferred to station 610 specifically to work with and be mentored by me. We shook hands and I told him we'd start working on everything the following shift. How was I to know that he would betray me worse than anyone in the fire department ever could have imagined? My dark space was about to get a hell of a lot darker.

Chapter 27
"The Betrayal"

———

LET'S GET THIS OUT of the way right off the bat. "DB" was, and forever will be, a coward. If this sounds hateful, you'll soon understand why. But I didn't know that until well after my relationship with him had begun. He had a long history of poor performance as a firefighter before he transferred to station 610 for me to mentor him and I knew this. I'd seen him work, but only on drills and it wasn't impressive. He was behind the eight ball from the start due to his small 5'2" 135 lb. stature. Normally when you see a firefighter with a small frame, they are able to make up for a lack of strength with superior physical technique and mental aptitude. DB had neither. He was a triathlete, which seemed to hold some merit with fire department staff here and there, but when I saw pictures of him finishing an Ironman race with arms triumphantly held in the air, something stood out. It was totally dark out when the picture was taken and he was clearly finishing somewhere close to DFL, or "dead fucking last" as the race organizers were taking down the finish line signage. I'm not shitting on his achievement of finishing the race, but I feel like the perspective of it is important, as is a person's representation of their sport and capabilities. I know what's involved in a long triathlon and have to admit that his ability to grind away all day and part of the night to finish was something that made me think that I could straighten him out and make a good firefighter/EMT/rescue tech out of the guy. I knew he must possess drive. Another plus was that he had some life experience and was about eight years older than me. In spite of the starting point, really thought he had some potential.

When I sat out front with him that night after the con space call and explained how and why I wanted to mentor him, he agreed with my only request, which was that he perform well in exchange for what would be my considerable outlay of time and effort. With that in mind, I made a mental plan of how to go about my new project. After we put our fire gear on the engine and checked our equipment on the first morning, I decided to begin with finding out what DB knew about Support 610, our TRT truck that is essentially a huge rolling tool box full of specialized rescue gear. At this point, DB had been on the TRT team for perhaps two years at the second-string station, long enough to become at least minimally familiar with the equipment stored in our truck's cab and 13 compartments. Although he hadn't been assigned to 610 before, his prior station, 614 was responsible for backfilling periodically vacant spots at our station and knowing everything about the TRT equipment was expected. The crews at 614 also took Support 610 with them to all of the same TRT training sessions we attended, so it wasn't as if he'd never had a chance to look things over and ask another firefighter for help.

Excited to begin the process, I asked him if he was ready to get started and after he said yes, we walked across the bay to the first compartment behind the driver's side door of Support 610. Standing there side-by-side, I pointed to the compartment door and asked, "What's in that first compartment?" Right away, he moved toward the handle to open the silver, 6' tall roll-up door.

I quickly said, "Hold it! Don't open it, just *tell me* what's in it."

"Uh, the water cooler?"

"Okay, good. What else?"

"Uh, I don't know", DB said with a chuckle.

"Well, can you picture it? Can you imagine what you'd see if you opened the compartment", I asked, trying to assess what kind of learner he was.

"No, not really."

"Okay, go ahead and open it."

He reached down, pressed the release button for the door and rolled it all the way up, exposing the huge, white Igloo water cooler he'd mentioned on the bottom shelf, along with four more shelves above it, all completely loaded with equipment. The compartment was about three feet deep, four feet wide and six feet tall. Each of the shelves is on rollers, allowing the shelf to be extended out from the cabinet for easier access to the equipment it holds. The top shelves tip downward as they're pulled out, which makes it easier to get to their contents. I helped organize nearly every piece of gear on this entire truck when it arrived new in Scottsdale over ten years prior, and this first compartment was mostly miscellaneous equipment, including the aforementioned cooler, two EMS backpacks full of medical equipment, clipboards, spare onboard communications headsets, traffic vests, spare batteries, eye and ear protection, EMS gloves of several sizes and a litany of other small items. It was the equivalent of the "junk drawer" in your kitchen. Hell, I even had scissors, pens and a screwdriver in there, too!

I asked DB to begin memorizing what was in the compartment on every shelf, and to write everything down as he looked at it to make an inventory. I was having him use written and visual learning skills to memorize the contents. I went inside the station to fill out my daily drug inventory on the computer and check in with Jim to let him know what I was up to. He seemed pleased to see that I was going to try passing on what knowledge I could, but I'm sure he was on some level glad to not have to do it himself! In the end, it really is the fire department tradition to have experienced firefighters mentor new members and I was known to be good at it. It had become a source of pride, knowing that my skills and experience would live on in those I'd mentored long after I was gone from active duty.

Back to the bay, about 30 minutes later, DB was just wrapping up the first compartment inventory. He handed me the clipboard and I looked it over, noting that he'd covered it pretty comprehensively, but there were a few things he found that he couldn't identify. One was a white PVC T fitting with a garden hose inlet on it. "That's a rope washer", I explained. Another was a remote push-to-talk attachment for our portable radios.

"Okay, bro. You can close that compartment."

He had to stand on the bottom shelf of the compartment, but was able to reach the handle to close the rolling door with a slam. He then went to open the next compartment to the right of the first.

"Hang on a second", I said, holding his inventory in my hand. Pointing back to the first compartment, I said, "Tell me what's in that compartment."

"What? What do you mean?"

"What kind of learner are you, D?"

"What are you talking about", he replied, confused.

"Do you remember what you hear, what you see, what you write, what you do, or some combination of all of these? I need to know how to teach you."

"Well, I guess I don't know."

"Well, then I guess we're gonna figure that out. Now tell me what's in that first compartment."

He did an okay job of rattling off some of the inventory and when he struggled, I told him to try and visualize the shelf and tell me what was on it. In all, I'd say he was able to remember about half or less of the very things he'd just spent the last 30 minutes writing down. I took the sheet of paper off of the clipboard and said, "Okay. We'll try again tomorrow." I put the inventory sheet in my locker and at the same time in the morning on the following shift, I asked him again to name every item in the compartment. And again, had to stop him as he went for the handle to open it. This time he could only name about a quarter of the inventory before opening the door. He'd actually gone *backward* from where he was last shift! I had him open it up and write the inventory again and later that afternoon when we got back from a call, had him try naming the inventory again before we went back into the station. And once more, he was only good for about half of it before opening the compartment door. "Okay, buddy. You know what to do", I said as I took his inventory sheet to my locker.

I'd never seen anything like this before. DB couldn't retain what he was looking at or what he was writing down. He couldn't seem to understand what everything in the compartment was, let alone what it was all used for. It was amazing, and for a moment I thought the crew might be playing a practical joke on me. But they weren't. His ineptitude was genuine and nearly complete from a practical standpoint. How, I wondered, could someone with this poor of a skillset get a job in the fire department, let alone keep that job. Thinking back to Billy McDowell's "Everyone passes" academy ethos answered the question. So my crew and I started asking some questions. It turned out DB had been a photographer for a local newspaper before he became a firefighter. He'd been testing for *years* in different cities all over the Valley to try and get hired, but always failed. I can't remember how many times he had tested for fire departments in the Phoenix area, but it was greater than five. When Billy took over as Chief in 2005, his biggest goal for the next academy was diversity. DB checked two of the diversity boxes and was hired. He struggled throughout that academy and was nearly thrown out multiple times due to poor performance. I was told by several company officers who supervised DB over the years that their concerns about his job performance laid somewhere between him being a danger to not only himself on fire and emergency scenes, but to the rest of the crew as well. Being able to make a hydrant connection, pull an attack line, raise a ladder or just keep up with the rest of the crew inside a burning building are expected, necessary skills that he was woefully deficient at. My goal was to turn all that around and make this wingless bird fly.

Behind the scenes, when we'd run calls with other units, firefighters and even a few company officers approached me about my trainee, joking and laughing about our new crew member. I was quick to assure them that we were going to "unfuck" him and turn him into a dragon slayer. I had my doubts, but I was sure going to try. What you have to realize is that the other three members of our crew had over 80 years of combined experience between us, and we could probably handle 99% of the calls on our own, something we'd done for years with Rural/Metro in the past with a crew of only three. DB wasn't really a necessary member of our crew the majority of the time, and we came to think of him as more of a member of the public doing a ride-along than a fourth firefighter.

During the next few years, I labored to bring DB up to speed on TRT, fire and EMS skills. And to some extent, I succeeded. He was actually starting to perform at the highest level he was capable of. What that amounted to is what I honestly think was about 60%

of what an average firefighter with the same amount of experience could do. There's this thing called "50 first shifts" in the fire department. It refers to people who can't retain information, making it seem like every day is their first shift. At one point I remember checking in with Jim about his progress. I was met with something just about like this: "You insisted that fucking guy come here in the first place. Fix him. And by the way, he needs to learn to drive the engine to the hospital when you and Don ride in with a patient. I'm getting tired of doing it myself."

I used every trick in my teaching book that I'd developed over the years. Some worked, most didn't. What ended up working best was repetition. And by that, I mean maniacal, obsessive, insane amounts of repetition. And even with that, the results were still barely passable. I'm quite sure that as I write this, he's on a call somewhere trying to remember how to put the 12-lead EKG electrodes on a patient or straining every muscle just to open a hydrant before someone's house burns down due to a lack of a water supply to the forward pumper.

Per Jim's "request", I began working with him on driving the truck, as did our engineer, Don. While the other guys were napping in the afternoon, I regularly had DB out on the front apron of the station in the engine, asking him for what I came to call a "basic". A "basic" involved pulling the truck up, setting the parking brake, then going through a procedure so well-known by engineers the world over that they can do it in their sleep. All that's involved is getting the pump in gear and sending water down an attack line for a firefighter waiting on the nozzle. This can be done by just about anyone in around one minute or less from the time the truck's parking brakes are applied. He did this dozens of times, with what seemed like some new and different problem every time. Again, it was amazing to me. But still we pressed on.

Over our time together DB and I actually became friends. I got him Christmas presents for two years, once giving him a stack of inner tubes for his bike, since he regularly got flats out on the road and another time a book on cycling called "The Rules". He'd been to my house for a crew dinner and I'd once driven out to an abandoned section of road in the desert an hour west of Phoenix to cheer him on during a long endurance relay running event. I'd tuned up his bike and glued race tires onto his wheels before a big triathlon. Looking back now, I got nothing in return. He either didn't like me or didn't care. I don't even remember any gratitude coming from him. Perhaps he felt entitled to the vast amount of time and effort I was paying out. It's hard to understand, but in the end doesn't warrant spending much time trying.

It was several months before this period of time that I went through my second divorce. My crew pretty much stayed away from the subject because they knew what was happening and surely it would've been uncomfortable to talk about. My ex was addicted to pain meds and had been for three years to my knowledge, but probably for a much longer time than that. And I'd been enabling her the whole time, which took its toll on not only our marriage, but my mental health as well. It was over between us and I started to check out at work, not spending time mentoring DB any longer and generally just feeling like shit was crumbling around me. I was starting to have nightmares about work again, and was isolating myself both at work and at home. I'd been going to therapy on a regular basis and trying to cope by using physical activity as self care. Coming out the other side months later, I had a new girlfriend, a Land Rover Discovery, a Porsche 911, a Ducati Monster and a giant house I'd remodeled and had up for sale. I was racing bikes again with some success and was still teaching TRT to the East Valley departments. I was also filling the positions of engineer and captain when either Don or Jim were off on vacation or out sick. Add to that the fact that I was regularly flying helicopter missions on mountain rescue calls and it quickly becomes clear that I looked to my friends and coworkers like the ultimate firefighter and general stud. I had also gotten a break from mentoring when DB was moved to 614 so that I could precept another new medic, Darren. It was awesome because Darren was a hard worker, knew his job and didn't have to be babysat every step of the way. Friction developed between Jim and I because he felt as though Darren was answering to me instead of to him. And he was right at least as far as being a medic went. Jim wasn't a medic and precepting Darren was my responsibility only. When it came to treating patients and making decisions regarding their care, my word was worth more than his and he didn't like that because I believe it made him feel powerless. I'm sure he also didn't like the absence of our little ride-along DB, who never asked questions and just did whatever he was told. After a few months, Darren had done a fine job of learning the real-world portion of being a medic and I would have let him work on me or my family without question as he finished up his training. Unfortunately our days together were numbered and DB came back to station 610 when Darren took his new medic position.

It's at this point in time that my personal life began to make me happy again; more so than work, which felt like more of an inconvenience lying in the way of my off-duty adventures. I had moved in with Lynn, who along with her daughter Deborah, took care of Lynn's mom, Sue (Grams). Yes, I moved in with three generations of women, and with three dogs and three cats, too! The house was a large tri-level floor plan near Old Town Scottsdale with a huge backyard and great access to recreation for Lynn and I, who were taking epic road trips and vacations to places like Manhattan, San Francisco, Mexico and at one point, the entire west coast of the United States. We backpacked, kayaked, climbed rock, rode bikes and eventually even took up Olympic recurve target archery. While we traveled and adventured, Deborah earned her keep by taking care of Grams, who over our first year together had been showing signs of Alzheimer's disease. In the three years leading up to meeting Lynn, I worked enough overtime to equal the pay rate of a Captain Paramedic, two ranks higher than me. After Lynn and I got together, that dropped to virtually no overtime hours at all. You see, I didn't like being at home very much during that earlier three-year period, so I worked a ton and got myself debt-free in the process. Even with the enormous change in living conditions, I was deep enough in love with Lynn to look past it all. Not working as much also seemed to help with my overall attitude at work, and I started to feel healthier from a mental standpoint. Overall, I'd say things were going great for me.

What happened next is a cascade of events that would set the stage for a very, very large change in my life and my mental wellbeing. Jim had been off sick for about three or four rotations, totaling nearly a month. I was moved into the captain's position for almost the entire time, and another firefighter/EMT was moved in to fill my normal spot in the backseat. Don and I would alternate riding into the hospital each time there was an EMS call, and when Don rode in, DB would take the wheel of the engine to drive to the hospital. One morning after wrapping up at the ER following a run of the mill EMS call, we walked out to the hospital parking lot and got in the truck. I heard the "psssssh" of air leaving the braking system as Don pulled the parking brake instead of pushing it in to release it. This was not normal, and as he and I looked at each other in the front seat, he said over the headset, "D, when you park the truck you have to set the fucking BRAKES!"

DB had pulled into the hospital parking lot, put the truck in neutral and gotten out. By not setting the brakes on a fire truck, it is free to roll on its own with no one behind the wheel. Imagine the damage that a truck weighing over 40,000 lbs. could do as it rolls across a hospital parking lot, then out into a street, not to mention what the headline would read. A few calls later, Don was riding in with a patient again, leaving me with DB and the other firefighter, Swifty. When DB went to climb into the driver's seat, I said, "Bro, you're in the wrong seat."

"Huh?" he replied, with a quizzical look on his face.

"Yeah dude, you're grounded until we can work on your driving some more."

"Huh?" he said again.

"I need Swifty to drive."

Swifty, our replacement firefighter, climbed up into the driver's seat and having been working on his engineer skills as well, did fine work of getting us to the hospital safely. He even set the parking brake when we arrived. I never heard a word from DB about the incident or how I'd handled it. No one on the crew said anything to me either. If DB had a problem, I never heard anything about it, and this just went down in my mind as one of at least a dozen times that he had made a mistake that we miraculously walked away from unscathed.

One afternoon in late October of 2017 as Lynn and I were getting ready to head to the gym for our workout, my phone rang. It was a representative from the City of Scottsdale HR department, who said that she had one other person present with her in the room. She told me that at 08:00 on the following morning, I was to report to fire headquarters instead of to my duty assignment at station 610 and that I was to bring my badge, city ID and any fire department equipment I had in my possession.

"I see. Can you tell me what's going on?"

"No." was the abrupt answer.

"Look, I know that things usually don't go well when guys are told to bring their stuff to HQ instead of going to their station. You're about to put me through the longest night of my life, and you can't even tell me why?"

There was a pause and it sounded like the ladies on the other end of the phone were having a sidebar.

"Alright. All I can tell you is that there's been a complaint filed and we need to speak to everyone involved."

"Okay, thanks. I'll see you in the morning."

The moment I hung up, Lynn walked into the room and could see something was wrong. I immediately called Jim, since he was my direct supervisor.

"Hey man, how ya feelin'?" I asked.

Jim summed up how his health was and that he'd be back on the truck soon. I then asked him why I had just gotten a call from HR, asking me to come to the office in the morning instead of going on shift.

"Oh, you haven't heard?" was his reply.

"Heard WHAT, that's why I'm fucking calling you!"

"Well, I'm not sure I'm even allowed to be talking to you about it right now, but DB filed a hostile workplace complaint against you."

"You've gotta be fucking kidding me."

"Nope. I tried to stop it, but he wanted to run it up the chain of command to Senior Staff and somehow it got over to HR.", Jim told me, sounding as if he was trying to sidestep the complete and total shit storm that was heading his way.

"Got it. Thanks. Catch you later." I said, hanging up the phone. I looked at Lynn and told her what was happening. The rest of that day is encased in a mental fog for me. I knew that when this process is started, it usually spells the end of one's career. And Scottsdale HR is pretty sensitive about the, at this point unknown to me, grievous accusations being made. My next call was to my IAFF union officer, Alex, to arrange for representation during the upcoming process.

I had plenty of time overnight to think about things while I was busy not sleeping. For the life of me, I couldn't think of anything that had happened between us that we didn't talk about either individually or as a crew. I still felt like his friend and mentor. And I didn't think we'd had any patient or customer encounter on a scene or otherwise while Jim was away that was even the least bit questionable. I was perplexed. I met Alex ahead of time in the lobby of fire department HQ and he outlined what he knew, which was by design, also very little. I decided to record the meeting on my phone and we went into "the fishbowl", a meeting room with a large table that sat about 10 and had two glass walls with the middle section frosted for an amount of imaginary privacy. We sat down on one side of the table, across from an HR representative and Cedrick, a member of fire department senior staff. They slid a copy of the administrative regulation (AR) I'd allegedly violated and told me that DB had filed a grievance against me. I was then asked for my fire department ID and badge. I pulled those items out of my wallet, slid them over to Cedrick and heard him say, "I'll keep these in a safe place and look forward to getting them back to you, Rick." I asked if they could tell me exactly what I was being accused of, or when this investigation was expected to end and was told that they couldn't tell me anything until they spoke to the other parties involved first. They also said that I was being placed on paid administrative leave in the meantime, with the expectation that I should be available for further meetings or phone calls at any point during the workweek. The staff on the other side of the table from me that day, and to some extent Alex also, seemed to look at me and speak to me like someone who had just received a cancer diagnosis. It was as if they all knew the end was near. Was it? How long did I have left?

To say that the rug had been pulled out from under me is a monumental understatement. I had a feeling deep in my gut that I was going to have to figure out what to start doing for work after they fired me for whatever this was about. I still didn't know, and had been told not to talk to anyone about the situation. Days went by with no news. Calls to Alex were helpful, but there wasn't any information coming from his side. I've rarely felt more alone. And I've rarely felt so sure that ending my life was a perfectly acceptable option in the event that I was to lose a 24-year career and my pension over some imaginary problem a butt-hurt crew member couldn't bring himself to talk about with his company officer or the crew around the day room table or privately in the captain's office. My emotions ran the full spectrum from rage at the injustice to hopelessness for the outcome. I experienced everything from the anxiety of foreshadowed loss to the serenity of my life-ending option and everything in between.

After eight days off, I was called to come in for another meeting. This time I'd be addressing each of the accusations against me. To say they were ridiculous doesn't really do them justice, and only other firefighters will truly understand this, but DB alleged that I had thrown a halligan tool at him during a fire, thrown a Pelican EMS box at him on an EMS call, sworn at him and told him that he was grounded. I set about having to explain these things to a city HR official who didn't understand that a halligan is a 12 lb., 36" long steel bar with sharp points on it for making forcible entry into buildings or vehicles, or that our Pelican EMS boxes weigh about 30 lbs. "Throwing" either of these things at another person would surely cause some sort of injury and that wasn't anything that I'd ever done. There was also no record of any injuries reported by him. I also denied swearing directly at DB, but acknowledged the fact that all of us on the crew, including him and virtually every other member of the fire department, used colorful language as a matter of course on a daily basis. He also said that I had struck him in the face during live fire training in blackout conditions, which is impossible to avoid during an interior firefight. We bump into each other regularly, but never purposefully hit each other in the face. I did admit to having told DB that he was "grounded" in reference to him leaving the truck without setting the parking brake in the hospital parking lot, and what I meant with the statement. Apparently that one single event was enough for him to sit down and inflate the other things in order to build some sort of a case against me. In closing, I explained that DB and I had been friends for some time and pointed out evidence of such a relationship, which the HR rep noted after I finished. She then asked about my relationship with my crew and I explained the chain of command to her, under which firefighters deal with problems between each other first before going to the company officer, battalion chief or anyone higher in rank. DB had not addressed any problem or accusation of hostility on a personal level with me before moving outside of our fire department chain of command, therefore keeping me from knowing that there was any kind of a personal problem between us. The line of questioning then shifted to her asking me about Jim, the crew and the work environment and how negative things were. When she focused in on Jim specifically, I asked to speak with Alex, my union rep, privately.

After she left the room, we had a sidebar confirming that she understood what I had covered about DB and about where her line of questioning was going, and then I told Alex that Jim had become super-negative and that he was killing us, but that I didn't want to sell him out. It was clear that others who were questioned had said negative things about pretty much everyone else involved. It was like a house of cards falling in on itself, but I still wanted to just go back to the way things were; to get back to normal and run calls. Clearly, that was never going to happen. When the HR rep returned, she asked more specific questions about a conversation we'd had as a crew in the station when we had approached Jim about his negative attitude, which was legendary around the department. He had told me flatly that the negative environment in the station was entirely my fault. She then asked a few more questions about other employees I had mentored and how we got along, seemingly trying to bait me into saying that I don't get along with people, which I didn't do. I felt like the HR rep had no earthly idea how interpersonal relationships in the fire service work. The city has no choice but to apply the same rules to firefighters as to garbage collectors, teachers and librarians. And that just doesn't make sense in every situation that firefighters run into. It's impossible for outsiders to comprehend, despite the best descriptions and explanations. She closed with the classic parent's question: "Is there anything else you think I should know?" I made a heartfelt closing statement pointing out that by nature I'm not a hostile or aggressive fighter and left the meeting feeling as though I was completely screwed.

Five days later, wondering and completely in the dark about the status of the investigation, something very unexpected happened. I was called back into HQ for a meeting with Bryan, the assistant fire chief of our department and an old friend of mine whom I'd gone through paramedic school with.

"Well, well, well..." Bryan said as he came out of his office and headed toward the fishbowl. We shook hands and exchanged pleasantries on our way in, then I sat down at the table after he said, "Have a seat, my man." As the door closed, the sound resembled that of a jail cell closing. I thought that this was the last time I'd wear navy blue as a firefighter. Monumental calls I'd run over the years flashed back through my mind in a flurry, as did Lynn's face and some of the scenes from vacations we'd been on together. This was it. I was about to lose everything I'd worked over two decades for. My "cancer" was about to take its final toll.

As my fire department ID and badge slid in slow motion from Bryan's outstretched hand, he said, "Let's give those back to you and get you back on the truck." I've never been more confused, but that feeling didn't last long. "This is the first step of the process of getting you back on the truck. The process isn't over, but you getting back on the truck should take some of the bellyache away. The rest of the process will happen later and we'll then pass it on to Jim and his BC to handle from there. But today is about getting you back on the truck. You're going to station 614 (our backup TRT station) today and probably for the next 48 hours and then we'll figure out what's next after that. So you can take a deep breath as you put your badge and your ID card back."

Next, Bryan advised me to be mindful about my interactions with people, especially in the next 48-96 hours because he felt like I had a "public perception problem" and that people could have an opinion about how I treated internal and external customers, and that at some point in the near future I'd be called back to HQ with Jim, our BC and HR to wrap things up with some paperwork. I was also told not to talk about the investigation and warned that at some point I would be questioned about the accusations at my station by other crewmembers.

So I went to 610, picked up my gear, bedding and some uniforms and headed up to 614 for my shift. Two shifts turned to three, then four, and after spending 24 days temporarily assigned to 614, the other shoe dropped. I was called back to the fishbowl for a third and final time. But it was different this time. Jim wasn't there, but just about everyone else was. The list included one rep from HR, Cedrick, Bryan, Alex, our BC Pete, and to top it all off, the Fire Chief, Leon Pano. I knew something was different; that something had changed. But I didn't know how, what or why.

Leon spoke first and said that he found the report disturbing and that he always found it ponderous when someone of my tenure and professionalism found themselves in a discussion such as this. And he also said the word "bullying" in reference to my relationship with DB. Before saying that, he said that he wasn't sure he wanted to hear anything from me and that I should just sit and listen. To sum up what he said, he felt as though my situation was a temporary one and that there was a perception that another employee was afraid of me. His message hit home and was about as positive as it could have been, but I still felt like shit. He was essentially telling me that I was getting a pass on this (whatever "this" was), but that it would be my only one. He then got up and walked out of the meeting, leaving the next person to speak.

It was Cedrick's turn. He said that I'd be getting a written reprimand for the situation regarding my interactions with DB. I signed the paperwork, signifying that the issue was closed and Cedrick and the HR rep left. At that point it became legal for me to talk about the entire investigation and its outcome to whomever I chose.

Bryan was up next and told me that he wanted me to "get back in the game" and take care of myself and that I'd be moving to B-shift. He said that I had some kind of a bad reputation and that he didn't believe that this was who I was. The next exchange took less than five seconds, but set off an unstoppable chain reaction within me that I could never have recognized at the time while it was happening:

"Where am I going on B-shift?"

"Rover pool."

"Am I still on TRT?"

"Nope."

After a long pause, Bryan said that if an opportunity arose, I was not prohibited from being on the team in the future. He also said that he thought that I'd wind up back on the team organically on my own at some point. The next five or ten-minute period with Bryan was pretty positive again, but I couldn't wrap my mind around what was happening. Bryan and I shook hands as he stood up, saying, "It's a punch in the gut, not a death sentence." He then left the room. It felt like watching a toilet flush as each member disappeared through the door. If only Bryan knew what was going through my mind when he said that one last thing. But I'm sure he didn't think twice about it. Who would have? Methods of committing suicide had actually been swirling through my mind since the moment he had delivered the news that I'd no longer be functioning as a technical rescue technician. That's how important that one seemingly small portion of my life was. And it evaporated into the air of that meeting room just as quickly as the sound of his voice saying the words had faded. It was just, gone.

That left me with Alex and my battalion chief, Pete, who spoke next. He had not been part of the investigation at all, and said that he agreed with my intent to keep DB at arm's length and to not interact with him at all. He said that in the future, I should be very cognizant of whom was in the station with me and that he had found himself in exactly the same situation ten years prior. He then left the room after telling me that it would be a pleasure to have me back in his battalion at some point and that he would help coordinate me moving my gear out of station 610.

I was devastated, symbolically abandoned one at a time by the most powerful people in the department walking out on me. Alex told me that something had obviously changed since my last meeting with Bryan when he'd sent me back to shift and active duty. No shit, really? Clearly in the two previous days, they had changed their tune about where things were going as far as my disciplinary action and station assignment. What had happened was far and away worse than what we had expected. I asked Alex if he'd played football in school. He said he had. I then told him, "I feel like I've been hit so hard that I can't get up, like I'm stuck on the ground and guys keep stepping on me." We then talked about how to proceed forward after this and about how DB could say whatever he wanted about anything at any time and it wouldn't be questioned. I then had to go to finish my shift on a truck I can't recall with a crew I can't remember running calls I've long since forgotten.

I reached out to everyone involved that I thought could shed light on the situation surrounding the investigation. Jim and Pete told me separately that DB had come to them after hearing that I was coming back to station 610 and said that he was afraid that I was going to hurt him. Both Jim and Pete had assured him that there was no possibility of him being in danger and dismissed his concern. Presumably moving on to a member of senior staff, DB took his concern to HQ, effectively forcing their hand in separating the two of us from working together ever again. What screwed me over was the fact that because he had been the one to move forward with the concern, I would be the one to have to leave the station and TRT along with it. There was no protection for the accused. But what he really was trying to do was get me fired. Jim later told me that one night, driving to the hospital to pick up the medics after an EMS call, DB had asked him directly, in no uncertain terms, why I hadn't been fired.

So that's it. There was no appeal to be had, and I had no recourse in the matter. I had lost a monumental part of my life, and my identity not only in the fire department, but to some extent, also as a man. Sure I still had a job, but a coward who I had trusted like a brother had irrevocably tarnished it. Someone I considered a friend had betrayed me. Simply removing the letter "r" from the word "friend" describes the situation poetically. DB was a wicked and cruel person, a fiend.

I felt absolutely wrong about this. I felt betrayed by the city, the fire department and by those I worked with and trusted for years. Wasn't there any justice here? Wasn't there anything I could do? Was he just going to get away with this? And as far as the department and the city went, the case was closed and everyone went on to live happily ever after.

Chapter 28
"The Only Constant: Change"

MY BATTALION CHIEF coordinated a time for me to go back to station 610 and clean out my locker after I got the bad news about having lost the technical rescue station assignment I'd had for well over 20 years. That's longer than many people even stay in the fire department before retiring. I'd be in a roving position for the foreseeable future and would essentially be living out of a couple of duffel bags when I went to work for my shifts. It was disturbing to the core to have to remove everything I had in two separate lockers, including lots of pictures and memorabilia I'd accumulated over the years. It was like being forced to move out of a house you'd lived in for years and not knowing where you were going because they decided to put a new freeway in and your home just happened to be in the way. It wasn't my choice. And there was no alternative. Such was the case here, because most of the time I didn't find out what station I was assigned to for a shift until an hour or two before that shift began. There would be no stability in this new roving life. I'd be working on up to ten different trucks with up to ten different crews (or 30 different people) per month, and perhaps even more if I were moved during a shift due to someone going home sick or getting injured. You'd be right to assume that I had a healthy dose of trust issues with everyone around me after what had just happened. I was trying to live down a betrayal of epic proportions.

Being a firefighter/paramedic who's also qualified to fill in as an engineer is a double-edged sword. The flexibility got me some extra overtime shifts, but as a rover it meant that I could be moved around in the middle of a shift should the need arise. Fortunately, most of the trucks and equipment are laid out similarly throughout the city, but innumerable subtle differences exist from one fire truck to the next, making it important to look everything over carefully every morning in the hopes that at 02:00 the next day you'll still remember where the size 4.0 uncuffed endotracheal tube is when it comes time to intubate a newborn in a crib who isn't breathing.

Fortunately, I'd roved before. It's just that it had been over 20 years since I'd done it. Be that as it may, what I had ahead of me amounted to a massive publicity campaign to hopefully re-establish my good name within the department and set the record straight in an organization with one of the most notorious rumor mills known to man. The scheduling staff worked me at every single station in the city over the next couple of months, which allowed me the opportunity to sit down with everyone on b-shift and explain what had happened between DB and me. Without fail, every single time I told the story at a dayroom table or on the front bumper of a truck, my audience dropped their shoulders, slumped a little and shook their heads, saying, "What a fucking piece of shit that guy is." or "How the fuck could the department not stand up for you?" And every single time I heard that, I felt a little more vindicated. It didn't take the pain of loss away, and it sure didn't get me my TRT assignment and pay back, but it shed a little more light on the fact that there was a traitor in our midst who would and could never be trusted by another firefighter, captain or chief within the Scottsdale Fire Department for the rest of his career.

I had good days and bad days during those months roving. I got to see and work with a lot of people I hadn't been around in many years. Frequently, at some point during a shift with old friends, the stories would start. "Dude, do you remember the time..." "Holy shit, you should have seen the look on your face when..." or, "Hey, can you make us that chili that you used to make at station 19 back in the day?" The ability of salty firefighters to spin a yarn is unrivaled by nearly anyone, and I was reminded of some pretty crazy and fun times. But I also was reminded of a lot of loss from years past, and calls I had swept under my mental rug were suddenly shaken out of that rug like dust that had been buried deep within the fibers, hidden from view.

Many of the ambitious young firefighters I'd worked with in the '90s were now captains or battalion chiefs with gray hair and a bit slower working pace than what I remembered of their earlier days and in most cases, a lot more wisdom about not only the job, but about life as well. And all of them were showing signs of becoming war-weary from our time in the fire service. It was in the way they climbed in and out of the rig. It was in the way they sat at the table for dinner. And it was in the way they each did many of the things I did at the time that were signs of PTSD. We'd all been through divorces, isolated ourselves from others, had periods of rage and anger, drank or did drugs to cope and avoided places and things that reminded us of our worst calls. That last part is what becomes very cruel as one spends more and more years at the same station. You're forced to drive through that intersection where the SUV ran over a baby stroller, or pass by the house where you pulled the skin off of a woman's arms as you carried her from the window of her burning home to the driveway for treatment. You might even regularly see the husband who drunkenly beat up his wife as you're shopping for dinner at the grocery store near your station. It all happened in your first-due area, in the same neighborhood where you work shift after shift, year after year. It's a worldwide, universal truth that the streets of every city are paved with reminders just like that for the firefighters who work nearby.

Eventually, a firefighter/paramedic assignment opened up at a station that would work out well for me. And it just happened to be about a mile away from Lynn's house near McCormick Ranch in Scottsdale and just down the street from Saguaro High School, where I had first seen, but never met her. The station was 603, and had been built in the 70's. The single-story, flat-roofed building was doing a poor job of hiding its age, and was full of history that I came to remember from having worked there off and on in the mid-90's. I remember working to relight the pilot light on the rickety old gas water heater with Captain Russ. He'd been holding down the pilot button for a while before he told me to light a match and get down there to put it in place next to the pilot nozzle. "WHOOSH!!!" There went the hair on my right arm. Russ was the same guy who years earlier had sauntered over next to me one day behind what was at the time station 14 on Shea Boulevard. I was standing there talking with two or three crewmembers when he put his finger in the left back pocket of my duty pants, standing uncomfortably close. I didn't miss a beat, looked over at him and said, "No thanks, buddy." before continuing on with the conversation with the guys, who all chuckled. The full time firefighters were just messing with me, but I guess I'd passed the test and spent a fair amount of time at station 14 back then as a reserve. It was the original TRT and HAZ MAT station for Scottsdale. But back to station 603. There was just a small amount of the old red paint that once covered the entire concrete bay floor and weeds now filled the planter out front where firefighter/paramedics Ray and Nate used to grow tomatoes and other vegetables. They're now at a station over 20 miles north and growing another garden up there at 616. What once was one big bunkroom at 603 without a single wall separating beds for privacy was now split into offices for the captain and firefighters. A long hallway now accessed separate, private bunkrooms in a wing that was added years earlier. You'll remember that back when I worked there in the Rural/

Metro days, a crew of eight staffed the station and there were a ladder truck, engine, rescue and battalion chief assigned there. Now, four people staffed one engine company and one person staffed a fire prevention pickup truck.

As much as I had bid on the position at 603 for its closeness to home, I'd mostly bid on the crew. I joined three people I knew I could trust to have my back and who I knew were in no way capable of hurting me the way I'd been hurt at my last assignment.

In the back seat with me, Kate was a young, ambitious firefighter/ EMT who had a handful of years full-time and was then working on getting into paramedic school. At about 5'6", she worked hard, more than pulled her weight and was a country girl at heart. She regularly ignored the fact that she stuck out like a sore thumb amongst three over-6' tall firemen as "that little blonde girl" and I admired her drive to be a great EMT and firefighter, but couldn't help feeling a bit pensive when it came to working as a mentor for her. I'd just been burned pretty badly by the last person I helped and wasn't interested in having that happen again any time soon. Add the female factor into that and it made sense to proceed with caution. Female firefighters have a bad reputation in department culture for filing claims against their male coworkers. The sad thing is that the few spoil it for the many in this case. If I had my choice now, I'd rather have the right female on my crew than the wrong guy for a lot of reasons and would have no fear of false allegations being made. It soon became clear that she was incapable of anything like that, and as the medic school talk became more serious, I offered to precept her once the time came for that. As we drove down Indian Bend Road one day, we passed a side street where she'd gone on a car fire a few years earlier. I still remember handing her the nozzle for fire attack that day and taking a picture with her phone after we wrapped up. It was the first real fire she'd been on, and I happened to be working at the station on an overtime shift. Kate dated and would later marry a police officer from a nearby city. They'd met years earlier at a burn camp for kids. Last I heard, they still volunteer at that camp every year and have started a family.

Up in the driver's seat was Jimmy. Widely known as one of the best engineer/EMTs in the city, Jimmy had entered the fire service back in the Rural/Metro days just a few years after me. He had extensive wildland fire experience and had just transferred from the insanely busy station 602 a couple miles south of us. His dad had worked for Rural/Metro also before retiring and then passing away a few years later. Like my old friend Greg, Jimmy grew up in Scottsdale and knew the streets like the back of his hand, something every fire captain relishes in an engineer because it takes one thing off of their plate when responding to an emergency and thinking of a dozen things other than how to get there. Jimmy paid equal amounts of respect to everyone around him, regardless of rank and I've not seen a more compassionate man when it comes to treating patients. He was the EMT glue that held the crew together, particularly when Kate began her medic education process, leaving him as essentially the only one performing EMT job tasks on every medical call we ran. He was more than up to the task and could do it with one hand behind his back and never complained. Jimmy had just added twin boys to his family, which also included two teenage girls. He and I had divorce in common and I think we related a bit on that level despite not talking much about it specifically. He and his ex had been friends with Lynn and her ex and one of their daughters was actually born in the same hospital on the same day as Lynn's daughter Deborah. Jimmy had witnessed firsthand the decline of Lynn's previous relationship and I believe he was very happy to see that she and I were in a new one together that was working out as well as his relationship with his new wife. Jimmy and I had massive respect for one another and I knew I could trust him with everything I held dear.

Leading us in the captain's seat was Stu Sommers. Having worked with Stu in the past, I placed a courtesy call to him prior to bidding into the spot at station 603, as was common practice and courteous behavior in the fire service. After all, we're talking about changing the crew that you live with for 33% of your life. I think he actually laughed at the fact that I was calling to ask and told me that of course I was welcome there. I knew how he would feel before I placed that call, but believed enough in tradition to show the respect he deserved as not only a captain, but as an old friend. Stu and I each had the longest hair in the department and just "clicked". I don't know what it was, but we were able to communicate on calls in a way that was similar to what I had with Jim in the past, but better because Stu was a paramedic also and as such, we spoke the same language. We worked very well as a team and had the same cunningly sarcastic wit and sense of humor. You may remember him from earlier as our first union president. He was ready to leave that position after being in it for years when he was essentially voted out by the membership. I wish that hadn't have happened, and I saw it take a toll on him, but all anyone could do was stand by and imagine how it must have felt. He had gone through that loss, but had also lost two crewmembers along the way over the years. One was lost to a helicopter accident and the other to suicide. His suitcase was certainly full. Stu was a roving captain, but had been assigned to 603 in a long-term spot for two years while the regular captain was working in an admin assignment. Knowing he would leave in a few months, we made it a point as a crew to enjoy "Papa" Stu, as Kate and Jimmy referred to him, while we could. They called me "Uncle Rick."

The funny thing about Jimmy, Stu and I was that we all lived in the same neighborhood, just down the street from 603. So to say that it was "our" area couldn't have been truer. Living and working in the same first due area is nice, but you're always left wondering somewhere in the back of your mind if one day the tones will drop and you'll recognize the address as your own. Will it be because one of your new twins isn't breathing? Will it be your mother in law lying on the ground after a fall? Or will you have to pull your family members out of a crashed car or worse, a fire that's engulfing your belongings as well as their lives. It's a heavy weight to bear. I think that the philosophy of that situation is that if those things ever did happen, we'd want to be the ones to deliver service.

It wasn't too long after I had arrived at 603 that we found out Stu would be leaving us and his replacement would be one of the newly promoted captains from the last promotional process. Before we knew the particulars, we amassed a fair few remarkable calls together. There was the house fire on Thomas where we had anticipated getting assigned to fire attack only to be presented with treatment of a critical burn patient instead. Stripping our airpacks off just as the interior crew was carrying her out of the kitchen door, I saw the situation, grabbed a backboard from the compartment of engine 603 and slid it 30 feet up the driveway and under the flaming eves of the house to the feet of the guys coming out. They placed her on the board, carried her out to the sidewalk where we'd gathered the required equipment for treatment, then turned around and disappeared back into the dark, smoky doorway like actors stepping out from backstage into a play. Meanwhile on the sidewalk, Stu and I knelt in our turnouts next to a woman who'd been burned to some degree over nearly all of her body. We got the cardiac monitor on her while the equipment for airway management and intubation was gathered. It was bad news. She was in asystole, or flat-line. She was dead. Her heart displayed no electrical activity. We could have called off resuscitative efforts right then and there. But we didn't. The hospital where we had responded from was just a few blocks up the road, and a chief who was on the scene came over and said, "I'll call Osborn and let them know you're coming." "Nope, we're going to County", I replied. He began to insist, but walked away as we carried on with chest compressions, IV/IO access and the most important thing in the given situation, Epinephrine. It's kind of ironic that the very thing that our bodies produce to adapt our physiological state in times of crisis, that chemical that makes us nervous, sweaty and shaky is what we were injecting into her to try and save her life. I've experienced adrenaline rushes by the tens of thousands in my life, but the ones I felt while rocking back and fourth in the back of an ambulance with the siren blaring on the way to a burn center or trauma hospital were always some of the best. It felt like being part of a rock band that's playing their hit song and hitting every note perfectly with the crowd singing along. We were in for about a 15-minute transport to the Maricopa County Medical Center Burn Unit versus the one-minute transport time to Osborn. Osborn is an amazing hospital, which specializes in trauma, but Stu and I knew that if this lady had a chance at living, she'd have to be treated by the incredible people down at Maricopa County Medical Center for burns of this magnitude. As we flew along down the road, oxygen was flowing through a bag-valve mask, down an endotracheal tube and into her lungs. We took turns doing chest compressions for two or three minutes each, attempting to circulate the oxygen and epinephrine to where she needed it most, but each time I looked at the monitor screen, there was nothing.

"County, it's Rick on Engine 603. We have a 12-minute ETA with a patient in her 50's with approximately 80% body surface area burns. She's in cardiac arrest, we have an IV and she is intubated. We're following ACLS protocols." Short and sweet, phone calls like that to a hospital's ER set off a cascade of action on the other end every time

I made them. The behind-the-scenes effort required to get ready for a critical patient inbound to a hospital is nothing short of remarkable. And so is what happened next.

During a change in chest compression shifts, I looked at the monitor and saw something other than the flat line characteristic of asystole. There they were, those magical little indicators of electrical activity. Nice, narrow spikes called QRS complexes. "Get back on the chest, please." I said and the compressions resumed. I didn't even check for a pulse because I didn't want to cause a delay in circulation. It had come into vogue to do another round of 200 chest compressions even after a patient started to have electrical function back in the heart after arrest. Electricity is one thing, but to have the muscle react to it is quite another. I was actually very surprised that her heart had skipped the normal ventricular fibrillation step that most codes go through at some point and skipped right to a normal sinus rhythm. 200 compressions later, a sweat-drenched firefighter still in his turnout gear from the fire scene rose up and away from the chest of our patient and as I watched the beautiful little complexes dance across the monitor screen I said four glorious words: "Check for a pulse..."

She wasn't out of the woods, but she had a pulse. Not only that, she had a very viable blood pressure on top of it and pulse oximetry actually looked good too, albeit probably being inaccurate due to smoke and carbon monoxide inhalation. We turned the patient over to a room full of hospital staff that would do their best in the following hours to keep this woman alive. And they did just that. But later that evening the phone rang at our station with the news. She'd died in the burn unit at County that night after her family arrived at her bedside to say a final goodbye. Firefighters do it all the time when they drop off a patient at the hospital. We essentially say goodbye to a person that we in all likelihood will never see again and we become callous to it out of necessity. If we allowed ourselves the freedom to feel sorrow and grieve over every lost patient, we'd surely go insane. I feel like I knew that woman would have no quality of life ever again when we drove away from County in Engine 603 that day. But I'm glad that she was still alive for that final goodbye with her family even though she wasn't conscious for it. At least they got to make the decision to not let her suffer any longer instead of a big fiery breath of superheated gas making the decision for them, then seeing her for the last time covered by a trauma blanket on the ground in front of her incinerated house. The relative peace of the burn unit downtown would have to do.

Chapter 29
"About To Give"

———

DURING MY TIME AT STATION 603, I worked for four different company officers over the course of just over 16 months, with each new captain averaging about four months on the crew. That's just about long enough to get settled in with someone new leading our team, and establishing workflow, expectations and responsibilities. And it's not easy to do in some cases. In my situation, I'd say that two of them went great, leaving the other two as, well, not so great. In any case, these changes are very stressful to all involved. And all the while, I was first precepting a paramedic student from outside our organization, then precepting Kate, or "K2" as she had come to be known after another Kate, "K1", was assigned as our captain, the second of the four. I have to admit, the K1/K2 thing was my idea and worked brilliantly to distinguish the two. Imagine being on a fire scene and referring to one of them as just, "Kate" in the heat of battle, only to have them both ask you, "Which one?" That first medic student turned out pretty well, and was the first person I had been assigned to train since the whole DB situation went down nearly a year prior. I went into that with a healthy dose of trepidation and a heap of trust issues, but in the end I wound up building up not only the confidence of this new paramedic, but my own confidence and faith in humanity in the process. I was beginning to heal. Weeks after I finished that assignment, I started my next with K2, but not before taking over the responsibility of overseeing the EMS standby equipment newly stored at station 603. It's the medical gear that's picked up by crews on overtime, assigned to one of dozens of special events that draw crowds in Scottsdale every year. These events range in size from as small as a city council meeting or block party all the way up to the largest event, the Phoenix Open golf tournament. I was responsible for keeping an inventory of equipment, supplies and drugs for six sets of gear, not to mention the other complete set of gear carried on Engine 603. It was a massive responsibility, and an even more massive time commitment. There were plenty of shifts where there just wasn't enough time to get to everything, when running calls and all other normal fire department operations were thrown into the schedule. Oh, and there was the not so little matter of precepting yet another new medic student. But I will say that precepting K2 was a delight, and one of the only things I enjoyed about my work at this point. I'd also volunteered for it.

When I begin teaching a student or mentoring someone, I always ask a few things. I need to know how they learn, what they're good at and what they suck at. And I've found it best to just come right out and ask them those things directly. But I also tell them what I feel my own strengths and weaknesses are. It's one of the things that define brotherhood and good leadership in the fire service. We must lead. We must follow. We must succeed. And unfortunately sometimes, we must fail. But we do all these things together as a crew. That's my leadership style and my teaching style, and it worked.

What you should know about precepting a medic student is that you and that student ride in to the hospital in the ambulance with each and every patient. And you and that student are responsible for documenting every patient encounter. The preceptor waits for the student to finish their chart, then reviews it and at least at first, points out corrections and additions that must be made to the chart. And all the while, the other two crewmembers are milling around the ER, snacking on whatever junk food has been laid out by the pre-hospital care coordinator, waiting for this process to come to a close so that we can get back to the station, available to start the whole thing over again when called to do so. In all, a normal, non-critical EMS call took about an hour to turn over while precepting was happening. But make that call a cardiac or respiratory arrest or anything requiring drug administration and you're looking at over an hour and a half to get back home. It taxed everyone on the crew, including the student. But to some extent, that was the point: to put them in real-world medical situations where they had a responsibility to uphold in the face of many outside factors influencing the process. Taxing as it was, it made me a better paramedic because it kept my skills sharp. And it's widely acknowledged that true masters of a craft have one very simple thing in common: mastery of the basics. That's what makes you an expert. But I was getting tired. And I mean really tired.

During this time, another change was happening. I had taken up Olympic recurve target archery, and was competing at a national level after only about a year in the sport. I had walked away from competitive cycling recently because it just wasn't as fun as it had been several years prior and there was a vacuum created by the void left by riding and racing. I won a race in the prior season, so I was still competitive, but the fire to be exceptional at it had died. This loss of joy went largely unnoticed to me because archery had filled cycling's place. I went about my training for shooting much the same way I had trained for cycling, including getting set up with a world-class coach by the name of Dick Tone, who lived not too far from me. We had begun working together during the indoor season, but as soon as the outdoor tournament schedule started to pick up, he had me shooting outside. If you watch archery in the Olympics, you know exactly what I was doing: shooting at a 4' diameter round target from 70 meters, or 230' away. The center 10-ring measures exactly the same size as a CD or DVD disk. An American named Jay Barrs won the gold medal in archery at the 1988 summer Olympics in Seoul, South Korea. And his coach was none other than Dick

Tone, or "DT" as I had come to call him. I was in the right place at the right time and asked for his help, and help he did. At the height of my shooting, I could put about 1/3 of my shots in the 10-ring if everything was going well and the winds were calm. And that shooting was good enough to find me in the middle of the national rankings after a handful of tournaments. It was also good enough for me to make the podium in the Arizona State Indoor Championships, just two months after starting training with DT. I was succeeding, but it was frustrating to me because I had been hitting a plateau recently and was not seeing the huge gains I'd had early on. So I doubled down on my training, sometimes shooting over 400 arrows in a single six-hour training session, often forgetting to even stop and eat. I was putting in nearly professional amounts of training, but I was also now beginning to feel like I was losing interest again in something that once brought me joy. This should have come as another red flag for me, but didn't. What I was really doing was seeking something that cycling had given me for thirty years when I was racing and training for that. What I wanted was to suffer. And considering that those long days shooting were happening during the Arizona summer, suffering was just what I got. Thinking back on it now, I feel like the time I spent suffering during training was necessary to perform at the highest of levels, but it was more likely a form of self-flagellation, rooted in a deep sense of self-loathing that I had kept to myself for many years. I really just didn't like who I was very much.

Despite outward appearances of success and accomplishment, I really hated myself. I hated that I didn't know who my real family was. I hated that my adoptive family and I had failed to get along. I hated that I'd gone through two divorces. I hated that there were people whose lives I wasn't able to save. I hated that I sometimes drank too much. I hated that I didn't race motorcycles any more. I hated that cycling wasn't fun any more. I hated that I'd lost my TRT assignment. I hated that I had to sell the huge house I had renovated with my own hands. I hated Scottsdale, with its fake tits and fake people. And I hated the fact that deep down, I really and truly never wanted to run another call in another fire truck ever again. Never another cardiac arrest with a family watching me steadily lose any hope of resuscitating their loved one as the chest compressions pounded on one after another. Never another house fire full of death and destruction and black soot coming out of my nose afterward in the shower at the station and the smell of smoke stuck to my hair for days. No more bloody car accidents with people trapped, dead or dying after innocently enough leaving their house just moments prior. No more wet, slippery, drowned kids lying limp on a pool deck while a mother wails and cries just feet away. No more getting startled by the red lights and station alert tones going off in the middle of the night as I try unsuccessfully to shield my eyes with a blanket pulled high on my face like a child hiding from the boogey man. No more stumbling home after another long night at work with little or no sleep, wondering just how much longer I can take this punishing work schedule. Where once I just wanted more of all of these things, I now wanted none of it. I was at the end of my rope, without enough slack left to tie a knot and hold on.

Something was about to give.

Everything was about to give.

Chapter 30
"The Clock And Regret"

———

THERE'S AN ANALOGY I use to describe my state of mind in September of 2019 and it goes like this. Picture a white Toyota pickup truck somewhere in the Middle East, loaded with 20 people, a goat, a chicken coup, and three donkeys tied behind it. The truck is barely making its way down the road, suspension overloaded, tires bulging and everything just barely hanging on. Put simply, it can't handle any more. Now a bird flies overhead and just one small feather falls onto the top of this heap of man, animal and machine. The weight of that one single feather is enough to cause the whole thing to collapse. In 2019, I had been the truck for a few years and the feather was a small argument at home over a nonexistent problem. The small weight of that argument was enough to collapse me, and the crash scene was going to be a big one.

I had actually looked upon suicide over the course of my life as a comforting option I could always take if my life didn't work out and I couldn't bear the burden of living any longer. I know that sounds odd, but I was actually that at peace with the concept, which had been present since I was a child. I didn't really have a serious plan or anything, but I always had the idea in the back of my mind. At one point a coworker of mine actually mentioned having the same thought. For a moment, I wanted to express to him that I felt the same, but didn't for fear of being seen as weak or worse, crazy. So I kept it to myself. But late in the evening on September 11, 2019, I found myself sitting in the backyard with my shotgun braced on the ground between my feet, contemplating whether to shoot myself in the heart or the head and what the outcome of each option would be.

Ten minutes into the process, I sat the gun down and held my head in my hands. I couldn't let Lynn and her family find me out here if I did it like this. I didn't want to traumatize them with that sight; one I'd seen a few times during my career. I knew that I was closer to making the decision to go ahead with this than I ever had been before, and it actually scared the hell out of me. I needed help.

I called the crisis line that had been provided to local firefighters for use in these circumstances, and promptly lied to them when they asked what was going on.

"Uh, yeah, I had this argument with my girlfriend."

"Okay, and then what happened?"

"I, um, well, I had thoughts of hurting myself."

"I see. Do you have a plan for that? Are you about to do something now that would cause harm?"

"Oh no, no. I'm not doing anything like that."

"Alright. If you're in crisis right now, we can send someone out to help you."

"No thanks, I'll be fine. I'll call back if I need you."

As I hung up the phone, I realized that what I was saying sounded absurd as the words were coming from my mouth. And the thought of telling that crisis counselor the truth sounded even more absurd to me, because I knew the cascade of events that would take place if I put those wheels in motion. I didn't want to sit and talk to anyone. And I didn't want to go through the mandatory 72-hour involuntary treatment hold in a mental facility for those threatening suicide. After sitting outside in the cool evening air for a while, all I wanted was to go to sleep and wake up the next day as though this whole thing had never happened. I put my shotgun back where I stored it, hoping that Lynn hadn't seen me with it, downed two double-shots of vodka from the freezer, chased by a beer and climbed into bed upstairs, next to Lynn.

Something felt seriously wrong with me. I found myself ruminating on every negative factor in my life at the time. Over and over, all night long, I laid there awake thinking of nothing but the bad things in my life and began rationalizing the possibility of going forward with the decision I'd fought off just hours prior. It began to make sense to me. I wanted the pain of my existence to end. I needed the pain of my existence to end. I couldn't take these lowest of lows any longer. My wheels were well and truly falling off before my very eyes. But I didn't understand why. I didn't understand what had been happening for years at that point. And at the time it didn't matter. I just wanted out. And then it came to me. I had a plan. I knew what I was going to do. And I knew it so deep in my heart as the best course of action that there was no stopping it.

When Lynn left for work the following morning, I had made her coffee like I always did and walked her out to the garage. Along the way, I told her, "I can't do this anymore."

"Okay, we should go to counseling. I'll talk to you later."

As she drove away, I realized that she had absolutely no idea what I was talking about and I suddenly felt irrevocably alone with my feelings. And the comfort of making the pain end began to wash over me. My vision narrowed. My path was clear to me. This was going to happen, and it was going to start right now.

I drove to my fire station, station 603 on McDonald Drive in Scottsdale, Arizona for one final time. I figured that if the engine was in the bay, I'd keep driving past the station. But Engine 603 was gone, out on a call. I turned sharply left off of the street and drove around to the back of the station and parked. Walking into the kitchen and day room, the only company I had was the morning news on the TV. Warm cups of coffee laid in wait on the table, to be finished by the crew when they returned, certain to be cold by then. Down the back hallway I walked. It was freezing back there, which was common practice by crews in nearly every fire station, who hoped to somehow get a good night's sleep the shift before. I went to the locker in my bunkroom and retrieved the key to the station's backup EMS equipment storage lockers. For a moment, I thought of leaving a note for my brothers and sisters, apologizing for being too weak to continue on in this life and begging them to take better care of each other, but thought better of it. I then considered taking my Class A dress uniform with me to change into for the occasion, hopefully to make a statement as to what had brought me to this desperate point, but decided against that as well. I walked back out and to the end of the hallway and arrived at a locked door. It's all that stood between the required items and me for the task at hand. I entered my six-digit security code and the electronic lock clicked. For a split second, I considered turning back. This was the last time I'd have that urge. Once in the storage room, I unlocked six of the metal cabinets and pulled the black, 6"x6" zippered drug pouches from six EMS backpacks that were used for special events in the city. All six were transferred into my backpack, and I put all the other gear back, closing the lockers and the door to the room behind me. It's about this time that I heard the familiar engine brake on the truck as it rounded the back corner of the station, just about ten feet from me on the other side of the wall. I was still inside, and waited about one minute, long enough, I thought, for the crew to walk into the day room from the apparatus bay, but not long enough to get all the way to the back of the station, where I was. I opened the back door and walked toward my truck, surprised to find that one of the firefighters was also headed to the back parking lot. Acting normal, I said, "Hi" from a distance, tossed my backpack onto the passenger seat and drove away.

I drove but a few blocks to a luxury resort and headed to the front desk, where I asked if they had a room available. As it was early in the day, they had to check on a few things, but within ten minutes or so, I had a room key card in my hand and went to the room. I'd checked into what seemed like hundreds of hotel rooms at that point in my life, but not like this. This was final. This was the last one. Walking into the nicely modern room, I set my bag on the counter, and remembered that I needed the EMS bag I carried in my truck and the IV supplies contained within it. I walked back out to get it, and then set it down on the bed. I noticed the mini bar right about then and poured two small bottles of red wine into the full-sized glass nearby. Three years earlier, I had told Lynn that at some point, I would probably call her from work, asking to just hear her voice. And what that meant was that I'd just seen something terrible on a call and needed her to help ground me again and stabilize my mood. I did that a few times since we'd been together for some tough calls and it always helped. All I needed was for her to talk about something, anything, so that I could hear her. So I called her one last time, thinking it would be calming to me. She was at her job as a school nurse and answered right away. The conversation was brief and she asked where I was. I told her not to worry about it and that I was okay. I told her that I loved her, and then told her a lie, saying that I'd talk to her later. After hanging up, I started some random country music playing on my phone and then set to work preparing what I needed to end the suffering once and for all.

Turning to the room, I found a floor lamp in the corner and took off the shade. I pulled it over to the side of the bed, and then set up a 1,000mL bag of normal saline with IV tubing. After purging the air from the line, I squeezed the little white plastic clamp, stopping the flow of fluid. That floor lamp would serve as my IV pole. On the inside jamb of the hotel room door, I placed a note that said, "Attention maids: DO NOT ENTER. Call police." I wrote another note asking the police to call Lynn and listed her phone number, then set my drivers license on top of it on the desk. My idea was to have the police find me about 24 hours later, long-deceased. They don't send the fire department for those calls and only request the coroner's office to respond to pick up the body after their investigation. I didn't leave a suicide note. Nothing and no one else mattered to me at that point. I was solely focused on the task at hand and didn't feel a need to explain myself. I wasn't trying to make a statement. I then unzipped each of the six black drug pouches, carefully lining up the vials of Morphine, Versed, Ativan and Fentanyl in rows like so many little soldiers, ready to march in and launch an all-out assault on my ability to breathe when I called them into action. Realizing that the liquid in all these vials would take up quite a bit of volume, I unwrapped two of the largest syringes I had in my pack, put a needle on the end of each, and began drawing up 120 mg of Morphine, 120 mg of Ativan and 50mg of Versed. There was no room left in the syringes for the Fentanyl on the table, so those soldiers would have to sit out this battle. The process took perhaps 20 minutes. Gathering the rest of my IV supplies, I tied the blue rubber tourniquet around my left bicep, causing the veins in my arm to bulge. Out of habit and ironically, I wiped my arm with an alcohol prep pad and then advanced an 18 gauge IV catheter into my antecubital vein, pulled the tourniquet, removed the needle, plugged the IV tubing into the green IV catheter hub on my arm and checked the flow of fluid. The clear liquid now contained in those two syringes I had prepared could easily kill ten people. This was my guarantee of success. They were now attached to the IV line at each of two ports. I laid down flat on the bed with a couple of pillows under my head, pinched off the IV tubing above the syringes and squeezed the plungers all the way down on both, forcing the lethal mix through the tubing and into my arm. I let go of the IV tubing, laid back and immediately lost consciousness. The pain was officially gone, the suffering officially over. I had begun dying and my life, remarkable as it had been, would soon come to a close. During this process of preparation and administration, I didn't feel afraid or apprehensive. I felt calm and resolute. The path ahead of me was crystal clear and unchangeable. I felt relief. I didn't think of anyone in my life and how this would affect them. I didn't think about what good I might have possibly done further along in my life. I didn't think about how others would look upon my decision. I didn't think about the first responders who would find me. I didn't think there were dozens, hundreds or tens of thousands of other firefighters who felt exactly the way I did that day.

I didn't think I had PTSD.

I didn't think.

———

WHAT I DIDN'T KNOW was that while I was drawing up those meds and preparing my IV, and just after I had hung up with Lynn, she had gone to the police officer stationed at her school and told him that something was wrong, that they needed to find me. He called PD dispatch and had the location of my phone pinged.

"Where would he be if he was near Scottsdale Road and Lincoln?"

Lynn named the hotel I was in, the hotel she and I had gone to for my birthday just days earlier. Police units responded to her house, my fire station and to the hotel to locate me. They found my truck, gained access from the front desk and found me lying in bed, barely breathing and realistically about three minutes from death. The two officers administered all of their intranasal Narcan, the antidote for Morphine, before any EMS units arrived. What happened next is one of several things from that day that I'll never be able to forgive myself for. The crew from station 603 arrived in the hotel room that fateful day. The firefighter I'd seen in the parking lot just over an hour earlier and his three partners set about resuscitating me. Four brave men at first and then a host of others after them, all of whom I had known for years, had to be the ones to try and save my life. And as the crew wheeled me out to the parking lot where an ambulance was waiting, Lynn pulled up in her car. If there's an image I wish I could erase, it's the one in her head of me on that black and yellow stretcher, with a crewmember squeezing a bag valve mask to breathe for me, and a swarm of people in blue shirts desperately performing life support functions on their brother firefighter. I know what the scene looked like because I have been on hundreds of calls very similar to it.

With all of the Narcan from two drug boxes and two PD officers gone, the crew still had a seven-minute code 3 run ahead of them to get me to the hospital. With amazing forethought, one of the fire officers on the scene requested that a truck from station 602 meet the ambulance and hand over another drug box, with more Narcan. That supply was also administered to me, with no change in my drive to breathe. There's no maximum dose for Narcan, and it sometimes takes several times the normal amount to get an effect, particularly if Fentanyl was in the patient. But all the Fentanyl was still sitting on the table in the hotel room. I remained unconscious thanks to the two benzodiazepines still coursing through my veins. I was taken into the ER at Honor Health Osborn, where I was treated for a massive drug overdose. I was placed on a ventilator and after no change in my level of consciousness for several hours; I was transferred upstairs to the Intensive Care Unit. Lynn faced hurdles trying to even get in to see me since we were not married and had made no power of attorney plans, but firefighters find a way, and with the help of my partner Jimmy and his wife Brianna (one of the nurses on staff) and the prehospital coordinator, Lynn made her way to my side.

Hospital staff spent the next three days trying to get me to breathe on my own. On the fourth day, they succeeded. Many hours later, I regained consciousness after they took me off of the sedatives meant to keep me from fighting the ventilator. Until that point, my hands and feet had been tied down to prevent me from pulling the ventilator tube out of my throat. I opened my eyes, realizing that I was in a hospital bed. I then looked at the wall above the foot of the bed and saw a clock hanging up high. I remember gradually gaining awareness of my body and questioning how that massive amount of drugs had not worked in doing what I'd asked of them. And then that's when it happened. I turned my head to the right and saw Lynn's face. She was sitting there next to the bed, looking at me with her big, beautiful brown eyes. I could hear other people in the room talking, but I couldn't draw my gaze away from her. At that moment, I felt the heaviest amount of guilt and regret that I ever had and ever have since. I knew that I had made an incredible mistake. But I had no idea what the path ahead of me was going to look like or how this event would affect my life and the lives around me, or how it would also affect people I hadn't even met yet.

One important thing was clear, though. I was alive.

Chapter 31
"Bagpipes In The Distance"

A REMARKABLE TURN OF events happened next. I could speak, but it felt like something was stuck in my throat. As it turned out, a nasal airway used during the resuscitation effort was still in place, but had slid down out of sight in my nose, coming to rest near my epiglottis, or the flap of tissue that keeps food and drink from going down your trachea instead of your esophagus. Hours later, the airway was removed but it was a couple of days before I could swallow food correctly, sending things "down the wrong pipe" into my airway. A radiologic study had to be done, and I sat inside an x-ray booth while a nurse fed me irradiated food of several textures while my ability to swallow was observed and recorded. I believe they called it "good enough" and there was no need to keep me in the hospital any longer for that issue alone.

There were immediate questions similar to "Now what?" going through everyone's minds, including mine. I didn't know where I would wind up, when I would be there and with whom. I didn't know if I would still have a job at the fire department after this. I didn't know if Lynn would stay with me after this event and all of the baggage that would be loaded up in my life moving forward. And I didn't know what the people in my life thought of me.

What I do know is that several firefighters made it through the theoretical barriers the hospital had set up in the interest of privacy and got in to see me. These weren't new guys on the department. They were some of the most senior, and were people I had known for decades at that point. Something sad was going on, and it was something so well hidden as to go largely unnoticed by everyone nearby in these people's lives. These firefighters all cried, gave me very long hugs and admitted that they had each at one point or another felt the same way I had in the hotel room that day. They all felt the same? I came to realize that I might not be alone in this. And that's the sad part. These people had all suffered the same way I had. We'd run the same calls, worked in the same stations, ridden on the same trucks and treated the same patients. But we had more in common than I had ever thought possible. And there were many, many more out there with the same issue. That fact would have to take a bit of a back seat for a while but was always on my mind afterward.

My fire chief came to the room on a couple of evenings and spent some time at my bedside. He was reassuring, and admitted that we all had our own demons to deal with in one way or another. Without coming right out and saying it, he'd let me know again that he knew I wasn't alone in this and I felt like he had my back. Another, but less than desirable, visit came from a Scottsdale Police Department Sergeant. He said that he was there to ask me some questions about what had happened and what I had done. He also told me that I didn't have to talk with him if I didn't want to. I invited him to take a seat and the questioning began, which essentially boiled down to this. He wanted to know if I had intended to use the drugs I took recreationally or if I had meant to hurt myself. I explained that the amount of narcotics I had injected was roughly ten times the amount required to kill a person and that my intent was very much to end my life. Less than five minutes after he had entered the room, he was gone.

Then Brett showed up. He was my contact from the local chapter of the International Association of Fire Fighters, or IAFF, which is our labor union. He had worked with that old favorite crew of mine at a few points during his start with the department and I had known him for nearly twenty years. He was a trusted friend. Brett let me know that there was a place in Maryland called the IAFF Center of Excellence (COE) that treated firefighters for mental health and substance abuse, and asked if I was interested in going. I immediately agreed to go and work started toward the logistics of getting me there, navigating the mandatory 72-hour custody required following a suicide attempt and lots more behind the scenes than I was aware of at the time. Lynn went home and called me on Face Time video. I guided her through my side of the closet and she packed a bag for me. Looking back now, I wish I had planned a little better for the cold east-coast autumn temps that were on the way, but this wasn't a vacation and I just needed some clothes to wear. There was guidance from the center regarding what to pack and what not to pack, and soon that bag was full thanks to Lynn. A local firefighter charity called The 100 Club provided round trip airfare for Brett and a one-way ticket for me to Maryland. Firefighters in Scottsdale donated their time to work my shifts when the sick and vacation time ran out. Firefighters even went to Lynn's house to assist when a monsoon storm flooded the basement while I was gone. In short, I had a lot of support from those around me, but I had absolutely no idea what I was getting into or where the road ahead would lead. I had reached the proverbial bottom and had nowhere to go but up. I was lost, hopelessly adrift in a sea of unimaginable sorrow and despair. I was scared, having done something so irrevocably damaging to not only my body, but to the relationships I had with absolutely everyone around me. I felt as though I would be forevermore though of as "That guy who..."

The night before I was to leave the hospital, I had a visit from another union officer. He had been on the department about the same amount of time as Brett, and had been treated at the COE a short time prior and gave Lynn and I priceless information on what to expect from my time there. He described the grounds, the buildings, and the staff and had inside information on how to communicate with the outside world, what the food was like and how the recovery program was delivered. It went a long way toward easing my mind and Lynn's before we were to be separated from one another for longer than ever before since we'd found each other.

The wheels touched down on our overnight flight from Phoenix Sky Harbor to Baltimore/Washington International Airport and I limped off the plane after a four-hour flight that felt like it took a decade. I was weak, having spent seven days in the hospital, largely immobile. I'd never been to Maryland before, and if you handed this Arizona boy a map, he would have had difficulty even pointing to where it was at the time. But I may as well have landed on the moon, because the treatment I was about to undergo would have me confined to a 15-acre facility that was purpose-built to resemble several fire stations, complete with bunk rooms, day rooms with recliners, classroom facilities and even kitchens. The administrative and treatment offices resembled fire headquarters, and the cafeteria was the equivalent of about ten fire station day room tables. But "confined" wasn't true at all. The front gates were always open, and patients could walk right out never to return any time they wanted.

Brett and I passed through that front entrance of the COE at around 07:00, just before the day was to get started for everyone there and it was still dark out. I was guided from the front entry back to an office where the facility's intake process would begin. Sitting next to a desk, I answered enough questions to provide a comprehensive medical, work and social history. After only a few of those questions, I started feeling extremely uneasy and anxious. I told the nurse that I needed to take a break and that I was having a hard time. She suggested we stop for a moment, put her pen down and said, "Okay Mr. Rick, I want you to imagine something for me. Can you do that?"

"I'll try."

She went on, after handing me a box of tissue, by telling me to close my eyes.

"You're at the beach, Mr. Rick, sitting on the sand and it's warm out. You can feel the sand under you and the warm wind on your face. You can hear the waves crashing in front of you, and you can see everything in crisp, clear colors. Can you picture that?"

"Yes, I can."

"Good. Just stay there with that for a minute."

The Technicolor scene in my mind flickered on and off, alternating between scenes flashing through my head. Things like Lynn, the confined space call, the hospital room, the hotel room, driving a fire truck to a fire, paddling a kayak, treating a cardiac arrest patient, riding a mountain bike, cooking dinner for my crew and all manner of other memories alternated with the beach scene. I couldn't make it stop and couldn't just keep the one thing visible, and decided to thank the nurse for her help in calming me and continued on with the intake process. Let's get on with it. After the interview, I was guided to an exam room, where my vitals were taken and an ECG was performed. Following that, and in the same room, my suitcase made it's way in. The staff opened and inspected the entire contents inside and out, then took inventory of everything valuable, including my wallet and phone. My suitcase was turned over to me and my valuables were stored in a safe, to be released back to me when I checked out of the facility. Brett came into the hallway where I was and we said our goodbyes. I was losing the last familiar face I'd get to see for a while. I was then guided to my first bunk assignment at the center, one of eight beds in the medical building. It truly looked just like a station, with a twin bed and tall locker in each of the room's four corners, one of which was occupied. A voice came from that corner, "Are you drunk or crazy?"

"Just crazy, I guess."

"Cool, I'm T."

"Hey, bro. I'm Rick."

I settled into the bed and closed my eyes, subconsciously hoping that the alarm didn't go off for a call for us to go on.

I believe I went to a couple of group meetings that first day, but mostly just spent the time wondering what I was getting myself into. The Center of Excellence runs a program that includes group therapy, psychiatric and psychological care, medicine administration, and a litany of topics covered in multiple classes during each day. The organization and the way it runs are nothing short of remarkable and the staff is second to none. But some of the best therapy took place after dinner and into the night. That was when firefighters from all over the United States sat around a campfire the size of which we could be proud, and shared information about how our departments worked, what brand of trucks we had, staffing types, uniforms and everything else imaginable. But we also shared our personal stories of triumph and tragedy, and our reasons for coming to this place. I sure wish I could keep telling you everything about the program, but the details will have to remain behind those front gates. Just know that what they do really works, and has not just kept me alive, but allowed me to thrive again.

In the evening of my first day there, I began having pain in the side of my chest that I couldn't seem to get away from. It was like a sharp stabbing sensation, and it was keeping me from taking a deep breath.

I asked for medical assistance, was given Ibuprofen and told to see how I felt later that night. The problem wasn't better in the morning. In fact, it was far worse. I could barely breathe at this point and my blood oxygen level was monitored. It was 84% and I was beside myself with anxiety. The decision was made to take me to the local ER, where I was treated. It turned out that a pulmonary embolism (PE) caused the chest pain I was feeling. That's the same thing that had killed my friend Eddie just a few years prior. Then more bad news came. I had not only one PE but two, one in each lung. After a day in the ER, I was admitted to the ICU upstairs for observation and was put on a medicine to help dissolve the clots in my lungs. This visit to an ICU bed was different, though. This visit was lonely and there would be no visitors or familiar faces. I felt so completely isolated and in the dark about what was going on and if I was going to recover from this or not. I was given blood thinners by injection into my abdomen again, which burned like hell, the same kind I'd had after my rock climbing accident. Within the first twelve hours at the hospital, I felt much better and was nearly pain-free. On the third day with steady improvement, I was picked up by the COE van and taken back to my new home, where people by this time had heard what happened. I had survived having a pulmonary embolism in each lung and a suicide attempt in less than ten days, and word of that story spread around pretty quickly in the center, with the gravity of the situation well-understood because the entire patient population was made up of EMTs and paramedics.

I soon had appointments with the physician, psychiatrist and psychologist on staff at the center. And I have Dr. Abby, my counselor Audra and Marc, the program director to thank for diagnosing and beginning treatment of my condition. I was kept on a blood-thinning medication for the duration of my time at the center and for two more months after release. In my first week there, and within 30 minutes of talking with the psychiatrist, I was diagnosed with severe anxiety, major depressive disorder and complex PTSD. And I had a hard time accepting that fact, but over time and as I began to understand what PTSD was and the signs and symptoms of it, I felt as though a huge curtain had been pulled back on a massive secret I'd unknowingly kept. I started to understand that I was checking all of the boxes and had been checking them for quite some time. If I had narrowed my eyes at the diagnoses at first, my gaze would soon widen as the truth became obvious. My mental health had been damaged by my time in the fire service, particularly over the last few years, and it was time to do something about it.

Part of doing something about it meant making a decision about running calls or ever even stepping foot on a fire truck again. As the days wore on and I pondered my career nearly nonstop, I started to accept the fact that going back to the job would not be an option for me. I called my chief and told him the news. I wasn't coming back to the fire department. He was very supportive and understanding. Behind the scenes, the union, the department and the city were handling the processing of my retirement paperwork. I had to sign some documents shipped to me overnight and once those hit the return mail, there was no turning back. My career was going to end. And I was about to have an identity crisis of epic proportions.

I remember having breakfast, lunch and dinner in the cafeteria and the food was actually great. I can remember the cooks and our conversations about motorcycle racing well. I can also remember the graduation ceremonies that were held every week and the woods on the property with hiking trails and what it was like to be on them alone or in groups. I can remember what it felt like to work out again every morning, and how cold it was on the late October mornings in Maryland. I can see the faces of every one there and remember spending time with all of them at some point or another, some scared and new, others reaching the end of their time at the center and appearing sorted.

Several people stand out and I'm still in touch with them, but the evening that I met David stands out a bit more. He was a Captain for another city in the western U.S., and had only been at the center for perhaps a day or less when he sat down next to me in front of the graduation bell, near the cafeteria. I was starting my second week and was getting into a rhythm each day, taking a few minutes to ponder what it would mean to me to be the one ringing that bell on my last day there. David came over and introduced himself. We made small talk for a few minutes, and then he told me why he was there. In return, I shared my story. The exchange probably took 30 minutes. And as I sat there in tears, right after I finished telling another person at the COE about the worst day of my life for the first time, another patient started playing his bagpipes from the other side of the property. It was one of those moments where something like a sign presents itself. Those bagpipes were speaking to me. They were applauding me for being able to share my story, and they were willing me to continue sharing it. But I wasn't in a place to receive their messages yet. That would come later. The haunting timing of their appearance however, lingered for a long while.

Patients at the COE could claim and use their cell phones for an hour on two days each week. During that time, I would check my email, respond to text messages and place a Face Time call to Lynn, who would always be in her office at work during that time of day. Those calls were difficult, to say the least. I felt like our relationship had been placed on hold for the time being, and it wasn't fun. Lynn's eyes more often than not looked cold to me. We had issues, and being so far away was a barrier nearly impossible to overcome. I could see that she was hurting, uncertain of our future together. After our calls were done, I would scroll through the pictures of us together in my phone, committing them to memory to carry me through the next day or so without them. I was afraid that we wouldn't make it through this and knew that we would have a lot of work ahead of us. I also knew that she had no idea what I was diagnosed with or why. The work of trying to explain these things to myself would pale in comparison to laying them before her for the first time.

It was at the COE that I started writing this book. We were issued composition books and pens and encouraged to start journaling as patients. I soon filled one book and requested a second. I finished filling it on my last day there. Passages, poems, thoughts and feelings all filled in the pages. In addition to those two journals, I would return to Arizona with a completely full 3" binder of handouts and notes. To put the amount of therapy into perspective, during my time in Maryland I received the equivalent of five years worth of one-hour per week sessions in about six weeks. And during my time there, I was entrusted to use the tools they gave me to protect my mental health and in this case, my own life. The goal of my treatment there was primarily to stabilize my mental condition to a point where my life was no longer in jeopardy. I would have plenty more work to do when I got home as I moved forward with treating my conditions, not to mention attempting to get my life in order without my previous career in it. If the fire of my suicidal action had been extinguished at the COE, the salvage operation to rebuild my life afterward would be up to me, with the support of those around me who loved and cared about me and help from a few professionals I would soon learn to count on.

I booked a flight home from Maryland and will never forget the trip to the airport with two of the other guys who were heading out that same morning. We were headed back to "The Noise", as one of our therapists had called it at the center and I was sure that I wasn't ready for it yet. As the seatbelt clicked for the four-hour return flight home, I did my best to keep my head together, but spent most of the next 2,200 miles with tears of fear and uncertainty streaming down my face. I had no idea what life was about to look like for me and it was terrifying. At points in the past, this would have seemed like some grand, new adventure. But now it just looked like a monumental restart, with no guarantee of a positive outcome regardless of how badly I wanted it.

I walked down the terminal back at Sky Harbor in Phoenix, searching desperately for the familiar face I needed more than anything in the world. It felt like forever as I neared the end of the walkway and entered the large, open area of the main terminal. And there she was. Lynn's golden blonde hair and beautiful face appeared like a lighthouse in the darkest, foggiest night and we were reunited. That first embrace was like none before and I knew that whatever work I had to do to move through this period of my life, she would be there with me. I also knew that I wanted to make her feel safe and loved in return for her giving me those same feelings.

As we walked hand in hand through the airport that day, in my mind I could hear those bagpipes playing off in the distance. Everything was going to be okay.

Chapter 32
"Who Do You Think You Are?"

OVER THE COURSE OF the next several months, I had a lot of settling in to do. I got set up with an amazing psychiatrist and an equally amazing psychologist for ongoing treatment, which took place once per week for each of them. My new job became recovery. The interesting thing was that I had a strong point of reference to compare these people to now, having seen so much treatment back at the center. These were two extremely powerful clinicians and I owe my continued recovery and mental health management to Dr. Adnan Celjo and Jennifer Cooper. Without them, I could never have continued successfully with my recovery.

Lynn and I worked out, went to yoga, cooked dinner together and generally tried to figure out what the new "normal" would be. I resumed shooting archery and made plans to go to some upcoming tournaments and started riding my road and mountain bikes again, but even with all this activity, there was one thing that was looming overhead the whole time. I was uncertain about my upcoming retirement and didn't know what my financial future would look like. This problem was two-fold. I had the public safety retirement and a work-comp claim with the city to get approved, which would require not one, but three independent medical examinations or IMEs. During these, I would have to sit down with psychiatrists and psychologists to be evaluated for my injury, and would consequently have to relive some key traumatic events from my career in order to explain the nature of my claim. They were spaced out over the course of nearly six months, and plenty of work was required after each appointment with my own mental health team to keep me on an even keel. It was grueling, but in the end, both the public safety and work comp claims were approved. To my knowledge, I was the first firefighter in Arizona to have a PTSD work comp claim approved, and I believe it was in no small part due to something called the Craig Tiger Act, which establishes PTSD as presumptively caused by service in public safety. It was a huge victory for those who have stepped forward after I did, but just as one stress was relieved, another appeared.

I heard from a credible source that there might be legal consequences for what I had done, because I did technically steal the narcotics I used to end my life that fateful day. Talk about something you never considered at the time, and why would I have. I wrapped up the conversation with my source by asking, "So, somebody might come-a-knockin'?"

"Yes, somebody indeed might do that."

The theories and possibilities started to build. Was I looking at the City of Scottsdale here, the State of Arizona or a federal agency? There was no way for me to tell, and several months passed with no sign of trouble.

In addition to settling in to a new life and seeing new treatment professionals, I was wrestling with something I hadn't experienced since the loss of my TRT assignment; the loss of my identity. I wasn't a firefighter anymore. I had no duty to uphold, no calls to run and no people's lives or property depending upon my skills and experience to come to the rescue. It's tough enough to transition into civilian life when you're expecting it at the end of your career, but to lose it abruptly is another story altogether. I decided to spend as much time shooting archery as possible to take my mind off of things, to make a run at the top of the national rankings through outdoor tournaments, and to go after a personal record at something called the "Vegas Shoot", which is the largest indoor archery tournament in the world, with competitors from 53 countries and all 50 states. I started shooting about 20 hours per week, which was the magic number for me when I was racing bicycles at the highest-level years earlier and I applied the same training principles to my archery. Gradual improvement started to happen and I was ready to roll when February of 2020 rolled around.

Lynn and I would be heading to Vegas after she got off of work on Thursday and the tournament was set to start late Friday morning. It was our first road trip since August of 2019. As I'd done dozens of times prior, I set about loading up my truck with archery equipment and our luggage for the trip. While doing so, I noticed a black SUV make a slow turn through our cul-de-sac and head back out away from the house. I thought nothing of it and wrapped up, ready to go pick Lynn up at work. As I drove down the street and turned right, two black, unmarked SUVs turned on their red and blue code lights and pulled me over. I immediately thought, "Fuck me. This is happening right NOW???"

"Rick Bucher, shut off your vehicle and put your hands out the window."

Officers approached the rear, driver's and passenger's sides of my truck. I rolled all my windows down, shut it off and put my hands out the window. The three officers from the Arizona State Attorney General's Office then conducted a felony stop, handcuffing me on the sidewalk three doors down from Lynn's house. I was actually more concerned about not being there to pick her up than I was about being arrested or having my neighbors see it all, and explained the situation to the officers. They agreed to call her with my phone on speaker, held up in front of my face. After she answered, I said, "Hey Lowie, do you remember the thing that I said might happen? Well, it's happening right now."

There was silence on the other end of the line.

"Lowie! The thing I said might happen one day is happening right now. Do you understand?"

"Are you serious?"

"Hello, this is an officer with the Arizona Attorney General's Office. We're taking Rick into custody and he'll be booked into the Madison Street Jail in downtown Phoenix."

"Okay, what should I do?" Lynn replied.

"Lowie, I need you to call the people I told you to call if this happened, okay? I'll be fine and I love you."

Lynn said she loved me too and I was taken to the back seat of the lead SUV. The officers helped me out by switching my shoes to sandals from the back seat because they knew my laces would be cut out during the booking process. They also agreed to park my truck back in the garage and we departed for downtown Phoenix.

I felt completely numb inside as the handcuffs cut into my wrists, trapped between my back and the seat. I went through the booking process, and spent time with some of Phoenix's finest for the next four or five hours until there were enough of us in the holding cell to be transferred two blocks to the main jail building in a white van. The day was full of firsts, including a remarkably unflattering mug shot. As the hours passed, I worked out the possibility of still going to Vegas and figured out the last possible hour we could leave in order to make the first round of shooting on Friday morning. I stayed up all night and paced non-stop in my cell for what seemed like several hours, calculating the distance covered with small pieces of peel from the two oranges I'd been given during the check-in process. After calculating my stride length and considering how many feet there are in a mile, I realized that I walked two and a half miles in that cell while I waited to get out. And then word came. I'd been released without bail or interstate travel restrictions on my own recognizance, and as the cold February air hit me after the door onto Madison Street slammed shut behind, I turned on my phone to order an Uber ride home. I called Lynn and told her I was on my way home to her and that I'd be there in about 45 minutes. When I arrived, it was about 4:00 AM. We still had two hours until it would be too late to make it and as Lynn repacked her bag, I showered and prepared for the four-hour trip across the desert to Las Vegas and archery glory. I needed this trip to keep my mind off of my legal predicament, if only for a weekend. As the hours counted down to just minutes, we were approaching the South Point Hotel and Casino. Lynn drove me right up to the front door, where I pulled my Pelican case from the back seat and jogged through the casino toward the convention center side of the property. At least there was no one in line when I went to check in, and then headed to the hall where I was assigned to shoot. I had shot in Vegas before and knew exactly where to go. I hastily but carefully assembled my bow, took about nine shots at a practice target and prepared for the first round of competition. And that's when it happened. The 10's started coming. And then, a couple hours later in the last end of competition that morning in Las Vegas, my personal indoor record fell. I had just shot better than ever, after being arrested, booked into jail, walking 2 ½ miles in a cell, getting released, driving four hours across the desert, watching the sunrise in the rearview mirror and running through a casino to shot a bow and arrow. Sometimes I even impress myself. But here's the best part: I had Lynn right there with me the whole time. She helped calm my legal concerns during our drive and was immensely supportive through an incredibly stressful number of hours. And while I was in jail, she did call the people I had planned for her to call ahead of time and even visited with the man who would become the first member of my legal team. I knew there was going to be some tough sledding ahead, but at least we were on the right track.

As the next two days of shooting wore on, my scores did begin to drop because my all-nighter and legal problems were starting to take a mental toll on me, somehow constantly entering my mind while I was at full-draw, ready to release the next shot. It didn't much matter to me any more, and I wound up 93rd out of 393 people, about 60 places away from my ultimate goal.

As we drove home on Sunday afternoon, I started to refocus my attention on what I was looking at for legal consequences should the worst happen. I had been charged with two counts of possession of narcotics, two counts of possession of a dangerous drug and one count of computer tampering (courtesy of my coded access to the storage room that day). These were all Class III felonies in Arizona, carrying a potential sentence of up to thirty years in prison. Let that sink in for a moment or two. Thirty years. I'd be released at age 78 if I served the worst possible sentence.

Suffice to say that the next six months were a living hell for me and for Lynn as we pondered the possibilities. A closed-door grand jury had agreed to the charges I was facing, and the thought of defending myself in front of twelve people who couldn't get out of jury duty was not a risk I was willing to take. So I agreed to a plea bargain and pled guilty to one count of possession of drug paraphernalia, which is a class VI undesignated offense. I was sentenced to one year of unsupervised probation and served six months before having my case closed. Looking back now, it seems like an isolated incident that happened long ago. But the reality is that the period of my life during that time was immensely stressful and had trauma all it's own involved. And I also had a felony on my record for the time being. Life was going to be interesting for me from this point on, for sure.

Good thing I had Lynn's love and support, and an excellent therapist to work with. Because I was going to need some help figuring out who I was now, and what my new normal was going to look like.

Chapter 33
"My Life's Greatest Mystery"

"WHO AM I?" I THINK anyone can ask that question figuratively, but having been adopted at four days old and never knowing anything about my natural family allowed me to ask that question in a more literal sense. There were plenty of times over the course of my life where I had tried to find Margaret Batura, the name under "mother" on my birth certificate, but none was ever successful. Back when I was traveling to race bicycles, I would pick up the phone book in different cities to look for her or just the same last name. On a few occasions, I actually worked up the nerve to call a few Baturas, but there were just no leads and I eventually gave up hope. When DNA testing websites started to arrive in the early 2000's, I justified the decision to not seek out my family history with the following reasoning. I thought that I had made it however many years without knowing, and what would that knowledge change now? I also considered the fact that finding my birth mother could open Pandora's box, since I didn't know who or what I would find, or if she would want to be found in the first place. This decision was going to affect at least one other person and I wasn't sure I wanted to do that.

But then I started to look at the issue from a different perspective; the perspective of a survivor who very nearly lost any possibility at all of ever solving this mystery, my life's biggest and oldest.

So for Christmas in 2019, Lynn ordered DNA tests to answer questions about our family trees, mine having only one single, solitary branch at the time. Sometime late in January of 2020, we sent in our tests and waited for the results. A few weeks later, they were emailed to us and the closest match I had was a fourth or fifth cousin. "Well, that went nowhere" I thought. But a few months later, Lynn ordered a DNA test from a different provider. And the box sat on the kitchen counter for a few more months while I presumed the results from it would be just the same as the other. It seemed pointless to submit another test only to see the same disappointing and depressing story. And with the year's trauma still freshly in place, I wasn't really prepared to experience another large life event. But at some point in July, I decided to go ahead with the test and mailed it in. Same story I thought, wait a few weeks for the results and probably find out nothing of interest or for that matter of any consequence.

A week passed, then two and I promptly forgot about the test altogether. But on the evening of July 31, before Lynn and I turned in for bed, I got an email from the DNA testing company. My results were in. And to my shock, astonishment and amazement, I had a 50% DNA match with another person, and that person was none other than my biological mother, Margaret Jordan. I couldn't move. I couldn't breathe. I couldn't even think. What did this mean, and where would I go with the answer to my life's greatest question? And why didn't the last name match what I had on my birth certificate? I then looked at her profile on the website and found her location: Chandler, Arizona, 30 minutes from our place! After a few moments, I turned my head, then my laptop toward Lynn and said, "I think I just found my mom." We were awestruck by the news and it took a bit of time before I could see the path clearly laid out in front of me. I was going to reach out and see what happened.

Through the messaging option on the DNA website, I sent her a message that said, "It appears we have some DNA in common! I'm sure you have as many questions as I do. Please reach out to me at your convenience." The reply came two days later, and it appeared as though she hadn't looked at how we were related because it was rather vague. My message back made things clearer, "I was born in Effingham, IL and adopted by the Bucher family in September of 1972. Is your first name Margaret? (She used an assumed name on the DNA site.) From this point on, we were both about to jump out of our skin and agreed to a phone call. The conversation lasted a couple of hours and started with a bit of a vetting process through which we confirmed that we each were, in fact, who we though we were and I provided all the details that I knew surrounding my birth and adoption. I also assured her that there was nothing that I wanted from her other than answers to some decades-old questions. A bit further into the conversation, Maggie told me that she had ridden Harley Davidson motorcycles around the United States throughout the 80's and onward, and that her father (my grandfather) had won the Colorado state bicycle road racing championship as a junior. These two pieces of the puzzle explained more than is outwardly imaginable. I had two wheels and competition in my blood! I always felt that way, but now I knew it to be true. I asked about the difficulty in finding her based on her name and she explained that Batura had been her previous married name, abandoned years earlier after a divorce. And then the other news came. I had six brothers and sisters! Maggie went on to tell me briefly about each of them, including Christina, closest in age to me, who had passed away in a plane crash in the 80's. The other five were all still living, and in various parts of the country, spanning from Washington to Florida, Texas, Utah and Arizona. I feverishly wrote down notes as she spoke, incredulous to the amount of information I had stumbled upon. If I had trepidation about the effect this news would have on one other person, it was quickly building because that number had now grown to at least six. This was going to be complex.

Four days later, on August 13, 2020, I met my biological mother, the then only blood relative I had ever seen in person. I was 47 years old. We had lunch and I couldn't take my eyes off of her, nor could I wipe the smile from my face, much the way I'm smiling right now as I type these words, just over two years since that first meeting. It's an absolutely amazing experience to sit across from the answer to a question you've had all your life, and in my case, for so long at that point. Maggie had my nose, my eyes, and the same smile that I couldn't contain. What I think sealed the deal for her was something I had brought along with me for that first meeting. It was a greeting card my adoptive father had given to me several years before he passed away, and after my adoptive mother had been placed in a memory care facility.

Dated September 10, 1972, that card said:

Some random thoughts-

Myself – as just a link in the chain of a child's life.

Baby – conceived in Love – that I might give it Life - to pass him on to a man and wife who will give him love and unite them into a family – a gift of God.

Parents – who have shared the last month of waiting with me – if only in thought and prayer. "Only?" It meant a great deal to me. And also to know that you "almost shared" his birth with me. Thank you.

I am thankful to God that Faith and Fate have brought us all together for the unique benefit of this child. The world is a beautiful place.

As I give him to you, I only ask that you teach him the values of Love, Truth, Understanding and Faith.

May God Bless All of You

M.B.

I told her that there was something I thought she should see, and slid the card across the table to her. She read it, and the note inside, and our bond was confirmed without question. That moment was one of the most significant of my life, and I'll treasure it forever.

As has become common practice for us, we met for lunch and stayed at the restaurant until we could have ordered dinner. Our conversations and the time we spend together seem to fly by so fast, and it's truly amazing to me to feel the connection I have with my mom. We continue to learn about each other and our histories more and more every time we're together, and even now at 86 years old, she has the spirit and mindset of someone my age or younger, but with every bit of the wisdom of an octogenarian. I find her fascinating, funny, beautiful and more than I ever could have hoped to find in the very best of scenarios and I love her with all my heart.

Two months later, I sat down across another table with my brother Marty. Then I met another brother, Pete. Cousin Tim was next, then my sister Kathryn. Some time later, I met my sister Julie and finally my brother Mike. They're all top-shelf, successful people who have welcomed me with open arms to the family I never knew I had and I somehow feel complete in a not so surprising way now. I've answered so many questions over the last two years and have come to value my family in a way I never could before. There's been much said about nature vs. nurture, and I think that each has it's own influence in one's life. But I can say from experience that nature is in most ways much stronger, as there have been things explained through conversations with my family that had nothing at all to do with nurture. My ethnic makeup is primarily Scottish and Irish, with Swedish and Danish also prevalent.

I did find out information about my biological father, but not before he passed away and haven't had any contact with his side of my family out of respect for circumstances. The wonderful people I've met to this point have more than satisfied my curiosity and I consider myself fortunate to have had these opportunities and connections. Where once I dreaded family events, I now look forward to them and have been so lucky to finally find some of the answers to my life's greatest question, "Who am I?" Who would have thought it would be this easy, or that every experience has been so positive?

There's more to that question than just my ethnicity and family members. Who I am is much, much more. Running over 16,000 calls for service as a firefighter formed some of it, but at points in my life, I've been an athlete, a student, a saxophonist, a bike racer, a firefighter, a paramedic, a mentor, an instructor, a rock climber, a motorcycle racer, a skier, a kayaker, a backpacker, a technical rescue tech, a loser, a winner, a survivor and now, a writer. But I can also add son and brother to the list, now that I've met blood relatives for the first time in my life. Another aspect to the question is who I will become from now on. What will I become now and what will I do with the rest of my life? What impact will I have on the world around me and how will I be remembered when I'm gone? Had I succeeded in ending my life in September of 2019, I'd never have found my biological family, would never have enjoyed another beautiful sunrise on my mountain bike or another sunset by Lynn's side. I would never have had the chance to cry tears of joy over something joyous, or feel the pain of loss followed by the strength and appreciation of recovery, for even those things are vital parts of going on living and growing in this beautiful life of ours. And who knows what the future will hold? That's perhaps the greatest mystery. But based on my past, it's going to be one amazing ride that I'm ready to tackle head-on and in high gear, bold as ever.

There's one more thing, though. I would also never have had the chance to be an advocate for those who have suffered trauma and I'd never have had the chance to share my story with you. From the bottom of my heart, thank you so much for hearing it.

RICK

[1] DUPONT NOMEX IS A heat and flame-resistant fiber

[2] International Fire Service Training Association

[3] Self-Contained Breathing Apparatus

[4] Firefighter

[5] S-130/S-190 is a federally mandated curriculum that addresses the foundational skills universal to all wildland firefighters.

[6] The Tonto National Forest is the ninth largest national forest in the United States, spanning 2,873,200 acres and ranging from 1,400' to 7,400' above sea level.

[7] A drip torch is a hand-held device that drips a mix of diesel fuel and gasoline over a lit wick, leaving a trail of fire when the torch is inverted. Fusees are road flares.

[8] Rope 1&2 are classes compliant with the NFPA 1006 standard on Technical Rescue Personnel training.

[9] A pressurized water extinguisher with 2.5 gallon capacity.

[10] Technical Rescue Team or Hazardous Materials

[11] Small utility truck used for medical and light fire responses, staffed by two people.

[12] Bag loaded with floating rope used to rescue people in water.

[13] Personal Floatation Device

[14] Estimated Time of Arrival

[15] Advanced Life Support

[16] Occupational Safety and Health Administration

[17] Intravenous Infusion

[18] A form of free climbing on low rocks without ropes or a harness

[19] Arizona Department of Public Safety Bell 407 rescue helicopter

[20] Thoracic- Lumbar-Sacral Orthosis

[21] The typical flow of water on a fire scene comes from a hydrant, through large-diameter supply hose, into a fire engine's pump, then out to hoses and nozzles tended to by firefighters.

[22] Large tarp used to protect property

[23] Nickname for a call coming into the station, with lights and an alert tone played over the intercom

[24] Medical tool used for endoscopy of the larynx, or breathing tube

[25] Common radio code for a dead body

[26] A one-day road race on a circuit course, often on closed city streets

[27] After joining the automatic aid system through Phoenix Fire Dispatch, Scottsdale stations and vehicles took on 600-series numbering.

About the Author

Rick Bucher was a firefighter, paramedic and technical rescue technician and is the author of "Flame And Fortune". He has appeared on the Cleared Hot Podcast with Retired Navy Seal Andy Stumpf and the Black Rifle Coffee Podcast to tell his story of trauma and redemption. He owns RB603, speaks to groups and advocates for survivors of trauma while travelling the United States.

Read more at www.rb603.net.